Writing Business Letters For Dummies®

Cheat Sheet

Start Up Sheet

Audience

1. Who's my primary reader? Do I have multiple readers?
2. What does my reader *need to know* about the topic?
3. What's in it for my reader?
4. Does my writing need a special angle or point of view? (managerial? technical? other?)
5. What's my reader's attitude toward the topic?

Purpose

6. My purpose is to _____ so my reader will _____.

Key Issue

7. What's the one *key point* I want my reader to remember?

Delivery

8. Who should receive a copy of this message?
9. What's the best way to deliver this message? Hard copy, e-mail, fax, phone, personal meeting, other?
10. When is the best time to deliver the message? When is too early? When is too late?

Six Steps to Writing Persuasive Business Letters

1. Getting Started
2. Creating Headlines and Strategic Sequencing
3. Writing the Draft
4. Designing for Visual Impact
5. Honing the Tone
6. Proofreading and Editing

Ten Reasons Letters Fail

1. **Where's the beef?** The message is so poorly written and the visual impact is so poor that the message is lost.
2. **Insensitive salutation.** The salutation is so impersonal, it's equivalent to yelling "Hey you" when you enter a room.
3. **I've been framed.** People often try to squeeze too much onto a single page, forsaking at least one-inch margins on the top, bottom, and sides.
4. **Your "John Hancock" please.** It's amazing how many people forget to sign their names.
5. **Spelling "errers."** Spelling errors pop out like zits.
6. **Grammatical goofs.** Grammatical faux pas make you sound illiterate.
7. **All about "Me."** The letter is focused on the writer, not the reader.
8. **Kid in a candy store.** The writer overwhelmed the reader with too many font styles and colors.
9. **Tinny tone.** The tone is stuffy (taxidermy), not conversational.
10. **The 500-word paragraph.** The paragraphs are so long that the reader tends to skip over them.

Letter-Perfect Checklist

❑ My subject line and headlines are informative to spark my reader's interest.

❑ My message is sequenced for the needs of my reader.

❑ My letter has visual impact, including

   ❑ 1 to $1\frac{1}{2}$ inch margins on the top, bottom, and sides.

   ❑ Sentences limited to 25 words.

   ❑ Paragraphs limited to 5 to 7 lines.

   ❑ Bulleted and numbered lists, when appropriate.

❑ My tone reflects my personality on paper.

❑ Spelling, grammar, and punctuation are correct.

❑ I didn't lay my cup down and leave coffee stains on the paper.

...For Dummies®: Bestselling Book Series for Beginners

Writing Business Letters For Dummies®

Cheat Sheet

Two-Letter State and Territory Abbreviations

Location	Abbreviation	Location	Abbreviation
Alabama	AL	Missouri	MO
Alaska	AK	Montana	MT
Arizona	AZ	Nebraska	NE
Arkansas	AR	Nevada	NV
California	CA	New Hampshire	NH
Canal Zone	CZ	New Jersey	NJ
Colorado	CO	New Mexico	NM
Connecticut	CT	New York	NY
Delaware	DE	North Carolina	NC
District of Columbia	DC	North Dakota	ND
Florida	FL	Ohio	OH
Georgia	GA	Oklahoma	OK
Guam	GU	Oregon	OR
Hawaii	HI	Pennsylvania	PA
Idaho	ID	Puerto Rico	PR
Illinois	IL	Rhode Island	RI
Indiana	IN	South Carolina	SC
Iowa	IA	South Dakota	SD
Kansas	KS	Tennessee	TN
Kentucky	KY	Texas	TX
Louisiana	LA	Utah	UT
Maine	ME	Vermont	VT
Maryland	MD	Virginia	VA
Massachusetts	MA	Virgin Islands	VI
Michigan	MI	Washington	WA
Minnesota	MN	West Virginia	WV
Mississippi	MS	Wisconsin	WI
		Wyoming	WY

Punctuation Basics

- ✔ Always place commas and periods inside quotation marks.
- ✔ Always place semicolons and colons outside quotation marks.
- ✔ Place question marks and exclamation points inside the quotes only when they apply to the quoted material.
- ✔ Place question marks and exclamation points outside the quotes when they apply to the entire sentence.

Note: Check out Appendix A for more punctuation.

...For Dummies®: Bestselling Book Series for Beginners

Praise For Writing Business Letters For Dummies

"*Writing Business Letters For Dummies* is a life raft in a sea of bad communication. Sheryl Lindsell-Roberts has compiled a guide that everyone — from the anxious beginner to the seasoned pro — can use immediately. But what makes her book such a delightful read is its light-hearted approach to a process that intimidates most of us but shouldn't! This book is a comprehensive road map to getting noticed in business."

> — Bill Lane, Business Editor

"Great business letter writing has become a lost art — until now. Thanks to *Writing Business Letters For Dummies*, the art of letter writing has been resuscitated. Armed with creative tips and strategies set forth in this book, you will give your business letters — and your career — new life. Get the book!"

> — Evilee Thibeault, Sr. VP/Publisher, Network World, Inc.

"Ms. Lindsell-Roberts has created a 'must-read' work for anyone entrusted with the art of written communication. Written in a form that is both easy to read and easy to implement, this book flies in a real world setting. Whether novice or expert, this book will greatly enhance your ability to communicate your ideas and get results."

> — Dr. Tony Palermo, Chiropractor and Success Coach

"This book offers straightforward advice for getting results and is packed with tips for communicating effectively in a fast-paced business world. Every reader will learn how to stand out better through their communications and leverage the power of the written word to their advantage. Whatever the purpose of your communication, this book shows you how to get your point across persuasively, in the best possible manner."

> — Bob Martel, President, JMB Marketing

"Sheryl Lindsell-Roberts has done it. Her simple-to-understand, easy-to-do exercises will have everyone (including me) writing business correspondence like a pro. The book is packed with great information. She answered questions I didn't even know I should ask. Well done!"

> — Debby Hoffman, co-author, *Find Something Nice to Say — the Power of Compliments*

"Sheryl Lindsell-Roberts has succeeded in crafting a results-focused, no-nonsense book written with the new and seasoned businessperson in mind. Lindsell-Roberts does a masterful job of addressing e-mail as well as "postal" snail-mail in directing people to achieve the results they want. In this cyber-communication age, delivering effective messages that people read is a coveted business skill necessary for success. With so much information coming at us, being able to write clearly and concisely in any medium has never been more important."

— Carol Szatkowski, CEO, Clear Point Consultants, Inc.

Writing
Business Letters
FOR
DUMMIES®

by Sheryl Lindsell-Roberts

IDG Books Worldwide, Inc.
An International Data Group Company

Foster City, CA ✦ Chicago, IL ✦ Indianapolis, IN ✦ New York, NY

Writing Business Letters For Dummies®

Published by
IDG Books Worldwide, Inc.
An International Data Group Company
919 E. Hillsdale Blvd.
Suite 400
Foster City, CA 94404
www.idgbooks.com (IDG Books Worldwide Web site)
www.dummies.com (Dummies Press Web site)

Library of Congress Catalog Card No.: 99-65874

ISBN: 0-7645-5207-4

Printed in the United States of America

10 9 8 7 6 5 4 3 2 1

1B/RV/QZ/ZZ/IN

Distributed in the United States by IDG Books Worldwide, Inc.

Distributed by CDG Books Canada Inc. for Canada; by Transworld Publishers Limited in the United Kingdom; by IDG Norge Books for Norway; by IDG Sweden Books for Sweden; by IDG Books Australia Publishing Corporation Pty. Ltd. for Australia and New Zealand; by TransQuest Publishers Pte Ltd. for Singapore, Malaysia, Thailand, Indonesia, and Hong Kong; by Gotop Information Inc. for Taiwan; by ICG Muse, Inc. for Japan; by Intersoft for South Africa; by Eyrolles for France; by International Thomson Publishing for Germany, Austria and Switzerland; by Distribuidora Cuspide for Argentina; by LR International for Brazil; by Galileo Libros for Chile; by Ediciones ZETA S.C.R. Ltda. for Peru; by WS Computer Publishing Corporation, Inc., for the Philippines; by Contemporanea de Ediciones for Venezuela; by Express Computer Distributors for the Caribbean and West Indies; by Micronesia Media Distributor, Inc. for Micronesia; by Chips Computadoras S.A. de C.V. for Mexico; by Editorial Norma de Panama S.A. for Panama; by American Bookshops for Finland.

For general information on IDG Books Worldwide's books in the U.S., please call our Consumer Customer Service department at 800-762-2974. For reseller information, including discounts and premium sales, please call our Reseller Customer Service department at 800-434-3422.

For information on where to purchase IDG Books Worldwide's books outside the U.S., please contact our International Sales department at 317-596-5530 or fax 317-596-5692.

For consumer information on foreign language translations, please contact our Customer Service department at 1-800-434-3422, fax 317-596-5692, or e-mail rights@idgbooks.com.

For information on licensing foreign or domestic rights, please phone +1-650-655-3109.

For sales inquiries and special prices for bulk quantities, please contact our Sales department at 650-655-3200 or write to the address above.

For information on using IDG Books Worldwide's books in the classroom or for ordering examination copies, please contact our Educational Sales department at 800-434-2086 or fax 317-596-5499.

For press review copies, author interviews, or other publicity information, please contact our Public Relations department at 650-655-3000 or fax 650-655-3299.

For authorization to photocopy items for corporate, personal, or educational use, please contact Copyright Clearance Center, 222 Rosewood Drive, Danvers, MA 01923, or fax 978-750-4470.

About the Author

My life involves wearing a lot of hats, just as yours does. First and foremost, I'm a wife and mother of two wonderful sons: Marc, a California architect; and Eric, a Maryland chiropractor. I live with my husband, Jon, in *Parnassus*, the splendid home in Marlborough, Massachusetts, that Marc designed.

I'm fortunate to have a job that would be my hobby if it weren't my profession. Between freelance writing assignments and business writing seminars, I've written more than a dozen books for the professional and humor markets. *Business Writing For Dummies* (my first book for the *...For Dummies* series) is a hot seller, and *The Office Professional's Quick Reference Handbook* (published by Macmillan) is in its 4th edition. My entree into the humor market was with *Loony Laws and Silly Statutes* (published by Sterling Publishing). *Loony Laws* continues to receive acclaim on nationwide talk shows and in magazines and newspapers. I recently finished a sequel, *Funny Laws & Other Zany Stuff*. Please look for it.

When my life gets more complicated than it needs to be, my warm-weather nirvana is my 30' sailboat — *Worth th' Wait*. Jon and I are aboard every weekend that the temperature rises above 60 and the seas aren't too treacherous. (We've also been out there when they were too treacherous, but not by choice.) I don't bring my suitcase stuffed with clothes because there isn't room to put too much, and I've learned to minimize. All I need is sunscreen, a few pairs of shorts, some T-shirts, and a good book. Columbus wanted to prove the world was round, Captain Kirk wanted "to boldly go where no man has gone before," Jon and I merely want to leave our obligations and harried lives on shore. Everyone needs a nirvana, even if it's a spot under a tree or the corner of a room.

When I'm not writing or sailing, I travel, paint (watercolors, not walls), garden, photograph nature, read, ski, eat strawberry cheesecake, and work out at the gym (after the cheesecake I really need to). I try to live each day to the fullest!

Sheryl Lindsell-Roberts, M.A.

ABOUT IDG BOOKS WORLDWIDE

Welcome to the world of IDG Books Worldwide.

IDG Books Worldwide, Inc., is a subsidiary of International Data Group, the world's largest publisher of computer-related information and the leading global provider of information services on information technology. IDG was founded more than 30 years ago by Patrick J. McGovern and now employs more than 9,000 people worldwide. IDG publishes more than 290 computer publications in over 75 countries. More than 90 million people read one or more IDG publications each month.

Launched in 1990, IDG Books Worldwide is today the #1 publisher of best-selling computer books in the United States. We are proud to have received eight awards from the Computer Press Association in recognition of editorial excellence and three from Computer Currents' First Annual Readers' Choice Awards. Our best-selling ...For Dummies® series has more than 50 million copies in print with translations in 31 languages. IDG Books Worldwide, through a joint venture with IDG's Hi-Tech Beijing, became the first U.S. publisher to publish a computer book in the People's Republic of China. In record time, IDG Books Worldwide has become the first choice for millions of readers around the world who want to learn how to better manage their businesses.

Our mission is simple: Every one of our books is designed to bring extra value and skill-building instructions to the reader. Our books are written by experts who understand and care about our readers. The knowledge base of our editorial staff comes from years of experience in publishing, education, and journalism — experience we use to produce books to carry us into the new millennium. In short, we care about books, so we attract the best people. We devote special attention to details such as audience, interior design, use of icons, and illustrations. And because we use an efficient process of authoring, editing, and desktop publishing our books electronically, we can spend more time ensuring superior content and less time on the technicalities of making books.

You can count on our commitment to deliver high-quality books at competitive prices on topics you want to read about. At IDG Books Worldwide, we continue in the IDG tradition of delivering quality for more than 30 years. You'll find no better book on a subject than one from IDG Books Worldwide.

IDG BOOKS WORLDWIDE

John Kilcullen
Chairman and CEO
IDG Books Worldwide, Inc.

Steven Berkowitz
President and Publisher
IDG Books Worldwide, Inc.

Eighth Annual Computer Press Awards ≥1992

Ninth Annual Computer Press Awards ≥1993

Tenth Annual Computer Press Awards ≥1994

Eleventh Annual Computer Press Awards ≥1995

IDG is the world's leading IT media, research and exposition company. Founded in 1964, IDG had 1997 revenues of $2.05 billion and has more than 9,000 employees worldwide. IDG offers the widest range of media options that reach IT buyers in 75 countries representing 95% of worldwide IT spending. IDG's diverse product and services portfolio spans six key areas including print publishing, online publishing, expositions and conferences, market research, education and training, and global marketing services. More than 90 million people read one or more of IDG's 290 magazines and newspapers, including IDG's leading global brands — Computerworld, PC World, Network World, Macworld and the Channel World family of publications. IDG Books Worldwide is one of the fastest-growing computer book publishers in the world, with more than 700 titles in 36 languages. The "...For Dummies®" series alone has more than 50 million copies in print. IDG offers online users the largest network of technology-specific Web sites around the world through IDG.net (http://www.idg.net), which comprises more than 225 targeted Web sites in 55 countries worldwide. International Data Corporation (IDC) is the world's largest provider of information technology data, analysis and consulting, with research centers in over 41 countries and more than 400 research analysts worldwide. IDG World Expo is a leading producer of more than 168 globally branded conferences and expositions in 35 countries including E3 (Electronic Entertainment Expo), Macworld Expo, ComNet, Windows World Expo, ICE (Internet Commerce Expo), Agenda, DEMO, and Spotlight. IDG's training subsidiary, ExecuTrain, is the world's largest computer training company, with more than 230 locations worldwide and 785 training courses. IDG Marketing Services helps industry-leading IT companies build international brand recognition by developing global integrated marketing programs via IDG's print, online and exposition products worldwide. Further information about the company can be found at www.idg.com.   1/24/99

Dedication

Dedicated to Louise Lodie and the Power of a Letter

My greatest moment as a writer and perhaps as a human being came from a wonderful woman, Louise Lodie. This is a real affirmation to the power of a letter.

A number of years ago I wrote a book and included a letter from Jay Lodie, an AIDS patient, who was soliciting funds on behalf of the AIDS Action Committee of Massachusetts. I never met Jay but was so moved by the warmth and conviction of his words that I was prompted to send a substantial donation. When my book was published, I contacted the AIDS Action Committee because I wanted to send Jay a copy. I found out that AIDS had claimed his life just a short time earlier.

Instead, I sent the book to Jay's bereaved mother, Louise Lodie, with a letter telling her how inspired I was by Jay's words and courage. I'd like to share a portion of the letter she sent back to me — the one that had such impact on both our lives.

(continued)

Dear Sheryl,

Your memorial to Jay is more than a "small comfort." I have read your letter and Jay's over and over. Tears flowed, but they were tears of pride that Jay will never be forgotten. He made a mark on so many lives in many ways. I wish you could have known him.

Several years ago he developed "Team Lodie" to raise funds for AIDS Action in the all Walks of Life with 60 family members and friends. Every year since then we have walked with him, increasingly in number and each year raising thousands of dollars... In 1994 we walked in his memory with over 100 in his team... He is still so loved and so missed. Using his letter in your book, you are keeping his words alive.

I close, hoping that someday we may meet as you hold a special place in my heart.

Sincerely,

Louise Lodie

(continued)

Louise and I met shortly thereafter. She greeted me with a big hug and warm smile. She's a remarkable and courageous woman, and we now share a warm friendship. (Her letter to me is framed and hangs in my office.) I knew from the first moment I met Louise that if my book never sold a single copy, knowing how deeply I had touched her life made it all worthwhile. *And it all started with a letter.*

Author's Acknowledgments

I want to express my heart-felt gratitude to my family (blood and extended) and my dear friends. Without their love and support I wouldn't be the person I am today and wouldn't have realized my dreams. I also want to thank all the folks at Dummies who made the vision of this book a reality — especially Mark Butler, for his incredible support; Andrea Boucher, for jumping in at the last minute (with a smile) and doing a bang-up job; and Corey Dalton, for his keen insights and wonderful humor.

Publisher's Acknowledgments

We're proud of this book; please register your comments through our IDG Books Worldwide Online Registration Form located at http://my2cents.dummies.com.

Some of the people who helped bring this book to market include the following:

Acquisitions and Editorial

Project Editors: Brian Kramer; Wendy Hatch; Andrea C. Boucher

Acquisitions Editor: Mark Butler

Copy Editor: Corey M. Dalton

Technical Editors: Lloyd Perell; Frances P. Capell

Editorial Manager: Jennifer Ehrlich

Editorial Assistant: Alison Walthall

Production

Project Coordinator: Maridee V. Ennis

Layout and Graphics: Angela F. Hunckler, Brent Savage, Janet Seib, Micheal A. Sullivan, Dan Whetstine

Proofreaders: Paula Lowell, Nancy Price, Nancy Reinhardt, Marianne Santy

Indexer: Infodex Indexing Services, Inc.

Special Help
Donna Love

General and Administrative

IDG Books Worldwide, Inc.: John Kilcullen, CEO; Steven Berkowitz, President and Publisher

IDG Books Technology Publishing Group: Richard Swadley, Senior Vice President and Publisher; Walter Bruce III, Vice President and Associate Publisher; Steven Sayre, Associate Publisher; Joseph Wikert, Associate Publisher; Mary Bednarek, Branded Product Development Director; Mary Corder, Editorial Director

IDG Books Consumer Publishing Group: Roland Elgey, Senior Vice President and Publisher; Kathleen A. Welton, Vice President and Publisher; Kevin Thornton, Acquisitions Manager; Kristin A. Cocks, Editorial Director

IDG Books Internet Publishing Group: Brenda McLaughlin, Senior Vice President and Publisher; Diane Graves Steele, Vice President and Associate Publisher; Sofia Marchant, Online Marketing Manager

IDG Books Production for Dummies Press: Michael R. Britton, Vice President of Production; Debbie Stailey, Associate Director of Production; Cindy L. Phipps, Manager of Project Coordination, Production Proofreading, and Indexing; Tony Augsburger, Manager of Prepress, Reprints, and Systems; Laura Carpenter, Production Control Manager; Shelley Lea, Supervisor of Graphics and Design; Debbie J. Gates, Production Systems Specialist; Robert Springer, Supervisor of Proofreading; Kathie Schutte, Production Supervisor

Dummies Packaging and Book Design: Patty Page, Manager, Promotions Marketing

◆

The publisher would like to give special thanks to Patrick J. McGovern, without whom this book would not have been possible.

◆

Contents at a Glance

Introduction 1

Part I: Making Your Mark in the Business World 7
Chapter 1: Catapulting Your Career 9
Chapter 2: Your Image to the World 17
Chapter 3: The ABC's of Letters 33

Part II: Writing Persuasive Letters 43
Chapter 4: Getting into High Gear 45
Chapter 5: Adding Spit and Polish 61

Part III: The Letter Carrier Cometh 91
Chapter 6: Spicy Sales Letters 93
Chapter 7: In the Course of Your Employment 107
Chapter 8: The Customer Is Always Right 127
Chapter 9: Cash or Charge? 139
Chapter 10: Ask (Nicely) and Ye Shall Receive 153
Chapter 11: May I Have Your Order, Please? 163
Chapter 12: Getting Personal in Business 169
Chapter 13: You Are Cordially Invited 183
Chapter 14: Professional Potpourri 193

Part IV: The Part of Tens 207
Chapter 15: Ten Hints for Writing Memorable Memos 209
Chapter 16: Ten Tips for Querying a Magazine 213
Chapter 17: Ten Things to Remember About Proper Forms of Address 219
Chapter 18: Ten Things to Know about Using the U.S. Postal Service 227
Chapter 19: Ten Tips for Cutting E-M@il Overload 235
Chapter 20: Ten Ways to Jettison Paper Piles 243

Part V: Appendixes 249
Appendix A: Punctuation Made Easy 251
Appendix B: Grammar's Not Grueling 263
Appendix C: Abridged Abbreviations 273
Appendix D: Spelling Superbly 279

Index 291

Book Registration Information ....Back of Book

Cartoons at a Glance

By Rich Tennant

"Yes, Mr. Van Gogh, now that I have your ear, so to speak, let me thank you for that enticing cover letter."

page 91

"Hey kid – dis is one nice business letter. I think you're the type of guy we can work with."

page 43

"Now take your time and see if you can identify the person who attacked you on e-mail."

page 207

"You're able to read the chicken bones just fine. It's the grammar you use when writing with them that needs work."

page 249

"We need someone to write our business correspondence. But I sense you have a tendency to dangle your participles. I also see a sentence in your future that will begin with a preposition..."

page 7

Fax: 978-546-7747 • E-mail: the5wave@tiac.net

Table of Contents

Introduction 1
    Why I Wrote This Book 1
    Getting the Maximum Benefit from This Book 1
    What's Hot in This Book 2
        Part I: Making Your Mark in the Business World 2
        Part II: Writing Persuasive Letters 2
        Part III: The Letter Carrier Cometh 2
        Part IV: The Part of Tens 3
        Part V: Appendixes 3
    To Whom Am I Talking? (Or Whom Am I Talking To?) 3
    Use the Icons Like Road Signs 3
    Don't Call the Gender Gendarmes 5
    Your Mantra Should Be, "Yes I Can" 5
    Making This Book Your Personal Reference Source 5
    Become a Registered Dummy 6

Part I: Making Your Mark in the Business World 7

Chapter 1: Catapulting Your Career 9
    Some Things Never Change 10
    You Are What You Write 12
    Gaining the Business Advantage 12
    Using the Six Steps 13
    You Be the Judge: Comparing Two Letters 14

Chapter 2: Your Image to the World 17
    Dressing Your Stationery in Style 18
        Seeing what's out there 18
        Creating your own 18
    It's What's Up Front that Counts: Designing the Letterhead 19
    Creating Your Image 20
    Letter Perfect 21
        Using your own laser or ink-jet printer 21
        Using a professional printer 21
    Your Calling Card 22
        Designing your card 22
        When a business card works better than a letter 23
        When in doubt, hand it out 24

The Envelope, Please 25
    What goes where 25
    Fabulous folds 26
Sample Letterheads 28
    Designing a better mousetrap 28
    Here's to your health 29
    Feel the burn 30
    Location, location, location 30
    Going Dutch 30
    Fiscal fitness 31

Chapter 3: The ABC's of Letters **33**
Dating American Style 33
Preparing the Carrier Pigeon 34
The Insider 34
    Naming names 34
    Who signs the addressee's paycheck? 35
    Is the company at 13 Elm Street? 35
    May I have your attention please? 36
Greetings and Salutations 36
    Forms of address 36
    A matter of style 37
While We're on the Subject 37
Body Beautiful 38
Roger and Out 39
Don't Forget Your John Hancock 40
Reference Initials 40
Stuffing the Envelope 41
You're Not the Only One Getting This 41
P.S. By the Way. 41

Part II: Writing Persuasive Letters **43**

Chapter 4: Getting into High Gear **45**
Determining Your Letter Writing IQ 45
Step 1: Getting Started 47
    Using the Start Up Sheet 47
    Understanding the Start Up Sheet 48
    Putting on your reporter's hat 52
Step 2: Writing Headlines and Strategic Sequencing 53
    Crafting attention-getting headlines 53
    Sequencing headlines for maximum impact 54
Step 3: Writing the Draft 56
    Before you begin 57
    Writing the draft 57
    Getting distance from your draft 58
    Returning to action 58

Chapter 5: Adding Spit and Polish 61

Step 4: Designing for Visual Impact 62
    It's a frame up 62
    A matter of style 62
    Don't crowd me 68
    Extra! Extra! Read all about it 69
    Listing key information 69
    Taking contractions out of the labor room 70
    Using great graphics 71
    Giving your letter visual impact 71
Step 5: Honing the Tone 72
    Letting your personality shine 72
    Sealed with a KISS 73
    Double trouble: Avoiding ambiguity 76
    Being positive and upbeat 77
    Think like an advertiser 78
    Using active voice 79
    Battle of the sexes 80
    Honing other tones 82
    Lost in the translation: Being globally aware 83
    Honing the tone 84
Step 6: Proofreading 85
    Avoiding boondoggles 85
    Putting out the fires before they start 86
    Striving to be letter perfect 87
    Using the Letter-Perfect Checklist 90

Part III: The Letter Carrier Cometh *91*

Chapter 6: Spicy Sales Letters 93

Establishing a Smiley Tone 93
Planning Your Sales Letter Campaign 94
The Envelope, Please 95
    Tempting teasers 95
    Looking personal 95
You're on a Roll 97
Adding Pizzazz to Your Sales Letters 97
    Stress benefits, not features 99
    The long and short of it 100
    Calling for action 100
    Using a postscript 101
    Sending a self-addressed, stamped envelope (SASE) 101
    Sales letter taboos 101
Seeing Is Believing! 102
Compiling a Mailing List 105
    Take advantage of trade shows 105
    Following up on a visit to a customer site 106

Chapter 7: In the Course of Your Employment 107

Separating the Gold from the Dross 107
Putting your personality on paper 108
Pumping up your professional image with letterhead 110
Hittin' them with all you have in three paragraphs 110
Broadcasting Yourself 114
Quantifying your accomplishments 115
Action words with pizzazz 115
Thanks for the Interview 117
Yes, We Got Your Resume 118
The Job Is Yours 119
Don't Shoot the Messenger 120
Declining an Offer 121
Welcoming a New Employee 122
Say "hello" personally 122
Spread the word to others 123
It's Time to Move On 124

Chapter 8: The Customer Is Always Right 127

Staking Your Claim 127
Gathering your information 128
Grin, don't grunt 128
Following up 130
Making Amicable Adjustments 130
Responding in a heartbeat 131
Yes, we can! 132
Don't stop there 134
Sorry, we can't 135

Chapter 9: Cash or Charge? 139

Credit is the American Way 140
Luring new customers 140
Yes, you're credit worthy 141
Better luck next time 143
Absence makes the heart grow fonder 144
Pay-Back Time: Collection Letters 145
Be gentle at first 146
Get a little stronger 146
Start a little arm twisting 147
Wage the final campaign 147

Chapter 10: Ask (Nicely) and Ye Shall Receive 153

Asking the "Write" Questions 154
Goodwill Responses 156
Saying "Yes" with a smile 157
Saying a friendly "No" 158

Chapter 11: May I Have Your Order, Please? 163

Ordering with Smarts 163
We're Pleased to Fill Your Order 165
    Brimming with customer service 165
    Gimme details 166
    Other times to get in touch 167

Chapter 12: Getting Personal in Business 169

Exposing Your Human Side: General Guidelines 170
Where Seldom Is Heard, an Encouraging Word 170
    Finding words for a colleague in distress 170
    Offering condolences 171
    Wishing a speedy recovery 172
    Bidding farewell 173
Just One Favor, Please 174
    Making a request 175
    Refusing a request 176
It's Better to Give than to Receive 176
    Offering a gift 176
    Acknowledging an appropriate gift 177
    Acknowledging an inappropriate gift 177
    Refusing a gift 178
Mazel Tov! 178
    Expressing kudos 179
Making Amends 180
Getting in the Holiday Spirit 180

Chapter 13: You Are Cordially Invited 183

Come One — Come All! 183
    Informal invitations 185
    Semi-formal invitations 187
    Formal, printed invitations 188
Responding to the Invitation 190

Chapter 14: Professional Potpourri 193

Beam Me Up, Scotty! 193
Who's Minding the Store? 194
Blame It on the Rain 195
    No, I can't accept your proposal 196
    Denying a request for an interview 196
Mixing, Matching, and Merging 197
We Want You Back 199
Welcome to my World 200
I Gave at the Office 201
Singing Your Praises! 202
On Bended Knee 202
Just Love What You Wrote 204

Part IV: The Part of Tens 207

Chapter 15: Ten Hints for Writing Memorable Memos 209
Know the Rules of the Road 209
Use a Header 210
Don't Use Memos to Share Bad News 210
Display a Sense of Humor 211
Complain Constructively 211
Use Proper Form When You Write a Memorandum Report 211
Sign on the Dotted Line 212
Proofread and Edit Your Memo 212

Chapter 16: Ten Tips for Querying a Magazine 213
Don't Procrastinate; Just Do It! 214
Know What's in It for You 214
Hook Up with the Right Publication 214
Test the Waters 214
Don't Take "No" for an Answer 215
Read the Masthead 215
Send Simultaneous Submissions 215
Become Intimate with the Journal You're Targeting 216
Know What Editors Look for in a Query Letter 216
Get a Copy of the Latest Writer's Market 217
Don't Hold Back Information 218

Chapter 17: Ten Things to Remember About Proper Forms
of Address 219
General Salutations: Formal and Informal 220
Military Might 221
Government Gurus 223
The Religious Realm 224
Campus Companions 225

Chapter 18: Ten Things to Know about Using the
U.S. Postal Service 227
Domestic Mail Services: In and Around the USA 227
First class 228
Certificate of Mailing 228
Certified Mail 229
Registered mail 230
Priority Mail 231
Express Mail 231
Mailgrams 231

International Mail 231
        Special services 232
        Addressing the envelope 232
    Other Carriers 232
    Cost-Cutting Tips 233

Chapter 19: Ten Tips for Cutting E-M@il Overload 235

    Don't Use E-Mail as a Shotgun 236
    Make the Subject Line Reflect the Message 236
    Use Another Program to Compose Long Messages 237
        Send as attachments 237
        Post to your intranet 237
        Post it on your Web site 238
    Tone It Down 238
    Don't Send Rambograms 238
    Save "Urgent" for Situations That Are 239
    Create an Electronic Filing Cabinet 239
    Notify Others When Your Address Changes 239
    Be Careful What You Write 240
    Break the Chain 240
    Proofread and Edit Your Message 241

Chapter 20: Ten Ways to Jettison Paper Piles 243

    Determine Whether You're a Clutterbug 244
    Know What Being a Clutterbug Costs You 244
    Clean Up the Burial Ground 245
        Create paper mountains 245
        Recycle: What goes around comes around 246
    Identify the Sources of Your Clutter 246
    Ditch Magazines 247
    Empty Your In-box and Out-box 247
    Toss Out Old Drafts 247
    Use Electronic Media 247

Part V: Appendixes 249

Appendix A: Punctuation Made Easy 251

    General Guidelines 251
    Commas 252
    Ending Punctuation 254
        Periods 254
        Question marks 254
        Exclamation points 255

Colons and Semicolons 255
   Colons 255
   Semicolons 255
Dashes and Parentheses 256
   Dashes 256
   Parentheses 257
Other Punctuation 257
   Quotation marks 258
   Apostrophes 259
   Hyphens 260
   Slashes 261
   Brackets 261

Appendix B: Grammar's Not Grueling 263

Adjectives 263
   Forms of adjectives 264
   Absolute adjectives 265
   Compound adjectives 265
   Articles 266
Adverbs 266
Double Negatives 266
Conjunctions 267
Nouns 267
Prepositions 267
Pronouns 268
   Singular pronouns 268
   Who and whom 268
Verbs 269
   Dangling participles 269
   Were and was 269
   Split infinitives 270
   Subject and verb agreement 270
   Gerunds 271
Commonly Confused Constructions 271

Appendix C: Abridged Abbreviations 273

Acronyms and Initialisms 273
Companies and Organizations 274
Compass Points 274
Latin Words and Phrases 274
Laws and Bylaws 275
Metric System 275
Periods 276
Postal Abbreviations 277

Appendix D: Spelling Superbly 279

    Plurals 280

    The Final E 281

    The Final Y 281

    IE and EI 281

    Doubling the Final Consonant 282

    Super Stumpers 283

    Booby Traps 288

Index...*291*

Book Registration Information ....*Back of Book*

Introduction

ear Reader:

Letter writing is the crux of business communications. Yet many people — even the brightest and most capable — aren't satisfied with their letter writing skills and would rather have root canal surgery than commit something to the (dreaded) written word. So, if you have trouble casting your letters in concrete, you're not alone. The good news is that everyone — no matter how uneasy — can learn to write clearly, effectively, and strategically.

Why I Wrote This Book

I wrote this book because I want to share with you the outgrowth of 20 years of successful business writing experience (and perhaps buy a 50-foot sailboat). I contribute to companies' bottom lines through marketing communications campaigns, video productions, reports, brochures, annual reports, white papers, user documents, and instructional design.

I also deliver business writing workshops in the business, academic, and government arenas. It's extremely gratifying when participants get in touch with me months after a workshop to tell me how my Six-Step Process helped them master what used to be one of the most frustrating parts of their job — writing. Many people relate how powerful their writing has become and how they cut their writing time in half and doubled, the impact. It's all right here.

Getting the Maximum Benefit from This Book

Writing Business Letters For Dummies walks you through an extensive variety of letter-writing experiences and abounds with letters you may use verbatim. However, you rarely find a one-size-fits-all letter that doesn't need tweaking. That's where Part II, my Six-Step Process is invaluable.

Part II shows you how to tweak any letter or prepare your own to suit your needs to a tee. It's the only section I recommend that you read sequentially. To get the most out of Part II, have in mind a letter, memo, or e-mail message you need to write. Apply the Six-Step Process to the writing you select, and you, too, will learn to write letters with confidence and competence.

Otherwise, jump around to whatever topic interests you. The book even has appendixes with simple and practical punctuation, grammar, abbreviation, and spelling guidelines. I recommend that you keep this book handy for easy reference and tell all your friends and colleagues to buy a copy!

What's Hot in This Book

Here's a preview of what's hot in *Writing Business Letters For Dummies*:

Part I: Making Your Mark in the Business World

Learn the secrets of the experts! In Part I you find out how effective letter writing can catapult your career and present a positive and lasting image to the world.

Part II: Writing Persuasive Letters

Part II introduces you to my Six-Step Process of effective business writing. You find out how to 1) get started, 2) create headlines and sequence for your reader's reaction, 3) write a draft, 4) design for visual impact, 5) use a conversational tone, and 6) proofread with ease.

Part III: The Letter Carrier Cometh

This section offers a cornucopia of business letters — everything from landing your dream job, to collecting money you had kissed goodbye, to writing personal business letters (condolences, apologies, and the like). Feel free to use whatever suits your needs. I won't sue you for copyright infringement unless you use my letters to write your own book.

Part IV: The Part of Tens

The Part of Tens is a ...*For Dummies* classic. Here you find a potpourri of tips and tidbits in a variety of specific areas such as energizing your e-mail messages, cleaning up your paper infobog, and submitting an article to a magazine.

Part V: Appendixes

The four appendixes give you the ability to make your letters *speak* your voice through punctuation, grammar, abbreviations, and spelling tips. For example, notice the difference in the two phrases:

Execution impossible: To be sent to Siberia.

Execution — impossible to be sent to Siberia.

To Whom Am I Talking? (Or Whom Am I Talking To?)

I'm talking to you if you . . .

- Would rather have root canal than write a letter.
- Wish to impact and influence your readers.
- Want your letters to be read ahead of the others vying for the reader's attention.
- Are interested in advancing your career.

Use the Icons Like Road Signs

To help you find the important stuff easily, I scattered icons throughout this book — somewhat like road signs. Each icon represents something vital to your letter-writing experience.

The Sheryl Says icon helps you benefit from my experiences: the blissful, the painful, and everything in between. Sometimes I use Sheryl Says because I want to talk to you. In addition to being a writer, I'm an avid talker and sometimes get lonely sitting in front of my computer.

The Remember icon represents little tidbits to tie around your finger. It can be something as simple as using a salutation and complimentary closing in an e-mail message to say "hello" and "good-bye" to your reader.

In the cyberworld, e-mail is the main stop on the information superhighway. This icon lets you know the rules of the road. E-mail is a serious business-writing tool and must be treated with the same respect as a letter or memo.

The Global Savvy icon gives you general tips for writing to people from around the world without getting pie in your face.

The Tip icon gives you handy hints to take on the road to effective letter writing. The paragraphs next to the Tip icon may be time savers, frustration savers, life savers, or just about anything else.

The Start Up Sheet icon reminds you to fill out the Start Up Sheet featured on the Cheat Sheet in the front of this book. You can only write effective business letters after you clearly identify your *audience*, *purpose*, and *key issue*.

The Checklist icon reminds you that before you send the letter to your reader, you should go through the Letter-Perfect Checklist (featured in Chapter 5 and on the Cheat Sheet in the front of this book). You don't want your blunders to stand out like a wart at the end of your nose.

The Caution icon calls attention to a pitfall you should avoid. If you pay attention to this icon, you may cure baldness and clear up the national debt.

The Success Story icon plays off the adage, "Nothing succeeds like success." You may find it helpful to read other people's success stories.

Don't Call the Gender Gendarmes

In Chaucer's day, any young person was a *girl* — male or female. Times have changed, however, so I searched for an elegant pronoun that would cover males and females. Unfortunately, I wasn't able to find one. Rather than getting into the clumsy he/she or him/her scenario, I opted to be an equal-opportunity writer. I tossed a coin and here's how it landed: I use the *male gender in the even chapters and the female gender in the odd chapters.* (If this offends anyone, please send up a smoke signal with a better suggestion.)

Your Mantra Should Be, "Yes I Can"

As you read this book and develop your letter writing skills, your mantra should be:

- ✔ Yes, I can.
- ✔ Letter writing beats having root canal surgery.
- ✔ Letter writing is essential for a successful career.

Making This Book Your Personal Reference Source

Here are a few tips for personalizing this book so that it truly becomes *your* reference source:

- ✔ Write your own notes in the margins; there's plenty of room.
- ✔ Highlight the stuff that's meaningful to you.
- ✔ Write your name in bold letters in some obvious spot in the front of the book. For example: *This book belongs to Ann Onomous. If you remove it from my desk, you'll be sentenced to serve for one year in an electronic chat room.* (I try to include hot tips on every page, and your coworkers will probably agree.)
- ✔ Get sticky notes or tape flags and tag the hot pages. (I put some of the good stuff on the Cheat Sheet in front of this book, but you can create your own cheat sheets with tags.)

Become a Registered Dummy

Please join the IDB Books Worldwide Book Registration. You can let me know what you think of this book and win a monthly prize giveaway. You find registration information on the last page of *Writing Business Letters For Dummies.*

With the greatest respect,

Sheryl Lindsell-Roberts, M.A.

P.S. For a great reference source on a wide array of documents — reports, proposals, presentations, speeches, and the like — check out my other *...For Dummies* book, *Business Writing For Dummies*, by IDG Books Worldwide, Inc. It's a red-hot seller!

Part I

Making Your Mark in the Business World

The 5th Wave   By Rich Tennant

PSYCHIC HOTLINE
NOW HIRING

"We need someone to write our business correspondence. But I sense you have a tendency to dangle your participles. I also see a sentence in your future that will begin with a preposition..."

In this part . . .

"**D**ress for Success," is a mantra of successful businesspeople. Successful people adorn their *birthday suits* to make statements about themselves, and their letters to make those same statements. A letter is often the first "meeting" you have with someone; so don't make your first impression your last.

This part includes everything from dressing your letterhead and business cards to your letter style. From conservative to contemporary — from artsy to formal — this part has it all!

Chapter 1

Catapulting Your Career

....

In This Chapter

▶ Overcoming your fear of writing

▶ Walking through the Six-Step Process that cuts your writing time in half and doubles the impact

▶ Seeing is believing

....

Writing good letters — communicating on the deeper level of thoughts, feelings, and ideas rather than on the shallow, superficial level of events — also effects our ability to think, to reason accurately, and to be understood effectively.

— Stephen R. Covey, *The 7 Habits of Highly Effective People*

*B*usiness letters account for 90 percent of all written correspondence, making the ability to write quality business letters a powerful instrument by any standards. How powerful, though, depends on how well the letter is written.

A well-written letter is golden. It achieves its purpose quickly, follows a logical path, is clear and to the point, and is courteous and positive. A dynamite letter can catapult your career by

- Landing your dream job.
- Bolstering your reputation.
- Influencing decisions.
- Providing leadership.
- Delighting clients and customers.
- Earning profit for your company.

Some Things Never Change

Letter writing is of noble ancestry (going back at least 3,400 years) and has been a key part of communicating for eons. The ancient kings of Egypt wrote letters to their vassal-princes. The kings inscribed letters on moist clay tablets, baked the tablets, and sent the messages on their way. If the king's writing wasn't concise, the messengers would collapse under the weight of the tablets, and the messages wouldn't be delivered.

Of course, methods have changed drastically from the demise of the clay tablet, the quill pen, and the manual typewriter to the advent of Bill Gates and electronic communications. But one thing hasn't changed — the need to get your point across *clearly* and *concisely*. Clear and concise communications help reduce the stress of our overloaded workdays.

Following is a scenario you may relate to: You start the morning off on the wrong foot. Your alarm didn't go off because of an evening storm that caused a power outage. After rushing to get the kids fed and off to school, you sit in bumper-to-bumper traffic for almost two hours because of the flooding and downed power lines. You arrive at the office — harried and stressed — only a few minutes before a big meeting with the CEO. You grab a cup of coffee to settle your nerves, open your mail, and this is the first letter you read:

> Dear Sir:
>
> On behalf of Ragged Bros., a client of my office, demand is heretofore made upon you for repayment of the $10,000 advance made by you on the 15th of October, XXXX. Such repayment duly became your obligation upon your failure to provide Ragged Bros. with a timely manuscript of *Legal Beagles* as deemed in your contract to be delivered no later than October 8th. If such payment is not made forthwith, we will find it necessary to institute legal proceedings on my client's behalf.
>
> We trust you that you will facilitate this matter expediently and that legal proceedings will not have to be instituted. Call me at your earliest convenience to arrange an amicable settlement of this issue.
>
> Very truly yours,

You scratch your head, wrinkle your brow, and ask yourself this question: On what planet did this person learn to write? Don't I have enough information overload without her wasting my time with such gobbledygook? Why can't she get to the point quickly? Maybe she gets paid by the word? Or better yet, by the syllable. Besides the irritation from the storm-related stress, you now have every reason to be irritated with the writer as well.

As a writer or reader, do you relate to any of the flaws in the letter?

- **The tone is so stuffy, it's taxidermy.** For example, ". . . demand is heretofore made upon you for repayment. . . ." Nobody speaks that way, and nobody should write that way.

- **The writer buried the key message in legalese.** For tips on using clear and simple language, check out Chapter 5.

- **The sentences are long and difficult to read.** Just reread the sentence, "Such repayment duly became your obligation upon your failure to provide Ragged Bros. with a timely manuscript of *Legal Beagles* as deemed in your contract to be delivered no later than October 8th" to understand what I mean.

- **The letter has a poor closing.** "Call me at your earliest convenience. . . ." As stifling as this person sounds, calling her will never be convenient. Who'd want to speak to that automaton?

Although this letter is an extreme example, many people write and receive letters and memos that are not much better. They lose the key issue in dense text; their tone is stiff; their sentences are too long to be clear; their message is full of antiquated expressions; and they never seem to get to the point. See this chapter's sidebar "E-mail messages need TLC" for a warning about making your correspondences too terse.

E-mail messages need TLC

E-mail messages tend to the opposite extreme of stuffy legalese. People often write them on the fly and use a terse tone. An e-mail message is a serious business document and should be treated with the same respect as a letter or memo. Would you send a letter written in ALL CAPS? Would you send a letter with a 500-line paragraph? Would you send a letter without proofreading it? Please check out Chapter 19 for handy tips on using e-mail effectively.

You Are What You Write

Business people associate communication skills with the ability to think clearly, examine alternatives, analyze information, and make decisions. Following is how you *can* write any letter, memo, or e-mail message to affect your reader as you wish:

- **Identify your audience, purpose, and key issue:** If you don't know to whom you're writing, why you're writing, or what you want to say, you're going to have a heck of a time starting the letter and an impossible time figuring out whether it communicates what you want. That's why the Start Up Sheet (found on the Cheat Sheet in the front of this book and fully explained in Chapter 4) is a quick way to identify these three important elements.

- **Sequence your message for the responsiveness of your audience:** Place yourself in the reader's shoes to understand the order in which to present your message. Deliver good news at the beginning and cushion bad news. Learn more about doing this in Chapter 4.

- **Create visual appeal:** When a letter is visually appealing, it invites readership. In Chapter 5 you find hints for presenting text and graphics for maximum impact.

- **Establish a conversational tone:** Take a look at Chapter 5 to learn how to keep your letters short and simple and create a conversational tone that "speaks" well for you.

- **Make sure there are no errors:** If you send a letter with even one error, it's the error your reader remembers, not your message. Chapter 5 outlines ways to avoid errors that can be as obvious as tarantulas on slices of angel food cake.

Gaining the Business Advantage

In an era where slipshod compromise is much too common, your well-crafted letter will make you shine. Because you often write business letters to people you have never met, the letter is somewhat like that first personal meeting; it becomes the reader's first impression of who you are. Don't make your first impression your last. Learn how to overcome your fear of writing and create letters that get priority attention.

If you feel some anxiety about writing a letter, relax. You're in good company. Most people don't like to put their thoughts into writing; they procrastinate and procrastinate. Perhaps you've mumbled these thoughts to yourself:

> ✔ I don't know where to start, so I'll wait 'til later. (Later never comes.)
>
> ✔ I've written the letter and realize that it's to-o-o long and so-o-o boring.
>
> ✔ I can't seem to get my point across clearly and concisely.
>
> ✔ I hate to say no to my customers. I'm afraid of losing their business.
>
> ✔ I saw a wonderful job advertised in the newspaper. How can I write a letter that stands out from the hundreds of letters the company will get?

People at all levels of the business spectrum — from the novice professional to the articulate CEO — experience self-doubts when it comes to letter writing. When you follow the Six Steps outlined in Part II, you're well on your way to conquering your self-doubts.

Using the Six Steps

Producing an effective letter takes planning and sensitivity toward your reader. In order for your letter to stand out from the myriad of others that compete for the reader's attention each day, you must unite the mechanics of writing with the human factor — the reader. You don't want your dynamic ideas to be diminished by mediocre writing.

By using the Six Steps that are explained in detail in Part II, writing becomes simple and effortless. After you learn to write persuasively by using this method, you'll never again revert to old habits. Here, in a nutshell, are the Six Steps:

Chapter 4

> Step 1: Getting started
>
> Step 2: Writing headlines and strategic sequencing
>
> Step 3: Writing the draft

Chapter 5

> Step 4: Designing for visual impact
>
> Step 5: Honing the tone
>
> Step 6: Proofreading and editing

You Be the Judge: Comparing Two Letters

Well-written letters are easy to read and understand. On the following pages are two letters, Examples 1-1 and 1-2. This is your chance to judge for yourself which you'd rather send and receive.

1. **Quickly scan — don't read, just scan — Examples 1-1 and 1-2. See whether you can find answers to these questions instantly, then continue with Number 2.**

   Are they merging?

   What's the date of the luncheon?

   What are the three lunch choices?

2. **After you find the answers, ask yourself these questions:**

   Which letter is more "reader friendly?"

   Which gives you the answers quickly?

   Which would you rather receive?

If you found answers instantly in Example 1-1, you have X-ray vision. If you write like this writer, however, I sympathize with your readers. They're victims, not beneficiaries, of your letters. If you found the answers instantly in Example 1-2, consider why. This is a true example of a letter that focuses on the reader. Some helpful aspects of Example 1-2 that make it easier to read include:

- ✔ The subject line delivers the main message.
- ✔ The headlines tell the story. Key information pops out without having to read the entire letter.
- ✔ The author included plenty of white space that provides contrast and a resting place for your eyes.
- ✔ Paragraphs are short, readable, and easy on the eyes.
- ✔ Sentences are short, simple, and easy to understand.
- ✔ A numbered list pops out key information.

March 1, XXXX

Ms. Terry English, President
Simpston, Inc.
One Haliston Drive
Spring Valley, NY 10977

Dear Terry:

Subject: Answering the question of the merger

Following through on our discussion last week, I'm pleased to let you know as of April 15 we'll be a wholly owned subsidiary of Amaco, Limited.

We've worked hard for this and know it comes as good news. There are two major advantages: First, we'll have added strength in terms of public acceptance and operating capital. Second, we'll be able to serve our customers more promptly, efficiently, and thoroughly. To help you learn more, we'll be sponsoring a company-wide luncheon on March 15 at noon, at the Holiday Inn in Suffern, NY. This will give you the opportunity to have all your concerns addressed.

Principals from Amaco, Limited will be on hand to answer questions and to let you know of their sincere intentions to continue operating this division autonomously. Please call Barbara Jenkins, my administrative assistant, at extension 232 by March 8 to let her know if you'd like chicken, fish, or vegetarian for lunch. This should be a worthwhile meeting and I hope you'll be able to make it on such short notice. We look forward to seeing you there.

Sincerely,

James Patterson

Example 1-1:
Where's the
message?

March 1, XXXX

Ms. Terry English, President
Simpston, Inc.
One Haliston Drive
Spring Valley, NY 10977

Dear Terry:

Subject: Yes, we're merging with Amaco, Limited

As of April 15, we'll be a wholly owned subsidiary of Amaco, Limited.
We've worked hard for this and know that it comes as good news. Here
are two key advantages we'll see immediately:

1. We'll have added strength in terms of public acceptance and operating
   capital.

2. We'll be able to serve our customers more promptly, efficiently, and
   thoroughly.

Learn More Over Lunch
We'll be sponsoring a company-wide luncheon so we can all get together
and address our concerns. Principals from Amaco, Limited will be on hand
to answer questions and to let you know of their sincere intentions to
continue operating this division autonomously.

> **When:** March 15 at noon
> **Where:** Holiday Inn, Suffern, NY
> **Lunch choices:** Chicken, fish, or vegetarian

Next Step
Please call Barbara Jenkins, my administrative assistant, at extension 232
by March 8 to let her know what you'd like for lunch. We look forward to
seeing you there.

Sincerely,

James Patterson

Example 1-2:
The same
message
with a read-
able layout.

Chapter 2

Your Image to the World

In This Chapter

▶ Making your statement with stationery

▶ Designing and handing out business cards

▶ Preparing the envelope

▶ Getting ideas from sample letterheads

I went to a recently opened supermarket looking to buy a package of envelopes. I spotted an aisle marked "stationary," and an oops! went off in my head. I found the manager and asked him if that was the only aisle in the store that doesn't move. He looked at me as if I had two heads. (So much for being a smart aleck.)

— Me

Your stationery (*ery* as in pap*er*) is your company's identity — the image you project to the world. Stationery delivers obvious and subconscious information at a quick glance. When you're starting your own business, you have the luxury of designing stationery that reflects *your* business and *your* philosophy. When you work for a company that's already established, you take what you get. This chapter gives you just what you need to "dress" your stationery for success.

Stationery is more than just a sheet of letterhead. It includes envelopes, business cards, note paper, and any other paper products that send your message. There are several examples of stationery products at the end of this chapter that reflect the personalities and professions of people (perhaps) just like you.

Dressing Your Stationery in Style

You want to dress your stationery, envelopes, and business cards to complement each other and reflect your tasteful image. There are three broad image categories:

- **Conservative:** The banking, insurance, legal, and finance industries reflect a very staid, three-piece-suit image. The stationery often has little or no texture. White or off-white (pale gray, ecru, or ivory) are the preferred colors, and traditional lettering is generally black.

- **Contemporary:** Industries in the design, communications, and arts and entertainment arenas can be more lavish. These industries foster textured or non-textured paper. The stationery can be in a variety of pale colors (blue, green, and the like). The typeface can be colored lettering in a contemporary font.

- **Glamour:** The sky's the limit in retailing, textiles, fashion, fragrances, cosmetics, and other glamour industries. They can get away with almost anything. Paper can be textured or non-textured and boast vibrant colors such as magenta, canary yellow, or violet. The typeface can be anything that makes a personal statement.

Seeing what's out there

You can find stationery to suit every taste, budget, and image. You can order stationery products directly from a professional printer or purchase blank stationery and do your own printing on a laser or ink-jet printer. Paper Direct, of Lyndhurst, New Jersey, has one of the largest paper selections I've seen with designs for all tastes and styles. You can call them in the U.S. at 800-4-PAPERS, or outside the U.S. at 201-507-5488. They'll be happy to send you a catalog and samples. You can also get good buys and selections at the large office supply chains.

Creating your own

If you're working with a professional designer, tell him about your business and the image you want to project. Save letterhead that appeals to you, so you and the designer may incorporate some of the ideas into your stationery. If you want to save money and not work with a designer, you can create your own stationery on your computer and save it as a template. Check your word processing software manual if you need help with font selections, templates, or anything else. Here's a simple design you may consider:

Marric Enterprises
One Bengal Lane, Monsey, NY 10952   (914) 356-7216

It's What's Up Front that Counts: Designing the Letterhead

The letterhead requires special care in the design so it has a balanced look. Some letterheads are centered at the top of the page; others are laid out across the top of the page from the left to the right margin. Letterhead should reflect your industry, but designs differ with taste. The following list describes the main elements for your letterhead:

- **Logo:** A logo isn't necessary but can add visual interest. If used, it should reflect the nature of your company. A logo can be your initials, name, or a graphic illustration of what you do. For example, a computer consultant might have a sketch of a small computer. A writer may have an ink bottle and quill pen. While clipart may be appropriate, be careful that you don't select a piece of clipart everyone is using; it will cheapen your letterhead.

- **Name and business title:** Write out your full name and business title. Don't include Mr., Mrs., or Ms. unless your first name could be either male or female, such as *Ms. Leslie Anderson*.

    Nicknames: If you're known by a nickname, fold that name into your formal name, such as Colson "Skip" Simmons.

    Professional titles: It's appropriate to include a professional title such as Ph.D., (someone who's earned a doctorate), Esq. (an attorney), C.P.A. (an accountant), M.D. (a medical doctor), or D.C. (a doctor of chiropractic).

- **Address:** If you have a street address and a P.O. box number, put the place you want your mail delivered directly above the city and state. Don't forget your ZIP code.

- **Phone and fax numbers:** Include both your telephone and fax numbers and identify which is which.

- **E-mail address:** E-mail has become a primary way to keep in touch in the business world, so be sure to include your e-mail address.

When to nix letterhead

You shouldn't use company letterhead for these instances:

- Charitable, fundraising, or political events, unless sanctioned by the company

- Controversial letters (such as "Letters to the Editor")

- Personal matters (such as lawsuits that aren't company related)

If you don't want clients or patients reaching you by e-mail, omit the e-mail address. Examples may be doctors, lawyers, or Neanderthals.

- **Web address:** If you went to the trouble of preparing a Web site, include your Web address on the letterhead. It's a wonderful way to advertise.

Large or diversified companies may have the names of a particular department, plant, group, or division printed on the letterhead. Organizations such as law offices or accounting firms often have the full names of the partners listed. High corporate officers supplement personalized or executive letterhead with their full names and business titles printed or engraved in small letters one or two lines beneath the letterhead at or near the left margin.

Companies that have international offices often list these offices on the letterhead.

Creating Your Image

Because the cost of stationery is less than five percent of the cost of the average business letter (when you factor in preparation and mailing), good quality paper is worth the expense. Paper is available in a wide variety of qualities that are commensurate with the prices. Although you don't need to break the bank on this investment, don't skimp. Image! Image! Image!

You have several qualities to consider when selecting paper: weight, rag content, grain, and finish.

- **Weight:** Paper is available in several weights. The weight is determined by the heaviness of four 8½-by-11-inch reams of paper. (A ream is 500 sheets.) The most common paper weight is 20- or 24-pound bond. The higher the number, the thicker the paper.

- **Rag content**: Stationery is made of cotton pulp combined with treated wood pulp. The most durable, best looking, and most expensive stationery is cotton fiber. This is known as "rag content."

A watermark — which is a translucent mark produced in the paper when it's manufactured — is elegant but costly. If you hold the paper up to the light, you can see the watermark. The manufacturers of fine paper often have their company names watermarked, but the epitome of class is to have your company's name or symbol watermarked. Be certain to feed the paper through your printer so that the watermark reads from left to right on the printed page.

✔ **Grain:** All paper has grain that comes from the process by which it's made, but the grain is not always obvious. When it is obvious, the grain should be parallel to the direction of the writing — left to right.

✔ **Finish:** The most common finish is linen laid. It's embossed with a linen design and has a fairly rough feel and appearance. A smooth finish works well and costs less.

Don't even think of using the paper from your photocopier or fax machine as stationery. That paper screams "poor quality" and diminishes your image and pearly words.

Letter Perfect

After you decide on the image and type of paper to use, you need to decide how you're going to print the stationery. This is called the lettering process. Which lettering process you choose depends on what tools you have available and how much you're willing to spend. You can find a variety of lettering processes — from inexpensive to selling your firstborn.

In addition to buying stationery with letterhead, purchase matching stationery without letterhead. When a letter runs longer than one page, subsequent pages should be on matching plain stationery.

Using your own laser or ink-jet printer

When you're on a limited budget, consider designing your own letterhead and running it through your own laser or ink-jet printer. Additionally, a scanner gives you a lot of versatility for adding logos and other stuff.

Using a professional printer

If you don't have access to a laser or ink-jet printer — or you don't want to use it, you can hire a professional printer to generate your stationery. When you use a professional printer, you have to specify which printing process you want to use. The following processes are from the least to the most expensive:

Thermography

This process is inexpensive and often called "poor man's engraving." Thermography is a heat process that causes the ink to rise slightly giving the illusion of engraving. (Before deciding on thermography, ask the printer for samples to see whether this process is for you.)

Engraving

This is a relatively expensive process and quite luxurious. You can actually feel the raised letters. In many companies, the CEO or president has engraved stationery.

Embossing

When you have letterhead embossed, you can actually feel the logo or printed word rise from the paper. This is truly a deluxe touch. Embossing is sometimes used on note paper where the person's initials appear raised.

When you have letterhead professionally printed, consider a lead time of up to three months, depending on the printer and what you select. When you're ordering blank stationery, the lead time is substantially shorter. It may even be available off the shelf so you don't have to wait.

Your Calling Card

Your business card says that you *are* someone of importance. It's literally your calling card, a visual statement of who you are and what you do. Your business card should entice the person you give it to want to get in touch with you. This section gives you tips on designing your card and how and when to use it.

Designing your card

A standard business card in the U.S. measures 3½ by 2 inches, or something close. European cards tend to be slightly larger — 4½ by 3 inches. You may opt for an odd size, but keep in mind that people put business cards in their wallets or card files; your card needs to fit.

For the most part, your business card should conform to your stationery in color, lettering, style, and information. For example, if your stationery has a logo, your business card should have the same logo. You can see examples of letterhead and business cards that match at the end of this chapter.

Creative business cards

I've gotten some unusual business cards over the years that didn't match the stationery. They worked!

✔ I saw a wonderful card from a lawyer. The card was a mini-legal pad (yellow with blue lines) with all the pertinent information. It was quite clever and I knew right away that the card came from a lawyer. His stationery was conventional — white with black lettering.

✔ I also saw a delightful, outlandish card in shocking pink from a design specialist. Not too many industries can get away with that, but it worked here. Her stationery was a lighter pink that complimented the card.

✔ Then I recall a business card from a landscape designer. The wallet-sized card was shaped and colored like a terra cotta flower pot; it really caught my eye at a home and garden show. The design on the card was also the logo on her letterhead.

Consider using the back side of your card for directions to your office, a pithy saying, appointments, or anything else you want recipients to know about you. Here's how I use the reverse side of my business card. Notice the page icons rather than bullets. After all, I am a writer.

🗐 *Marketing Communications*

🗐 *Documentation, User Manuals, and Reports*

🗐 *Video Productions*

🗐 *Business Writing and E-Mail Seminars*

🗐 *Annual Reports and Newsletters*

When a business card works better than a letter

Consider jotting a note on the back of your business card (instead of sending a letter) in situations such as these:

▸ **You're sending flowers as a thank you to a hostess**. You may write, *"Thanks for the wonderful dinner last night. Please enjoy these flowers. Bert"*

When in Rome . . . or Japan, that is!

I know this chapter is about design, but I'd feel remiss if I didn't include this tip on global savvy. When you're in a foreign country, find out whether there's a formality for giving out business cards. Ask someone who's visited the country on business or look in a guidebook. For example, here are some tips for distributing business cards in Japan:

1. Be certain your name, company name, and address appear in Japanese on the reverse side of your card. (*Meishi* [me-she] is the Japanese word for business card.)

2. After the initial introduction and bow, present your card.

3. Say, "*Watashi no meishi desu, Dozo.*" That means, "This is my business card, please."

4. After you present your card, bow once again.

Be prepared for a shower of business cards. If you attend a meeting with 30 people, you may exchange business cards with all 30.

As a little side note, if you receive a card from a senior-level Japanese businessman, it may have no title beneath his name. The blank space means everyone "should know" who he is. So don't even think of asking!

✔ **You're forwarding material such as a relevant magazine or newspaper article to someone.** Attach your business card and write, "*Perhaps this may be of interest. Regards, Jennifer*"

✔ **You're introducing a friend or colleague to a business associate.** Attach your business card to the person's resume and write, "*Donna Comeau may be a likely candidate for your MIS position. Here's her resume. Bill*"

When in doubt, hand it out

Always have plenty of business cards on hand, and offer them face up. If you're giving your card to someone in a non-English speaking country or to a visitor to this country who doesn't speak English, write your name, company, and address on the reverse side of the card in the language of the host country. Offer it with the native-language side showing.

I can still remember the pride I felt for my first business card, which I received while working as a technical writer for a small start-up computer company — my first job in the business world. I sent my new card to all of my friends and relatives to let them know that I had become someone of professional importance.

The Envelope, Please

The envelope should match the stationery in terms of quality and color. For example, if your stationery is white and the lettering is in block form, your envelopes should be white with lettering in block form.

To save costs, some companies skimp on the envelopes because envelopes usually wind up in the trash. I don't necessarily agree with doing that because the envelope is what invites the reader to look inside. It must be appealing and reflect the essence of the letterhead.

What goes where

The following envelope illustrates how the post office requests that you address your envelopes. This method of labeling makes it easier for the optical character readers (OCRs) to recognize names and addresses. Here are some suggestions for easy recognition:

✔ Type the address in block style — everything aligned at the left.

✔ Place special mailing notations under the stamp, and personal mailing notations under the return address. (Check out Chapter 3 for the scoop on personal and special mailing notations.)

✔ If the address has a suite number, put it next to the street address, and separate it with a comma.

✔ Use at least the five-digit ZIP code. (Use the nine-digit ZIP code, if you know it.)

Boulder Rocks, Inc.
233 Shard Blvd.
Talbotton, GA 31827-5423

STAMP

Personal

Registered Mail

Lester Strong, Esq.
One Robin Way, Suite 402
Bird In Hand, PA 17505-2344

When you send a letter overseas, be sure you put **U.S.A.** on your return address. If your letter gets lost in Outer Mongolia, the postal workers there may not know that Cairo, IN is part of the United States.

Fabulous folds

The most commonly used envelope size is the No. 10, which measures 4⅛ by 9½ inches. When a reader opens the envelope, he should open to the letterhead. Example 2-1 shows how to fold a letter for a No. 10 envelope.

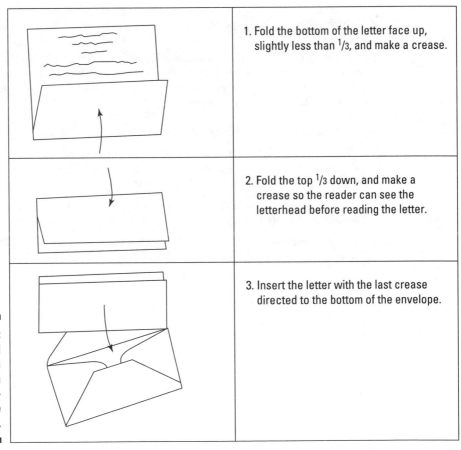

1. Fold the bottom of the letter face up, slightly less than $1/3$, and make a crease.

2. Fold the top $1/3$ down, and make a crease so the reader can see the letterhead before reading the letter.

3. Insert the letter with the last crease directed to the bottom of the envelope.

Example 2-1: Folding and inserting a letter into a No. 10 business-size envelope.

Example 2-2 shows how to fold a letter for a smaller envelope.

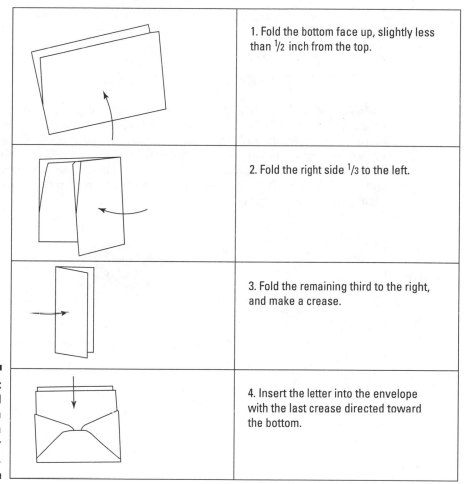

	1. Fold the bottom face up, slightly less than $1/2$ inch from the top.
	2. Fold the right side $1/3$ to the left.
	3. Fold the remaining third to the right, and make a crease.
	4. Insert the letter into the envelope with the last crease directed toward the bottom.

Example 2-2:
Folding and
inserting a
letter into a
smaller
envelope.

Check out Chapter 18 for U.S. Postal Service tips on sending letters nationally and internationally.

Sample Letterheads

Following are several examples of letterheads. In each, you can see how the design of the letterhead conveys an intended message to the reader.

Designing a better mousetrap

Marc A. Lindsell is a talented architect who uses the design of architectural vaults as his logo. The four vaults in the logo represent a progression of increased complexity and richness. Marc carries two of the vault elements onto the letterhead to create a "watermark" behind the text of his letters. Although the color of his letterhead isn't visible in the black and white version you see here, the unique design is in wine colors and is contrasted on cream-colored stationery.

561 Banks Street   San Francisco, California 94110-6111   Tel/Fax 415|826.5459   mlindsell@earthlink.net

This letterhead was designed by Jack Jackson, Square Peg Graphics, San Francisco, CA

Here's to your health

Dr. Eric Lindsell uses stick figures as his logo to highlight at a glance that Essential Family Chiropractic is a family practice. Dr. Lindsell doesn't include his name on the letterhead (but does on his business card) because he wants the letterhead to represent any of his staff members. Notice how Dr. Lindsell uses the back of his business card as an appointment card. A great use of space!

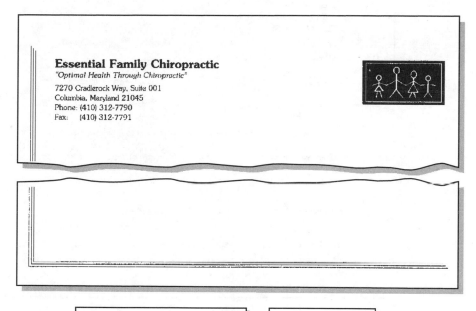

Feel the burn

The Aerobics Stop is a women's-only health club that uses the graceful swirls of its initials to replicate willowy body motions. The swirls are in deep pink, and the rest of the lettering is in aqua. You know at a glance that this is a women's-only health club for graceful (and not-so-graceful) women.

500 Boston Post Road • Marlboro, Massachusetts 01752 • (508) 481-4877

Location, location, location

Steve M. Tove, doing business as Noel-Lane/Retail, reflects his corporate real estate company by casting his logo as an A-shaped chalet-style home.

Going Dutch

Rick Manganello was stationed in Holland when he retired from the U.S. Air Force. When Rick was asked to do some consulting in Holland, he needed a company name. Rick had always been fascinated with windmills — "the science of draining a swamp without being eaten by alligators." Therefore, Windmill, International became an apt name for his Acquisition Management company, and the logo reflects the international flavor.

2 Robinson Road
Nashua, New Hampshire
03060-5830 USA
tel 603.888.5502
fax 603.888.5512

Fiscal fitness

Richard and Michael Hodge are a father-and-son team. Richard, a Certified Public Accountant, helps you stave off the IRS. Michael, a Certified Financial Planner, helps you invest what's left. They've chosen a very conservative letterhead, which reflects the traditional image of the financial world.

HODGE ASSOCIATES, Inc.
Richard L. Hodge, CPA
Michael J. Hodge, CFP, CLU

Income Tax Planning & Preparation
Retirement Planning
Financial Planning

291 Main Street
Northborough, MA 01532
(508) 393-8200 • Fax: (508) 393-3529

HODGE ASSOCIATES, INC.

Richard L. Hodge
Certified Public Accountant

291 Main Street
Northborough, MA 01532
rlhodgecpa@aol.com

(508) 393-8208
(800) 339-8208
Fax: (508) 393-3529

HODGE ASSOCIATES, INC.

Michael J. Hodge, CLU, ChFC
CERTIFIED FINANCIAL PLANNER

291 Main Street
Northborough, MA 01532
mjhodgecfp@aol.com

(508) 393-8208
(800) 339-8208
Fax: (508) 393-3529

1st GLOBAL CAPITAL Corp.

Securities offered through 1st Global Capital Corp. Member NASD, SIPC.
Investment Advisory Services offered through 1st Global Advisors, Inc.
8150 N. Central Expressway, Suite M-1000 Dallas, TX 75206
(800) 959-8440

Chapter 3

The ABC's of Letters

In This Chapter

▶ Fashioning the header

▶ Building a better body

▶ Signing off

All things began in order, so shall they end, and so shall they begin again. . . .

— Sir Thomas Browne, *On Dreams*

From the time we're born, we learn the natural order of things. We crawl before we walk. We wash our hands before we eat. We eat our meal before dessert. And we learn our ABC's before we read or write. Business letters also follow a natural order. First comes everything before the body, then the body, and, finally, everything after the body.

This chapter gives you the natural order of letters. Example 3-1, at the end of this chapter, lists all the possible parts of letters. (Although you'd probably never use all the parts in any one letter, you see where everything goes.)

This chapter gives many tips on the ABC's of e-mail messages. Always remember that e-mail messages are essentially letters; they need the same tender love and care.

Dating American Style

Every letter opens with a *date*. The horizontal position of the date line depends on the letter style you use. Check out Chapter 5 for the four styles of letters. Here are some tips for writing the date line:

✔ Use Arabic numerals (2, 1, 8), not ordinal numerals (2nd, 1st, 8th).

✔ Never abbreviate the month or use its numerical equivalent.

> ✔ Never spell out the year. (You do that only in formal invitations.)
>
> ✔ April 1, XXXX (not April 1st, XXXX; April 1st; or 4/1/XX).

People in Europe and in the military write the day first. People in Japan write the year first.

> 15 December XXXX (European or military style)
>
> XXXX December 15 (Japanese style)

Preparing the Carrier Pigeon

When you plan to send your letter using a special method of delivery, write the *mailing notation* (special delivery, certified mail, registered mail, air mail, by messenger) or *in-house notation* (personal, confidential) in all caps at the left margin two lines below the date.

The Insider

The *inside address* on your letter ultimately appears verbatim on the envelope. It consists of the addressee's name and title, company name, and full mailing address. Start the inside address at the left margin, four lines below the date line. If you're using a mailing notation or in-house notation, place the inside address two lines below the notation. Check out Example 3-1 at the end of this chapter for an example.

Naming names

The name and business title of the addressee goes on the first line of the inside address. Following are some things to keep in mind:

> ✔ If the person's name and title are short, place both on one line. Separate the name and title with a comma.
>
> > Mr. Patrick Jackson, Vice President
>
> ✔ If the name and title are long, break them into two lines and ditch the comma.
>
> > Ms. Mary Jane Mitchell-Jacobson
> > Manager of Human Resources

✔ If you don't know whether the addressee is a male or female, use the complete name only. For example, the first line of the inside address may read "Leslie Jackson, MIS Director."

Who signs the addressee's paycheck?

After the name and title of the addressee, include the company name. Treat the company name the way the company does. For example, if the company writes out the word *Corporation* or *Company*, you should, too. If the company uses "The" as part of its name, you should, too. Check the company's letterhead or Web site if you're unsure.

Is the company at 13 Elm Street?

The company address follows the company name on the next line. The list below shows you how to write the address portion of your letter:

✔ **Building number:** Don't precede the building number with the # sign. Use Arabic numbers for building numbers other than *One*.

> One Main Street

> 115 Smith Boulevard

✔ **Street name and/or post office box:** Use words for street numerals between one and ten. Use numerals for streets 11 and above, not ordinal endings — 1st, 2nd, and so on. And don't abbreviate the street directions (East, West, North, or South) unless you need to shorten a very long street name.

If you want your letter delivered to a post office box, place the box number underneath (or in place of) the street address.

> 222 North Fifth Avenue

> P.O. Box 4564

✔ **City and state:** Never abbreviate the name of the city, but always abbreviate the state with the two-letter state abbreviation. In the rare instance when you have no street name or post office box, put the city and state on separate lines. For easy reference, the state and territory abbreviations are on the Cheat Sheet in front of this book and in Appendix C.

✔ **ZIP code:** You must use at least the five-digit ZIP code on all addresses. The post office will soon be requiring you to use the additional four digits, which indicate the house number and street address.

May I have your attention please?

When you write to a specific person, using the standard form of address, rather than an attention line, is preferable. Save an attention line for the rare occasions when the addressee is a company or department and you want the letter directed to a specific person. For example, it's the end of August (heavy vacation season) and you want to send a letter to the Bandrell Company. You'd like your issue brought to the attention of the Manager of Customer Relations. If the manager is on vacation, however, someone else in the company may handle your issue and not wait until the manager returns.

Type the attention line at the left margin and use any of the following styles:

ATTENTION SALLY MITCHELL

Attention Vice President of Purchasing

Att: MIS Department

Here are two ways to sequence the attention line. The choice is yours.

Marlborough Arts League
100 Spruce Street
Montezuma, KA 67867

Att: Bev Rinck

Marlborough Arts League
ATTENTION BEV RINCK
100 Spruce Street
Montezuma, KA 67867

Greetings and Salutations

The *salutation* is a greeting — a way of saying "hello" to the reader. Place it two lines below the address, flush with the left margin. The salutation corresponds directly to the first line of the inside address. For example, if Ms. Jane Smith is the addressee, the salutation is Dear Ms. Smith. If the Human Resources Manager is the addressee, the salutation is Dear Human Resources Manager.

Forms of address

Check out Chapter 17 for proper forms of address in different walks of life. Here are some quick tips for saying "hello" to your reader:

✔ Avoid the cold and impersonal salutations *To Whom This May Concern* or *Dear Sir or Madam*. Instead, try to find the name of the person you're writing to. If you can't, use the person's job title (*Dear MIS Director:*).

- Use *Ms.* as the courtesy title for females. If the woman is a doctor or high ranking official, use her specific title.

- Use *The Honorable* for elected officials, judges, and other high-ranking people.

- When you're writing to more than one person of the same sex, use the French plurals — *Messrs.* for males and *Mmes.* for females (*Dear Messrs. Hahn:*).

- If you can't determine the sex of the person you're writing to, the salutation may be *Dear Pat Jenkins.*

To personalize the salutation, say "hello" in the addressee's native tongue. For example, if you write to Jergen Lehnert in Germany, *Dear Herr Lehnert:* is a nice touch. (*Dear* is recognized internationally.)

A matter of style

The salutation has its own punctuation style. Here are a few tips for using punctuation correctly. (See Chapter 18 for specifics.)

- Capitalize the first word of the addressee's name or title.

- End with a colon when you address the person by her last name.

- End with a comma when you know the reader well enough to use her first name.

- Write out titles unless you use *Mr., Ms.,* and *Dr.*

Etta Kitt (the netiquette guru) in my book *Business Writing For Dummies* (IDG Books Worldwide, Inc.) tells you to start each e-mail message with a salutation. If you're writing to a group, "Hello Everyone:" is a nice touch. According to Miss Kitt, "People who don't start [e-mail messages] with a greeting are the same ones who come into the office and bark out orders before they remove their coats."

While We're on the Subject

The *subject line* expresses the theme of the letter. Sometimes it can deliver the message itself, such as in the following examples. (Check out Chapter 4 for a full discussion of how to deliver subject lines with impact.) Place the subject line two lines below the salutation, capitalizing the first letter of each key word.

Although each of the following subject lines has a different style, notice how each tells the story:

> SUBJECT: Agenda for February 5 seminar

> Subject: New Rate Schedule Effective Immediately

> Subject: 15% Profit Expected for Next Year

In an e-mail message, the subject line is the *most important* part of your message. It's the reader's first and only clue as to what your message is about. If the subject line doesn't jump off the screen and shout "read me!" the reader may not open your message. Check out Chapter 4 for ways to make your e-mail subject lines seductive.

Body Beautiful

The *body* supports the theme of the message. You may expect this section to be longer than the others in this chapter because the body is the longest part of a letter. The body, however, differs greatly from one letter to another so this is just to show you where it fits into the natural order of a letter. (Part III deals with the body of letters for a wide variety of occasions.)

Single space the body of the letter, double space between paragraphs, and use headlines to introduce your paragraphs. For more information about writing paragraphs that have visual appeal, check out Chapter 5.

In this chapter, I mention using headlines to focus on the essence of your message and take your reader through the key issues. Although you may not be accustomed to using headlines in letters, memos, and e-mails, companies who want their messages to stand out use them.

Here are some suggestions for breaking down the body and using headlines:

✔ **Make the *opening paragraph* relatively short.** The opening paragraph introduces the reason for the letter. Use a headline to sum up the opening paragraph. When your letter is short (one or two paragraphs), your subject line may serve as the headline.

> **Insulating older homes**

> Our research staff has successfully solved the problem of insulating older homes, which you asked about in your May 10 letter.

✔ **Support the *opening paragraph* with one or more supporting paragraphs.** Use a headline to stress each idea.

We'll be in your area the week of February 18

If you'd like to see our line of new personal computers, we'll be at the Personal Computer Trade Show. It runs from February 18 to 23 at the Newbury Trade Center. Please stop by and say "hello."

✔ Make the *final paragraph* short. It serves as a summation, request, suggestion, or look to the future. Headlines such as *Next Step* or *Action Requested* let the reader know at a glance what, if anything, she should do.

Action Requested

If you'd like to take advantage of this order, please sign the enclosed form and return it to me in the enclosed envelope.

One of the hot things about word processing programs is that you can key in standard paragraphs that you use frequently and retrieve them when you need them. These are known as *boilerplates*. (Check out your software's user manual for the "how to's.") You can keep your boilerplates from sounding cold and impersonal by inserting information that's applicable to your reader.

The body of an e-mail message is equivalent to the body of a letter. Unless your e-mail message is a let's-do-lunch note to a close friend, treat it with the same respect as a letter. E-mail is a serious communications tool!

Roger and Out

Just as the salutation says "hello" to the reader, the *complimentary closing* says "good-bye." Always type the closing two lines below the last line of the body. Capitalize only the first letter of the first word of the closing and end with a comma. (Check out Chapter 5 for where to place the complimentary closing horizontally; it depends on the style of the letter you use.) Consider these good-byes:

Formal closing: Yours truly, Very truly yours, Yours very truly, Respectfully, Respectfully yours,

Informal closing: Sincerely, Sincerely yours, Cordially, Cordially yours,

Personal closing: Best wishes, As always, Regards, Kindest regards,

You wouldn't hang up the phone without saying "good-bye" to the person at the other end, so don't end e-mail messages without saying good-bye to your reader. End e-mail messages with a complimentary closing. Because e-mail messages are generally less formal than letters, people tend to keep the closings personal.

Here's another way to add a personal touch. Say "good-bye" to the addressee in her native tongue. Why not use *Shalom* for someone in Israel, *Hasta luego* for someone in a Spanish-speaking country, and *Auf wiedersehen* for someone in Germany?

Don't Forget Your John Hancock

It's amazing how many people send letters and forget to sign them; don't be one of them. To prepare your *signature block,* type your name and title in the block format. Following are guidelines that apply to all signature blocks:

- Leave four to five lines for your signature, depending on the size of your handwriting.
- Don't forget your John Hancock (your signature).

Sincerely yours,

Jack Spratt

Jack Spratt, Treasurer

Sincerely yours,

SPRATT & RATT, INC.

Jack Spratt

Jack Spratt, Treasurer

 If you forget to sign your name, your reader may wonder. . . .

- Was this merely an oversight or did you forget to take your daily dose of ginkgo biloba?
- Do you often forget critical things such as deadlines and your mother's birthday?

 Most e-mail programs let you set up a *signature file* that automatically adds your signature to the end of the messages you send. You may also include your telephone number, fax number, or any other contact information you want the reader to know. If you can't figure out how to set up a signature file, check with a guru at your company or look on the Help screen.

Reference Initials

If someone other than the writer prepares the letter, use *reference initials* to identify the typist. Place the initials at the left margin, two lines below the signature block. You can use any of the following styles or combinations. In each example, ARC is the typist:

BSmith/arc   BS:arc

BS/arc   BS:ARC

Stuffing the Envelope

When you're enclosing anything in the envelope, include an *enclosure notation* on the letter itself. Place the enclosure notation on the line directly below the reference initials. (Check out Chapter 2 to see the proper ways to fold letters for different size envelopes.)

When you enclose checks, receipts, or the like, staple or clip them so they don't fall out when the reader opens the envelope. Consider typing the word *Attachment* instead of *Enclosure*. You may use any of the following styles:

Enclosure	1 Enc.
Attachments: 2	Encls.
Enc. (2)	Enclosures:
	1. Check no. 345
	2. P.O. No. 3456-23456

You're Not the Only One Getting This

When you send a copy of the letter to a third person, make a notation directly below the enclosure notation (or reference initials). The *cc* notation is a holdover from the days when people made carbon copies and sent them with eraser crumbs. Today, *cc* is known as *courtesy copy*. You can also use *pc* for *photocopy*. If you don't want the addressee to know you're sending a copy to a third party, use *bc* for *blind copy*.

Use the bc notation sparingly because it clearly indicates that you're going behind someone's back. Place the bc notation on the *office copy* and *third-party copy only*, otherwise it's no secret from the addressee. You can use any of these styles for either of these notations:

pc: Vic Torian	bc: Vic Torian
CC Vic Torian	Copy to: Vic Torian

P.S. By the Way . . .

A *postscript* is a wonderful way to emphasize something you didn't include in the body of the letter, such as *Remember that our one-day sale is on May 12.* If you write the postscript in your own handwriting, it has even more impact. Place postscripts at the left margin two lines below your last notation.

Use postscripts sparingly because you don't want the words to appear as an afterthought, indicating a lack of organization.

Brian & Jill, Incorporated
11737 Ferrick Lane, Lakewood, NJ 08701-2344
(908) 234-5654

December 27, XXXX Date

PERSONAL In-house notation

Ms. Dawne Roberts
Columbia Housing Association Inside address
One Cradlerock Way
Spring Valley, NY 10977

Dear Ms. Roberts: Salutation

Subject: Letter of recommendation for Eric Laurence Subject line

It's with great pleasure that I write this letter on behalf of Eric
Laurence. He was employed by me as a Contracts Manager for five
years and left to pursue his Master's Degree full time. We told Eric
that the position would be waiting for him when he finished, but he
now wants to pursue opportunities with a larger company.

I'm enclosing a copy of an award Eric received while he was with us.
Eric is a person of the highest integrity, who works efficiently and
tirelessly to get the job done. He's creative and delightful to work
with. You'd be most fortunate to have him join your staff.

Body

Sincerely, Complimentary closing

Anna Katherine Boucher Signature line

AKB/stl Reference initials
Enclosure Enclosure notation
cc: Eric Laurence Copy notation

P.S. Please send Eric my warmest regards. Postscript

Example 3-1:
It's unlikely
you'd use all
these parts
in one letter.
This is just
to show
you where
they go in
the natural
order
of letters.

Part II

Writing Persuasive Letters

The 5th Wave   By Rich Tennant

Dear SIR
Thankyou FO
TAKING The
time Jr

"Hey kid – dis is one nice business letter. I think you're the type of guy we can work with."

In this part . . .

No longer do you have to wrack your brain trying to write a letter. The Six Steps in this part walk you through the tried-and-tested writing process thousands of people rave about. The Six Steps include:

1. Getting started

2. Creating headlines and strategic sequencing for impact

3. Writing the draft

4. Designing for visual appeal

5. Honing the tone

6. Proofreading and editing.

This part even focuses on the three things you need to identify before you start to write: your audience, purpose, and key issue(s).

Chapter 4

Getting into High Gear

In This Chapter

▶ Karate chopping your way through writer's block

▶ Identifying your audience, purpose, and key issue

▶ Asking the "write" questions

▶ Crafting dynamic headlines and subject lines

▶ Sequencing to affect your reader as you wish

▶ Drafting the letter

Success is not a doorway; it's a stairway.

— Dottie Walters, speaker, agent, and writer

Masterful letter writers aren't born, they're developed. Like anything else, writing is a process — approached one step at a time. After you learn the Six Steps outlined in this chapter and Chapter 5, writing is actually quite simple. Participants in my workshops often ask, "Can anyone learn to write great letters?" My answer is unequivocally "Yes."

Determining Your Letter Writing IQ

We all have preconceived ideas about what it takes to be a great business letter writer. Test your knowledge of business letter writing and answer the following questions:

	True	False
1. Writing a business letter is difficult.	❏	❏
2. Just about anyone can write business letter.	❏	❏
3. Business letters are dull no matter how you cut it.	❏	❏

Answers

1. **Writing a business letter is difficult.** *False*. When you plan properly using the Six Steps, writing business letters is actually a piece of cake. It's somewhat akin to taking a car trip across the U.S. If you don't plan your trip, you drive around and around without a clear idea of where you're going. The key word is "plan."

2. **Just about anyone can write a business letter.** *True*. The trick in this question comes in the wording. Anyone can write a business letter, but how many people write letters that drive action and get the results they want? The real answer is that anyone can *learn* to write effective business letters. When you plan, you *do* drive action and *do* get the results you want.

3. **Business letters are dull no matter how you cut it.** *False*. Perhaps some people who write business letters are dull, but the letters themselves can avoid this fate. With the proper planning, you can write letters that are energized and interesting.

Planning is the hallmark of effective letter writing. By following this tried-and-tested Six-Step Process, writing business letters is a snap.

This chapter explains the first three steps of energized letter writing:

Step 1: Getting started

Step 2: Writing headlines and strategic sequencing

Step 3: Writing the draft

Chapter 5 explains the final three steps of energized letter writing:

Step 4: Designing for visual impact

Step 5: Honing the tone

Step 6: Proofreading and editing

To make this chapter and the next truly meaningful, think of a letter, memo, or e-mail message you need to write. Follow the Six Steps and learn while you lighten your in-box.

Step 1: Getting Started

Everyone suffers from writer's block at some time. You sit and stare at a blank piece of paper or computer screen hoping something materializes. Even the prolific writer Mark Twain had trouble getting started. At the end of each day, he'd leave one sentence unfinished so that when he sat down for his next day's writing session, there would be a point from which to begin. Step 1 gives you several ways to karate chop your way through writer's block — quickly and simply.

As a professional writer, I never commit one word to my computer until I've identified these three critical elements — my audience, purpose, and key issue. These elements must be crystal clear in my mind in order for me to write a clear message to my reader.

Using the Start Up Sheet

The Start Up Sheet walks you through these three elements, plus something else to consider — the best method of delivery.

- **Audience:** Is my reader a butcher, baker, or candlestick maker?
- **Purpose:** What's my real motive?
- **Key Issue:** If my reader remembers only one thing, what should that be?
- **Delivery**: What's the best way to deliver this message?

For each letter you write, fill out a Start Up Sheet like the one that follows. After the first time, filling out the sheet only takes you a few minutes and makes you wonder how you ever lived without it. You can find a copy of the Start Up Sheet on the Cheat Sheet in the front of this book. Keep it handy for all your letters, memos, and e-mail messages.

You get more out of the Start Up Sheet if you relate it to a particular letter, memo, or e-mail message you need to write. Here's how I suggest you proceed:

1. **Read through the following Start Up Sheet.** Don't attempt to answer any of the questions yet.

2. **Read the explanations that follow the Start Up Sheet.** They offer useful clues to get you into high gear.

3. **Fill out the Start Up Sheet.** Answer each question as it relates to your letter, memo, or e-mail message.

Start Up Sheet

Audience

1. Who's my primary reader? Do I have multiple readers?

2. What does my reader *need to know* about the topic?

3. What's in it for my reader?

4. Does my writing need a special *angle* or *point of view?* (Technical? Other?)

5. What's my reader's attitude toward the topic?

Purpose

6. My purpose is to _____ so my reader will _____.

Key Issue

7. What's the one *key point* I want my reader to remember?

Delivery

8. Who should receive a copy of this message?

9. What's the best way to deliver this message? Hard copy? E-mail? Fax? Phone? Personal meeting? Other?

10. When is the best time to deliver this message? When is too early? When is too late?

Understanding the Start Up Sheet

Here are the questions on the Start Up Sheet broken out in detail:

1. Who is my primary reader? Do I have multiple readers?

Why is it so easy to send a letter to someone you know well? Because you know his preconceived ideas, level of expertise, probable reaction to your message, reaction to slang or jargon, and so on.

When you send a letter to someone you don't know, try to imagine that you actually do know him. Close your eyes and ask yourself these questions. What color eyes and hair does he have? How is he dressed? Try to make him real, even if you have to invent him. Don't write to a faceless person.

If you write to multiple readers, rank them in order of seniority. Ask yourself this question: "Who is my primary reader and who will take action on the basis of this message?" Then write to that person.

E-mail messages are often sent to groups of people, so the tone must be appropriate for all your readers in the United States and abroad. Check out Chapter 5 for tips on honing the tone when writing to people outside the United States.

2. What does my reader need to know about the topic?

Think of what your reader needs to know — not what he already knows. You don't want to give too much or too little information. Consider these questions:

- What is his level of knowledge about the subject?
- What preconceived ideas does he have?
- What are the barriers to his understanding?
- What about his style of dealing with situations should drive your tone or content? (You'll learn about tone in Chapter 5.)

3. What's in it for my reader?

When you receive a message, you mentally ask yourself, "What's in it for me?" Your reader asks that same question. Maybe what's in it for him is an opportunity to make his job easier, to look good to his superiors, to be more knowledgeable, to propel his career, or to jump on a wonderful opportunity. Make it clear what's in it for him!

4. Does my writing need a special angle or point of view?

You determine the point of view by understanding the needs of your reader. Managers, for example, are big-picture people. They want to know the key issue. Technical types want the details.

5. What's my reader's attitude toward the topic?

You may not always tell the reader what he wants to hear, but you must tell him what he needs to know. Will his reaction be responsive, neutral, or unresponsive? Your reader's reaction determines the way you present (sequence) your message. (Step 2 talks about sequencing.)

- **Responsive:** You're telling him he's getting a promotion or won a free trip to Tahiti.
- **Neutral:** His magazine subscription is about to expire.
- **Unresponsive:** He's relegated to the midnight to noon shift.

6. My purpose is to _____ so my reader will _____.

Whether you think your purpose is to communicate, inform, sell, or whatever, chances are you're trying to persuade the reader to do something. More letters are written to persuade than for any other purpose. Do you want the reader to refund your money, send a check, write a new lease, stop the shipment, or do nothing? When your reader knows exactly what action you expect, he can digest your message more intelligently. Following are examples of writing to persuade:

✔ Are you writing to let your reader know his warranty has expired? Or are you trying to persuade him to extend his warranty because that's where you make your money?

✔ Are you writing to disallow a claim for a medical procedure? Or are you trying to persuade the reader that your reason is valid and he should continue to be a loyal customer?

The Greek philosop er Aristotle — one of the first people to write about persuasion — said that if you want to win people over, you must state your case in their *thoughts*, their *beliefs*, and their *attitudes*. That process is what mimicking is all about. People are more likely to accept messages that mimic what's already in their heads.

7. What's the one key point I want my reader to remember?

Business readers want the key issue, so they can get to the point immediately. Put on your advertising hat. Pretend you have to write a 15-second commercial. If your reader forgets everything else, what one key point should he remember? Thinking about this very carefully is critical.

8. Who should receive a copy of this message?

Are you copying people because they need to see the message or is this for CYA purposes? (You know, cover your anatomy.)

In an e-mail environment this decision must be thought through carefully because people have a tendency to press the *Send* button, delivering copies to everyone in the immediate world. With everyone screaming about information overload, be considerate and send messages only to people who need them, just as you would with a letter or memo. If you send people only the information they need to do their jobs well and don't contribute to their overload, they'll approach anything you send with respect. Chapter 19 is chock-full of tips for using your e-mail effectively.

E-mail is not for emergencies!

This past winter my husband was working on a research project and was sequestered (like Igor) in his lab. An unexpected ice blizzard hit, threatening to immobilize the area. The president of my husband's company sent an e-mail message to everyone announcing that they should leave work immediately before the roads became too treacherous. My husband, who was oblivious to the situation, remained in his lab for several more hours.

When he finally emerged, everyone was gone, the phones were out, and the parking lot was so slippery he couldn't get to his car. (I won't go in to the anxiety I experienced not knowing where he was; suffice it to say my hair is a lot grayer than it was.) Luckily, the vending machines at his office were stocked with chocolate candy so he didn't go hungry.

The moral of the tale is simple: *Don't use e-mail for emergency situations.* You can't assume people will read the message in time. If the company president had made the announcement on the loudspeaker, everyone would have known to leave — including my beloved.

9. What's the best way to deliver this message?

Consider the best method of delivery. Is it by letter, memo, e-mail message, fax, in person, by phone, at a meeting, or some other way? Use your judgment as to the best way to deliver your message.

I recently received an e-mail message from a woman, asking me to attend a meeting at 9:00 the following morning. She sent the message at 6:30 in the afternoon, and I had already turned off my computer for the day. The following morning when I downloaded my e-mail, there was the message. It was too late for me to attend the meeting, which was one hour from my home. If the woman had telephoned me, rather than sending an e-mail message, I would have made arrangements to attend the meeting. This is a typical example of how people use e-mail messages incorrectly.

E-mail doesn't always substitute for telephoning or making personal contact any more than frozen food substitutes for naturalness and nutrition. Don't forget to talk to people face to face or call them on the phone when it's appropriate.

10. When is the best time to deliver this message?

Timing is everything. Think about how much time you would need to react to the message. Give the reader that much time.

Putting on your reporter's hat

By filling out the Start Up Sheet, you take the first step toward writing your letter, memo, or e-mail message. Now, think like a newspaper reporter. They use the *who, what, when, where, why,* and *how* approach to guide them through stories. (Who needs to act? What action should they take?) The answers to these questions provide the information the reader needs to know.

Of course, not all the questions apply to your letter, so decide which satisfy your reader's needs. Be sure the answers to your questions are specific, not vague. Following are a few examples:

When? What?

> **Specific:** Please send us the June issue of *SCIENCE* magazine by December 1.

> **Vague:** Please send us the June issue of *SCIENCE* magazine ASAP. (As soon as possible isn't a date. If you want results by a certain date, be sure to state it.)

Who?

> **Specific:** Feel free to call Glen Richards, manager of our MIS Department, if you have any questions.

> **Vague:** Please feel free to call the manager of our MIS Department if you have any questions. (Does he have a name?)

How much?

> **Specific:** You can buy our software for just $398, which is 15 percent less than our competitor's price.

> **Vague:** Our software is less expensive than our competitor's.

Where?

> **Specific:** I'll be in Washington, D.C. next week. Can you meet me there?

> **Vague:** I'll be in Washington next week. Can you meet me there? (Washington is also a state.)

When? Where?

> **Specific:** The monthly staff meeting will be on Monday, June 3, from 1:30 to 2:30, in the Delta room.

> **Vague:** The meeting will be on June 2 from 1:30 to 2:30. (Which meeting? Where will the meeting be?)

After you fill out the Start Up Sheet and answer the questions your reader will have, you're ready to prepare your headlines and sequence them for maximum impact.

Step 2: Writing Headlines and Strategic Sequencing

Headlines are powerful! Notice how newspapers and magazines use headlines to tell the story and direct the reader's eye to what's important. Companies apply the power of dynamic headlines to their business letters. Here's how both the reader and the writer benefit from headlines:

- *As a writer*, you direct your reader's attention to what's important and control the flow of information.

- *As a reader*, you get the gist of the message and find key information at a glance.

Crafting attention-getting headlines

The subject line in a letter, memo, or e-mail message is the most important headline that you write. It gives your reader the big picture. Look at question 7 on your Start Up Sheet: "What's the one *key point* I want my reader to remember?" Why not make your subject line the reader's key issue? Here are a few examples of subject lines that integrate their key issues:

> **Subject:** Sales soar 25%
>
> **Subject:** Yes, we can honor your request
>
> **Subject:** Staff meeting 2/15 in Room 100 at noon

In an e-mail message, the subject line gives your reader the *only* clue as to what the message is about; therefore, it must be seductive. If the subject line fails to grab the reader's attention, the message may sit in his in-box for all eternity.

Perhaps you're not accustomed to seeing headlines used in letters beyond the subject line. However, I've started to look carefully at the mail I receive and notice that more and more companies are including headlines in their letters. If you want to get your point across, you should use headlines also.

Following are both basic and expanded headlines. Although both serve as headlines, which ones give the reader information he needs to know? These are just a few of many headlines that add punch to a letter. Feel free to use these basic headlines and expand them to get your message across at a glance.

Basic headline:	*Expanded headline:*
Action requested	Action requested: Please fill out the questionnaire
Action required	Action required: Send your check immediately
Deadline	Deadline: June 15
Next step	Next step: Please call us
Meeting information	Meeting information:
	Date: Monday, October 15
	Time: 3 to 5 PM
	Place: Room 333

Sequencing headlines for maximum impact

Being mindful of where to put your key issue is one of your challenges as a writer. The secret to effective communication is to sequence your ideas for maximum impact. It's critical to put yourself in the reader's shoes to understand how he'll react to your message. Question 5 in the Start Up Sheet asks: What's my reader's attitude towards the topic? Is my reader responsive, neutral, or unresponsive? The following examples explain how to sequence your information, based on the reader's likely reaction:

- ✔ For a *responsive or neutral reader,* put the key issue at the beginning of your letter. Perhaps the key issue can serve as the subject line.
- ✔ For an *unresponsive reader,* cushion the key issue between buffers — a positive opening and friendly closing.

The next two sections take you through sequencing strategies for two different scenarios — being the bearer of good news and sequencing for bad news.

Being the bearer of good news

When the reader is responsive, the message is easy to write because everyone likes to be the bearer of good news. Your message is also easy to write when the reader is neutral, because you're giving information the reader may find useful. So, when you sequence a good-news message, focus on the primary piece of information the reader needs to know. Why hide it?

✔ **Be direct and to the point.** Briefly expand the main topic in terms of who, what, when, where, and how. If your reader needs background information, perhaps you should include it in the opening paragraph.

✔ **Include the necessary details in the supporting paragraph(s).** Address the supporting issues in whatever order they make sense for your reader. Think of the questions in the order in which your reader will ask them.

✔ **End on a friendly, positive note.** Conclude with a sentence or two stressing your appreciation, your willingness to help further, the next step, and so on.

Don't shoot the messenger

Sometimes you have to send distressing information, offer a compromise, or just say "No." You need special planning if you have to disappoint your reader. You intend to keep the customer (or client) happy while sending unfavorable information.

Following are a few tips for letting the reader down gently:

✔ **Create a buffer.** You're trying to persuade the reader that your news is fair, even if it's not what he wants to hear. Following are some tactful openings that don't hit the reader between the eyes:

> We agree with you.
>
> Thank you for bringing this to our attention.
>
> You have an excellent record.
>
> We're happy to grant part of your request.

✔ **Put yourself in the reader's shoes:** Include honest, convincing reasons why you can't grant the reader's request. Consider some of these positive-sounding expressions:

> This is how we may help you. . . .
>
> With your best interests in mind. . . .
>
> Won't you accept this as a substitute?
>
> May we offer this suggestion?

✔ **End on a friendly, positive note.** Your intention is to maintain goodwill and keep the reader as a customer. Here are a few suggestions:

> You're a valued customer.
>
> Won't you try. . . . (Offer a sales promotion if you think it's appropriate).
>
> We look forward to helping you the next time.

Twisted headlines

Have you ever noticed errors in the headlines of major newspapers? Here are some classics:

"Two Convicts Evade Noose: Jury Hung"

— Oakland Tribune (CA)

"Six New Families to be Connected to Sewer"

— Clinton Morning Times (OK)

"Doctor Compiles List of Poisons Children May Try at Home"

— Buffalo Times (NY)

"Avoid Having Baby at Dinner Table"

— Minneapolis Daily Herald (MN)

"Illinois Man Pulls Needle from Foot He Swallowed 66 Years Ago"

— Greenville Democratic Times (MS)

"Case of Stolen Whiskey Expected to Go to Jury"

— New Brunswick (NJ) Sunday Home News

Here are just a few more thoughts:

- ✔ **Take caution when you're the bearer of bad news.** Consider eliminating the subject line or using a neutral one such as a claim number.

- ✔ **Don't cite company rules.** Company policies won't soothe the reader. Customer-benefit reasons will.

After you write your headlines and sequence them for maximum impact, you're ready to write the draft.

Step 3: Writing the Draft

You probably expect this step to be long and cumbersome because that's how you view drafting a letter. However, this is where your planning in Steps 1 and 2 pays off. You should be able to write your draft by filling in the blanks below your headlines.

A draft isn't a finished letter. It's a first pass — your initial thoughts. The draft is your chance to express yourself without being critical of anything you write. You polish your letter later, as outlined in Steps 4, 5, and 6 in Chapter 5. Your task right now is to transfer your thoughts from your head to the computer (or paper.) Get all your information down.

Before you begin

Don't wait for inspiration. Perhaps these suggestions will help you get started:

- ✔ **Create a comfortable environment.** If possible, create an environment that encourages concentration. If you try to write between phone calls and walk-in visitors, you'll be distracted. It takes time to reorganize your thoughts after each interruption. Everybody has a different comfort level. What's yours?

    Do you work best with or without music?

    Is the lighting good for you?

    Do you like to snack on munchies?

    Do you like to kick off your shoes?

- ✔ **Gather your materials together.** When you stop to look for things, it breaks your concentration.

- ✔ **Set time limits for yourself.** Set reasonable and attainable time limits for yourself based on the time you have available. Your goal can be to write for 15–30 minutes or to expand one or two headlines. Write continually until your goal is met, no matter how good or bad your writing seems to be. The point is to keep writing.

Writing the draft

After your environment is comfortable and you've gathered all your stuff, you're ready to begin drafting. Look at questions 1 and 2 on your Start Up Sheet. "Who's my primary reader?" and "What does my reader need to know about the topic?" Keep in mind your assessment of the reader's background, knowledge, and preconceptions to include only those facts he needs to know. Get ready, on your mark, get set, go! Begin writing your draft:

- ✔ **Start expanding one headline at a time.** Start with the headline that seems easiest. Don't worry about starting at the beginning. (Your reader will never know where you started.) After you finish the easiest headline, move to the second easiest, and continue until you meet your allotted time.

- ✔ **Keep writing.** Avoid the temptation to go back over what you wrote. The important thing is to keep moving. If you can't think of the right word, use another word and keep going. Or leave a blank space and fill it in later.

If you're drafting on a computer, consider darkening your monitor so you're not distracted by typos. However, be certain you fingers are on the right keys or you'll wind up with gibberish.

If you're on a roll, don't stop. On the other hand, if you're on overload, stop or take a break. (This may be a good time to pop some popcorn or munch on a carrot stick.)

Getting distance from your draft

After you finish writing the draft, get some distance. It's difficult to be objective about your writing when you're too close to it. It would be nice to put your draft down for a day or two and revisit it later, if you have that much time. Following are some tips for taking a 10–15 minute break — even when you're pressed for time:

- Go for a short walk.
- Get a cup of coffee.
- Make a quick phone call.
- Pat yourself on the back.
- Complete another brief task.

Returning to action

After a reprieve, revisit your draft. (You're still not ready to edit; that's Step 6.) Ask yourself these questions:

- **Are my headlines informative?** Do they tell the story? If not, how can I pump them up?

    Informative: New interest rates are 7.6%

    Uninformative: Announcing new interest rate

- **Did I use paragraphs appropriately?** A paragraph is a grouping of sentences that develops a single idea in support of a headline. Limit paragraphs to *no more than seven lines* (not sentences, lines). Each paragraph starts with a *topic sentence* that supplies the direction of the sentences to follow.

- **Did I explain the problem or situation clearly?** Your wording must be clear so the reader understands the significance of the problem, solution, or conclusion.

    Clear: Mr. Smith and Mr. Jones won't be able to attend the meeting together. Mr. Jones will be in Arizona that week.

    Unclear: Mr. Smith and Mr. Jones won't be able to attend the meeting together. He'll be in Arizona that week. (Which one?)

✔ **Should I re-sequence?** After you write the draft, you may want to re-sequence some of your headlines and paragraphs for greater impact.

> Do the headlines tell the story?

> Do the paragraphs support the headlines?

> Did you cushion bad news?

✔ **Does the reader need background information?** Most backgrounds are dull, and people don't read them. Refer to question 2 on your Start Up Sheet, "What does the reader *need* to know?" Include only the information the reader needs to know — not information he already knows.

✔ **Did I provide closure?** Look at question 6 on your Start Up Sheet, "My purpose is to _____ so my reader will _____." Exactly what do you want the reader to do? The action item may be for the writer to do something specific, to wait for your action, or to do nothing. Whatever the action item is, make it clear. Consider expanding a headline such as *Action Requested* or *Next Step*.

When you finish your rough draft, you're ready to polish your text. Chapter 5 shows you how to give your letter visual impact, hone the tone, and proofread like a pro.

Chapter 5

Adding Spit and Polish

· ·

In This Chapter
▶ Looking elegant on paper
▶ Building instant rapport with your reader
▶ Blotting out mistakes

· ·

The difference between the almost right *word and the* right *word is really a large matter — 'tis the difference between the lightning-bug and the lightning.*

— Mark Twain, *The Art of Authorship*

Okay. You've gone through Chapter 4. (Or at least I certainly hope you have because it offers the three steps to getting your writing into high gear.) Here's quick recap:

1. You filled out the Start Up Sheet and identified your audience, purpose, and key issue. You also answered the questions your reader may have.

2. You wrote an attention-getting subject line and headlines that tell your story. Then you sequenced them for the reaction of your reader.

3. You developed the draft, which was a piece of cake after having completed Steps 1 and 2.

But don't stop there! You're already in high gear; now you need to polish what you wrote. Your letter, memo, or e-mail message must have visual impact and a conversational tone that "talks" to your reader. It must also be free from sticky-wicket blunders.

Step 4: Designing for Visual Impact

When your letter, memo, or e-mail message has visual impact, it attracts attention, invites readership, and establishes the credibility of your message. Visual impact organizes your letter by breaking the message into bite-sized chunks of information. It also lets the reader see at a glance what's important. Visual impact includes white space, letter style, bulleted and numbered lists, graphics, and a whole lot more.

It's a frame up

Every letter should have ample *white space,* which includes all areas on the page where there's neither type nor graphics. (White space doesn't have to be white. If your stationery is ivory, gray, tan, or electric green — that's white space.) Here are some tips for using white space effectively:

- ✔ Use no less than 1- to 1½-inch margins on the top, bottom, and sides. These margins create a visual frame around the text and graphics.

- ✔ Limit paragraphs to five or seven lines. (That's lines, not sentences.) Double space between each paragraph.

- ✔ Place the parts of your letter according to the guidelines outlined in Chapter 3.

Although e-mail messages don't have margins around the text, allow for ample white space by keeping the paragraph length between five and seven lines of print. Use headlines to break up the text and tell your story. And use bulleted and numbered lists, when appropriate. (These elements appear later in Step 4.)

A matter of style

Choosing a *letter style* is a big step in delivering your message because it may be an indication of how "fashionable" your company is. The examples that follow show you the four most popular letter styles:

- ✔ **Full block:** The full block letter, shown in Example 5-1, is quickly becoming the style of choice in the modern office. Everything starts at the left margin, so there's no need to set tabs or wonder where to put the date and complimentary closing. This letter style is efficient, businesslike, and very popular.

✔ **Block (or modified block):** The block style, shown in Example 5-2, is quite similar to the full block style. The key difference is that the date and complimentary closing are slightly to the right of center, so you have to tab over. Everything else is flush with the left margin. The block style is very traditional and quite popular. Because this letter style has traditionally been the most commonly used, it's the one most people are comfortable seeing and using.

✔ **Semiblock:** The semiblock style, shown in Example 5-3, is quite similar to the block style. The key difference is that the paragraphs are indented one tab stop. Therefore, you need to use two tabs: one for the indented paragraphs and one for the date and complimentary closing. This is also a familiar-looking style and people are comfortable with it. It is, however, playing second fiddle to the full block or block styles. Many people consider this style somewhat dated.

✔ **Simplified:** The simplified letter, shown in Example 5-4, is quite streamlined. Although not commonly used, it is expected to become more popular because it's the least time-consuming to write of all the letter styles. If you use this letter style, remember these guidelines:

- Eliminate the salutation and complimentary closing.

- Eliminate the Subject: or Re: notation. Just type the subject.

- Type the SUBJECT LINE and NAME OF SENDER in all caps.

- Leave three line spaces above and below the subject line.

Some letterheads lend themselves to one style over another. For example, at the end of Chapter 9, there's a series of collection letters. Notice how the block style is more appropriate than the full block because the placement of the date helps balance the graphic.

Regardless of the style you use and the length of your letter, center the text vertically and horizontally so that the margins form an imaginary frame around the text.

Letterhead

Date

Addressee
Street Address
City, State ZIP

Salutation:

Subject: Full Block Letter Style

Characteristics
The full block letter is quickly becoming the style of choice in the modern office. Everything starts at the left margin, so there's no need to set tabs or wonder where to put the date and complimentary closing. The full block letter style is efficient, businesslike, and very popular.

Benefits
We live in a fast-paced society and people are constantly trying to simplify their cluttered lives. The full block letter style will— over time—increase the flow of paperwork and save time.

Complimentary closing,

Justin Case

P.S. Some critics feel that the full block style looks somewhat crowded.

Example 5-1:
Full block style is chic. Right off the fashion runway.

Letterhead

Date

Addressee
Street Address
City, State ZIP

Salutation:

Subject: Block (or Modified Block)

Characteristics
The block style is quite similar to the full block style. The key
difference is that the block style's date and complimentary closing
are slightly to the right of center, so you have to tab over. Everything
else is flush with the left margin. The block style is very traditional
and quite popular.

Benefits
The block letter style has traditionally been the most commonly used
of all letter styles. Therefore, it's the one most people are comfortable
with.

Complimentary closing,

Justin Case

Example 5-2:
Block is
sophisti-
cated and
always in
good taste.

Letterhead

Date

Addressee
Street Address
City, State ZIP

Salutation:

Subject: Semiblock Style

Characteristics
    The semiblock style is quite similar to the block style. The key difference is that the semiblock style's paragraphs are indented one tab stop. Therefore, you need to use two tabs: one for the indented paragraphs and one for the date and complimentary closing.

Benefits
    The semiblock style also looks familiar and people are comfortable with it. It is, however, playing second fiddle to the full block or block styles. Many people consider the semiblocked style somewhat of a dated look.

Complimentary closing,

Justin Case

P.S. This letter style is a throwback to the days when June Cleaver was the standard-bearer of domestic righteousness.

Example 5-3: Semiblock style is slightly dated but still functional.

| Letterhead |

Date

Addressee
Street Address
City, State ZIP

SUBJECT OF LETTER

Characteristics
The simplified letter is quite streamlined. Here are some
characteristics to remember if you use this letter style:

- Eliminate the salutation and complimentary closing.
- Eliminate the Subject: or Re: notation. Just type the
  subject.
- Type the SUBJECT LINE and NAME OF SENDER in all
  caps.
- Leave three line spaces above and below the subject line.

Benefits
The simplified letter style isn't commonly used. It is, however,
expected to become more popular because it's the least time-
consuming of all the letter styles.

JUSTIN CASE

P.S. Critics say this style lacks warmth and is unconventional.

Example 5-4:
Simplified
style is
futuristic.

Don't crowd me

Never crowd your letter onto one page if doing so means narrowing the margins, decreasing the font size, or compromising the visual impact in any way. There's nothing wrong with an occasional two- or three-page letter when it's *absolutely* necessary. For great tips on keeping your letter as short and simple as possible, check out "Step 6: Honing the Tone," later in this chapter. Here are some tips for presenting multiple page letters:

- ✔ When a letter runs more than one page, use letterhead for the first page and *matching plain paper* for subsequent pages.

- ✔ When you divide a paragraph between pages, leave at least two lines on the current page and carry at least two lines to the next page. If you can't do that, don't divide the paragraph. Therefore, you should never divide a three-line paragraph.

- ✔ Never carry a complimentary closing over to a separate page without having at least two lines above it.

Following are examples of how to head the second page of a two-page letter:

Example: Full Block Second Page

Ms. Alex Stark
Page 2
April 1, XXXX

Example: Modified Block, Semiblock, and Simplified Second Page

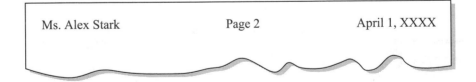

Ms. Alex Stark   Page 2   April 1, XXXX

When you send an e-mail message that's more than two or three screens, consider sending the message as an attachment. If the message has wide appeal, consider posting it on the company's intranet and creating a link that takes the reader directly to the message.

Extra! Extra! Read all about it

People don't read letters word for word; they scan them. Therefore, companies that want their message to stand out use headlines to direct the flow of information by letting the reader know what's important.

Here are a few tips for giving your headlines oomph:

- **HEADLINES IN BOLD CAPITAL LETTERS JUMP OUT**
- **BOLD SMALL CAPS ALSO MAKE A STRONG STATEMENT**
- ***Bold Italics Add a Nice Slant to Headlines***
- <u>Underscores Are Useful But Dated</u>

Listing key information

Lists save the readers time by drawing their attention to key pieces of information. Lists also break up complex sentences. Check out these tips for listing information:

- Don't overuse lists; save them for key points. If you have too many lists, you lose the impact of breaking out key pieces of information.
- List only similar items (such as items in a shipment).
- Use words, phrases, and short sentences.
- Consider grouping items with sidelines if the list has more than five items. (Otherwise, the list looks like a laundry list.) Following is an example of groups of hardware items with sidelines:

  Computer Hardware:
  - Central processing unit
  - Monitor
  - Printer

  Construction Hardware:
  - Hammers
  - Nails
  - Chisels

There are two types of lists: bulleted and numbered. Which type of list you use depends on what you're trying to convey.

Bulleted lists

Use a bulleted list when rank and sequence aren't a factor. Bullets give everything on the list equal value. In the following list, all items are of equal importance:

Don't forget to pick up the following:

- One box of No. 10 envelopes
- Two reams of ivory paper
- One package of black thin-line markers

Numbered lists

Numbered lists show steps in a procedure such as you see in directions to assemble a kid's bike. Numbered lists also set the priority. Notice that the following example lists the same items as the preceding one. By using numbers instead of bullets, however, the writer stresses the importance of each item in order or priority. Number 1 is the most important, and Number 3 is the least important.

Don't forget to pick up the following:

1. One box of No. 10 envelopes
2. Two reams of ivory paper
3. One package of black thin-line markers

All items in a list should be parallel in structure. Parallel structure means that when elements function alike they should be treated alike. When lists aren't parallel, they stand out like black eyes. Notice that the word *preparing* in the second column isn't parallel.

Parallel:	*Not Parallel:*
• Call the caterer.	• Call the caterer.
• Send the fax to the ad agency.	• Send the fax to the ad agency.
• Prepare the agenda for tomorrow's meeting.	• Preparing the agenda for tomorrow's meeting.

Taking contractions out of the labor room

Years ago contractions belonged only in labor and delivery rooms — they were taboo in letters. Today, however, contractions are preferable because they add a personal and a conversational tone quality to your writing. Plus, they make your intention more readable. Notice the visual impact of the following sentences:

Seeing through punctuation

Punctuation also helps your reader *see* your message. (Check out Appendix A for using punctuation to express your message.) Following are two sentences with the same words. Notice the difference in the way you see the person because of the punctuation.

Short brown hair and goatee. (We envision the length and color of a man's hair and his hairy chin.)

Short, brown hair, and goatee. (We envision the man's height but know nothing about the length of his hair. We still see his hairy chin.)

> ✔ *Prominent:* Mr. Jones doesn't plan to be at the meeting.
>
> ✔ *Not prominent:* Mr. Jones does not plan to be at the meeting.

Some people don't like to use contractions. So, you three-piece-suit types don't have to.

Using great graphics

If a graphical element — such as chart, table, figure, or photo — will enhance your letter, include it! After all, why use a thousand words when a picture will do? For a great explanation of how to prepare and use graphical elements, check out my book *Business Writing For Dummies* (IDG Books Worldwide, Inc.).

When you send an e-mail message, always err on the side of simplified graphics because not all e-mail systems are created equal. If your system has all the bells and whistles and your reader's doesn't, your beautiful formatting and clearly expressed message may be garbled on her screen. If you do have a wonderful graphic that your e-mail software won't support, send the graphic as an attachment.

Giving your letter visual impact

Take a look at the letter you're working on. Ask yourself the following questions and look for ways to improve its visual impact:

> ✔ **Is there ample white space?** If not, add some. Make sure you left a visual border and your paragraphs are no longer than seven lines.

✔ **Did I stick to one letter style without mixing and matching?** Mixing letter styles makes you look like you 1) don't know what you're doing, 2) can't make up your mind, or 3) forgot to proofread before you sent the letter. That's not exactly the impression you want to create.

✔ **Do my headlines tell the story?** If not, try expanding or re-sequencing them.

✔ **Would a list be more appropriate than a sentence?** Look for opportunities to create bulleted or numbered lists.

Step 5: Honing the Tone

By honing the tone of your letter, you can build instant rapport with your reader. When you speak to someone, you talk slowly, loudly, calmly, or emotionally. Your tone reflects your ability to be sincere, understand a situation, demonstrate distress, show consideration, or a wide array of other emotions. Your letters need the same astuteness.

Take a look at the Audience section of your Start Up Sheet to understand the needs of your reader. Once you know your reader better — even if only on paper — a rapport akin to magic occurs.

Letting your personality shine

One of the greatest professional compliments people pay me is telling me that when they read my writing, they feel as if I'm talking to them. I always try to write in a conversational tone. For people who don't know me, they can get a sense of who I am through my "paper" voice. For people who do know me, my letter substitutes for my dulcet tones.

When you speak to someone face to face, much of what you say is interpreted through nonverbal cues (gestures, voice, inflections, eye contact, movements, and so on) This type of "reading between the lines" isn't possible with the written word, so it's critical that you choose your words carefully.

Always remember that a real person reads what you write. Put yourself in the reader's shoes and try to experience her reaction. Use a natural and relaxed writing style and a positive tone. The tone of your message influences your reader as much as the message itself. Use words that are simple, not complex; concise, not wordy; positive, not negative; and active, not passive — all explained in Step 5.

For A's or a raise

In school we write to get good grades, not to get good results. Can you recall an instructor saying, "Write a ten-page paper on 'The Fractal Geometry as it Applies to Nature'" or whatever? So you do your research, gather your information, and come up with nine and a half pages. You know you're not going to get that "A" because your paper isn't long enough. (Some instructors don't read papers; they weigh them.)

So you rehash some of what you already said and eke out another half page of gobbledygook.

Voila! You reach ten pages. The instructor tosses the papers down the stairs, your paper weighs enough to land at the bottom, and you get that "A."

What's wrong with this picture? Business people don't have time for the gobbledygook you put into your school assignments. *The essence of good letter writing is shaving everything down to the bare essentials.* Get to the point in the shortest possible way. If information doesn't add value, leave it out.

The tone of your letter falls into one of three categories:

- **Formal:** This is a stilted style that may be appropriate for academic journals and such, but not for letters. Take a look at the following sentence. It's so stuffy it should be mounted on a wall next to a boar's head.

    Enclosed herewith please find the brochure for the sales training program you requested from us in your letter dated March 15.

- **Personable and conversational:** This is the preferred style for letters — writing the way you speak. (Notice the difference in tone between the sentence above and the one below.)

    I'm please to send you the brochure you requested for our sales training program.

- **Chatty:** This is a very loose and "talky" style that you should save for writing a two-line message to your best friend.

    Here's the brochure you asked for.

Sealed with a KISS

As a young girl, when I sent a letter to a friend or relative, I blotted lipstick on the back of the envelope to show that the letter was sealed with a kiss. As an adult, I still seal my letters with a KISS — only now the kiss is an acronym for "Keep It Short and Simple." *The less I say, the more impact my words have.* Keeping it short and simple is the epitome of conversational tone. Check out the following sections for tips on how you can achieve a conversational tone in your letters.

Tell it to me in 25 words or less!

Well-known people tell it in 25 words or less. Ann Landers, World War II correspondent Ernie Pyle, and Sir Winston Churchill all share an average sentence length of 15 words. Even Churchill's blood-sweat-and-tears radio speeches and his journalism from the Boer War average 15 words. If they can say it in 25 words or less, so can you. Limit *your* sentences to 25 words or less.

Whether a sentence is long or short, it should be concise. Concise isn't the opposite of long; it's the opposite of wordy. Following are two letters that were KISS-ed successfully:

Perhaps the shortest letter ever written that most effectively expressed the writer's intentions was the one received by Victor Hugo from his publisher on February 26, 1802. Mr. Hugo had written to his publisher asking how he liked the manuscript, *Les Miserables*. Following is the publisher's entire response:

> **!**

Here is another punchy letter — one that keeps things short and simple. I don't know who the recipient of the letter was or the circumstances that provoked it, but I wouldn't want to be on CV's bad side.

> Gentlemen:
>
> You have undertaken to cheat me. I won't sue you for the law is too slow. I'll ruin you.
>
> Yours truly,
>
> Cornelius Vanderbilt

Toppling the tower of babble

Avoid wordy, repetitive, repeated, and repetitious redundancies. After all, why use several words when one will do? Check out Table 5-1 for some examples that will raze the tower of babble.

Table 5-1	Toppling the Tower of Babble		
Use	**Instead of**	**Use**	**Instead of**
agree	come to an agreement	group	group together
apply	make an application	have	are in receipt of
as soon as	at the earliest possible	investigate	conduct an investigation
breakthrough	new breakthrough	invite	extend an invitation
can	are able to	loan	temporary loan
concluded	at the conclusion of	meet	hold a meeting
consensus	general consensus	now	at the present time
consider	give consideration to	opposite	completely opposite
costs	total cost of	outcome	final outcome
developments	new developments	refer to	make reference to
enclosed	enclosed herewith please find	result	end result
essential	absolutely essential	return	arrange to return
examine	make an examination of	save	realize a savings of
experiment	conduct an experiment	show	give an indication of
fact	true fact	status	current status
factor	contributing factor	thank you	I wish to take this opportunity to thank you
first	first and foremost	truth	honest truth

Cutting unnecessary words

Imagine that every word you write costs $100. That gives you a motivation to cut to the bare essentials. Every word that doesn't add to the effectiveness of your message wastes the reader's time, reduces her interest, and costs you money. The examples below show how to make your sentences concise, not wordy. At $100 a word, how much money could you save?

Concise: Our Fall Festival will run from October 12 through 18. We hope to see you there. (16 words)

Wordy: We have scheduled this year's fall festival to span the dates of October 12 through October 18. We would very much enjoy seeing you and your family at the festival during one of those dates. (35 words)

Concise: We're looking into why you didn't receive check No. 234 dated March 12. If you need to follow up, please reference Case No. 114. (24 words)

Wordy: We will conduct an investigation to determine why you did not receive the check in question, No. 234 dated March 12. If you need to follow up on this matter in the future, please make reference to Case No. 114. (40 words)

Concise: Thanks for your good wishes. I hope to make you all proud. (12 words)

Wordy: Thank you for your letter extending good wishes that arrived on my desk this morning. I assure you that I will do everything that is in my power to prove myself worthy of the trust you and your colleagues have placed in me and my abilities. (46 words)

It's okay to be redundant when you want to emphasize or strengthen a thought. But use this technique sparingly and strategically. Consider the following example:

Strong: Keep it short. Keep it simple. Keep it flowing.

Weak: Keep it short, simple, and flowing.

Double trouble: Avoiding ambiguity

Be alert to situations where something you write may be ambiguous, especially in our global community where things may be lost in the translation. (Later in this chapter are guidelines for writing to people in other countries.) Here are examples that may make you scratch your head.

> A Japanese real estate company built 150 homes in Michigan hills. The head of the company, who spoke no English, needed to tell the building contractor that the dirt around the finished houses needed to be leveled. The translator told the builder that "the houses needed to be leveled." The building contractor, who was paid by the hour, bulldozed all 150 houses.
>
> —Sheryl Lindsell-Roberts, *Funny Laws & Other Zany Stuff*

A gentleman received the following invitation from a colleague: "I'd like to have you and your wife for dinner next Saturday. (The writer intended to invite the man and his wife to join him for dinner. Instead he invited them to *be* the dinner.)

Brain drain

Can you simplify the following sentences into commonly known expressions? The answers appear at the bottom of the sidebar. Turn the book upside down to read them.

1. Similar sire, similar scion.

2. A feathered creature clasped in the manual member is equal in value to a brace in the bosky growth.

3. Every article that is coruscated is not fashioned from aureate metal.

3. All that glitters isn't gold.

2. A bird in the hand is worth two in the bush.

1. Like father, like son.

Being positive and upbeat

Presenting yourself as an optimist is a winning strategy. ("The glass is half full, not half empty.") Let the reader know what you *can and will do*, not what you can't and won't do. Positive words engage the reader's goodwill and enhance your tone. Negative words trigger negative responses.

The following sentences send the same message, but notice the difference in tone:

> *Positive:* Your order should be shipped next Tuesday.
> *Negative:* It's not likely that your order will be shipped before next Tuesday.

> *Positive:* I hope you'll be delighted with our new line of merchandise.
> *Negative:* I hope our merchandise won't fall short of your expectations.

> *Positive:* I appreciate the suggestions you sent about ways to improve our software.
> *Negative:* We're disappointed that you found that our software fell short of your expectations.

The following words pack a positive punch:

Benefit	Bonus	Congratulations	Convenient
Delighted	Excellent	Friend	Generous
Glad	Guarantee	Health	Honest

Immediately	I will	Of course	Pleasant
Pleasure	Pleasing	Proven	Qualified
Right	Safe	Sale	Satisfactory
Save	Thank you	Vacation	Yes

The following words pack a negative punch:

Apology	Broken	Cannot	Complaint
Impossible	Inconvenient	Loss	Damages
Delay	Difficulty	Disappoint	Discomfort
Failure	Guilty	Mistake	Problem
Regret	Sorry	Suspicion	Trouble
Unable to	You claim	You neglected	Carelessly
Your failure	Your inability	Your insinuation	Your refusal

Think like an advertiser

Advertisers know that talking to the reader creates a very persuasive tone. Notice how often they include the words *you* and *your* in ads. When you write a business letter, you're also selling something — whether it's your product, yourself, or your idea. Talk to *your* reader.

In the following examples, you can see subtle differences in tone. The reader-focused sentences stress *you* and *your*. (For example, notice the subtlety of referring to Richard Smith as *your* sales representative.) The writer-focused sentences concentrate on *I* and *our*.

> ***Reader focused:*** Thanks for <u>your</u> interest in our new product line. The enclosed spec sheet should answer a lot of <u>your</u> questions. If <u>you</u> need more information, please call Richard Smith, <u>your</u> sales representative. He'll be delighted to help <u>you</u>.

> ***Writer focused:*** <u>I'm</u> sorry that <u>I</u> cannot answer your questions, but <u>I've</u> enclosed one of <u>our</u> spec sheets. <u>I've</u> also taken the liberty of forwarding these questions to <u>our</u> sales representative, Richard Smith. <u>I'm</u> sure he can answer any of your questions.

Here are some more writer- and reader-focused snippets:

Reader focused:	You'll be happy to hear. . . .
Writer focused:	I'm happy to tell you. . . .
Reader focused:	By now you should have received. . . .
Writer focused:	On May 2 we sent you. . . .
Reader focused:	This is in answer to your. . . .
Writer focused:	I'd like to respond to. . . .

Using active voice

When you use the active voice, you focus the sentence on the doer (or actor). (*Voice,* by the way, is the grammatical term that refers to whether the subject of the sentence or clause acts or receives the action.) Using the active voice is a major factor in projecting a tone that's alive and interesting.

To understand the difference between active and passive voice, picture this: You're on a Caribbean vacation with your loved one sailing aboard a 100-foot yacht. You're sitting on the deck and the fiery crimson sun is slowly sinking into the distant horizon. The waves are gently rolling over the craggy shore, while you sip a glass of your favorite wine. The special someone you're with leans over and whispers tenderly in your ear the words you've been longing to hear:

- ✔ **"I love you."**

   Doesn't that make you want to melt? "I love you," is probably the most wonderful example of the active voice. It's animated and alive!

- ✔ **"You are loved."**

   By whom, the dog? The dolphin that just swam by? This passive sentence is dull, weak, and ineffective.

- ✔ **"You are loved by me."**

   If I heard that phony and stilted line, I'd immediately check the singles ads and pack my bags.

Passive sentences are also more wordy because they include helping verbs. Therefore, when you see *is, are, was, were, will be, have been, should be,* and so on, the sentence is probably passive. Notice the underscored helping verbs in the following passive sentences:

Active: People interpret things based on their own experiences.
Passive: Things <u>are</u> interpreted by people based on their own experiences.

Active: The payroll department issued the checks on Monday.
Passive: The checks <u>were</u> issued by the payroll department on Monday.

Active: Conversational tone builds rapport with readers. (In this case, the doer isn't a person, which is fine.)
Passive: Rapport with readers <u>is</u> built with conversational tone.

There are times people deliberately hide the doer (if there is one). For example, whenever someone says to me, "The check has been sent," I always ask, "Who sent it and when?"

Battle of the sexes

Sexism is a hot topic these days. The English language, as rich as it is, has no clear-cut solution. Without getting into absurdities (such as changing *man*hole cover to *person*hole cover), the key is to be

✔ Aware of hidden and overt meanings.

✔ Sensitive to your reader.

Following are some tips that may help you bridge the gender gap:

Reword the sentence

Gender neutrality is often a matter of rewording the sentence. The examples that follow show a number of ways to say the same thing:

Sexist: Each person did *his* work quietly.

Grammatically incorrect: Each person did *their* work quietly.

Acceptable: Each person did *the* work quietly.

Acceptable: Each person *worked* quietly.

Acceptable: Everyone worked quietly.

Avoid gender judgments in job titles

When you're speaking of someone's job title, don't make a gender judgment. Judges aren't necessarily males, and nurses aren't necessarily females. If you can, identify the person by name.

Use gender-neutral terms

Someone who's employed in a stockroom isn't a stockboy, but a stockclerk. You no longer have a postman, but a letter (or postal) carrier. Table 5-2 shows other gender-neutral terms worth considering.

Table 5-2	Subtle Sexisms
Rather Than Saying	*Try*
Anchorman	Newscaster, Anchor
Cameraman	Cinematographer
Chairman	Chairperson, Chair, Moderator
Clergyman	Member of the clergy
Delivery boy	Delivery person, Messenger
Fireman	Fire fighter
Forefather	Ancestor
Insurance man	Insurance agent
Layman	Nonprofessional
Man-made	Synthetic
Mankind	Humanity, Human race
Newsman	Reporter, Journalist
Policeman, Policewoman	Police officer
Repairman, Repairwoman	Service technician
Salesman	Salesperson, Sales representative
Spokesman	Spokesperson
Steward, stewardess	Flight attendant
Weatherman	Meteorologist
Workman	Worker

Think plural

In some cases you can make a sentence plural to avoid the clunky he/she or his/her situations.

> *Plural:* Doctors are trained to heal their patients.
> *Singular:* A doctor is trained to heal his/her patients.

> *Plural:* All candidates for the human resources position must file their applications no later than June 5. They should include their educational backgrounds.
> *Singular:* Each candidate for the human resources position must file his/her application no later than June 5. He/she should include his/her educational background.

Apologize in advance

When all else fails, consider using *he* or *she* to refer to both sexes. State your intentions (and apologies) at the outset of your writing.

Notice how I address this delicate issue in *Writing Business Letters For Dummies.* I explain early in the book that I use the male gender in the even chapters and the female gender in the odd chapters. (I didn't determine that women are odd; the penny I tossed did that.)

Honing other tones

There are a few other areas where you may hone the tone: euphemisms, humor, clichés, and jargon.

Euphemisms

Euphemisms are word associations. Tone plays a part in the unspoken meanings that words and expressions invoke. For example, notice the difference between *opportunity* and *problem, direct report* and *subordinate, supervisor* and *boss.* The first of each set creates a more positive association.

Humor

Will Rogers once said, "Humor is funny as long as it is happening to somebody else." Humor is a sensitive area. Using humor in your letters, memos, and e-mail messages may be appropriate, however you must be sensitive to the way the reader will perceive what you say. If in doubt, leave it out!

Stop yelling at me!

PEOPLE OFTEN SEND E-MAIL MESSAGES IN ALL CAPITAL LETTERS. THIS IS THE EQUIVALENT OF YELLING AT YOUR READER AND CREATING A VERY HARSH TONE. IF YOU WANT TO GET SOMEONE'S ATTENTION, DON'T YELL AT HER. ADDITIONALLY, ALL CAPITAL LETTERS ARE MORE DIFFICULT TO READ THAN A COMBINATION OF UPPER- AND LOWERCASE LETTERS.

by the way, the reverse is true. if you use all lowercase, the effect is the opposite of shouting. the tone is weak and wimpy.

Clichés

Clichés are worn-out expressions that have little, if any, meaning. If you've heard the cliché "crazy as a bedbug," have you ever wondered why bedbugs are crazier than tsetse flies? Avoid cliches like the plague.

Jargon

Jargon (sometimes referred to as slang) is specialized "shop talk" that's effective when you write to people in your industry. When you write to people outside your industry; however, avoid jargon. The tone may become tangled in abstract words that the reader may view as exclusionary.

Don't confuse jargon with street slang. Stay away from expressions such as *cool, dude, awesome*, and other slangy expressions.

Lost in the translation: Being globally aware

We adapt our tones for different people and situations. We use one tone for our friends and family, another for peers, another for managers, and yet another for people whose primary language isn't English. With e-mail allowing you to write and instantly send messages to people or groups of people in most parts of the world, global savvy is a must. Always be sensitive to how a foreign reader may interpret your message.

Geographic expressions

Be attuned to geographic references. If you write "I'll be visiting the West Coast next week," someone outside the United States may not understand your frame of reference. If you're writing to a person in another country, consider saying, "I'll be visiting the West Coast of the United States next week." Or be specific and say, "I'll be visiting California next week."

Dates

It's good business practice to write out the month, date, and year because you never know who may read your message. If you do abbreviate, remember that people in different parts of the world abbreviate dates differently. For example, to Europeans, April 5, XXXX is 5/4/XX; to Japanese, it's XX/4/5; and, to people in the states, it's 4/5/XX. So, if you use numerals to abbreviate the date for a critical meeting, people from different parts of the world may arrive in different months.

Metric measurements

The United States is of the few countries in the *galaxy* that doesn't use the metric system. Therefore, it's wise to write metric measurements with American equivalents in parentheses, so measurements are clear to anyone reading your message.

Idioms

Idiomatic expressions have meaning only in certain parts of the country and world. For example, if you told someone from outside the United States that "the judge threw the book at the defendant," you're not saying that the judge physically tossed *War and Peace* in the defendant's face. Therefore, avoid idiomatic expressions because they're often misinterpreted.

Honing the tone of your letter

Take a look at the letter you're working on. Ask yourself the following questions and look for ways to hone its tone:

- ✔ Did I cut to the quick — KISS the letter?
- ✔ Did I use positive words, not negative ones?
- ✔ Did I turn the focus from myself to the reader?
- ✔ Did I liven up my tone with the active voice?
- ✔ Did I change sexist terms to gender-neutral ones?
- ✔ Did I misuse euphemisms, humor, clichés, jargon, or idioms?

Step 6: Proofreading

We hear a lot today about total quality and quality management, meaning that everything that ships should be free from defects. Software shouldn't have bugs; the door handle shouldn't fall off your newly purchased car; and business correspondence shouldn't have errors. It's your responsibility to control the quality of every letter, memo, and e-mail message you send. Proofreading and editing aren't innate talents; they're skills you can learn quite easily.

Although the terms *proofreading* and *editing* generally refer to checking the quality of your writing, there's a slight difference in meaning.

- **Proofreading** refers to the systematic method of finding errors and noting them for correction.

- **Editing** refers to modifying words, sentences, paragraphs, and the general structure of your writing. (In Step 5 you honed the tone, which is a step in the editing direction. However, there's more to editing — as you'll see.)

Avoiding boondoggles

When people don't review the essence of what they write, the results can be boondoggles. Sometimes they're larger than life and haunt us for all eternity. For example, there was a Bible published in England in 1716. It was a gift to the colonies from the wife of King George II. Instead of the Bible reading, "Parables of the Vineyard," it read "Parables of Vinegar." (That was prior to the revolution, so perhaps there was a subtle message in those words.)

Following are two laws that are actually on the books. U.S. lawmakers, in their infinite wisdom, didn't carefully proofread or edit what they wrote.

- A law in Kansas reads: "When two trains approach each other at a railroad crossing, both shall come to a full stop and neither shall start up again until the other has gone."

- Belvedere, California, has this law on the books: "No dog shall appear in public without its owner on a leash."

Even a punctuation mark put in the wrong place can dramatically alter the meaning of a sentence, as you see below.

Woman without her man is a savage.

Woman: without her, man is a savage.

Putting out the fires before they start

Proofreading and editing are skills that you can learn quite easily just by following these guidelines:

- **Check all names, including middle initials, titles, and company distinctions.** Are you spelling *Glenn* with two n's instead of one? Are you writing *Corp.* instead of *Co.?*

- **Double check numbers.** Are you telling the reader she'll receive a check for $15,750.00 and the check reads $15,570.00?

- **Keep an eye out for misused or misspelled homophones (words that sound the same but are spelled differently.)** Are you writing *affect* instead of *effect*? (Check Appendix D for others.)

- **Be on the alert for small words that are misused.** Perhaps you typed *it* instead of *at* and didn't notice the error. (We tend to read what we expect to be there.)

- **Make sure you're consistent with terminology.** For example, do you typically do business with dealers, distributors, or manufacturers? Do you have customers, clients, or accounts? If you use *customers* in one place and *accounts* in another, the switch in terminology may confuse your reader.

- **Check dates against those on the calendar.** When you type Monday, September 15, be sure September 15 is a Monday.

- **Check for omissions.** Perhaps you left off a ZIP code, policy number, or other critical piece of information.

- **Check spelling, grammar, and punctuation.** Check out the appendixes for nifty tips on spelling, grammar, and punctuation.

- **Re-read the hardcopy.** Don't take the letter from the printer and put it in an envelope. Re-read it first. Face it, despite the hours you spend in front of your computer, you're still more used to reading hardcopy. Therefore, you tend to see errors on hardcopy you may miss on the screen.

- **Don't turn on your computer and turn off your brain!** Although electronic tools are wonderful, they don't replace human intervention. If you write "I am now available" instead of "I am not available," the computer won't know the difference. Yet, you deliver the opposite message.

- **Read the letter aloud.** Can you mumble it to yourself just once and thoroughly understand it? If not, re-write whatever parts may be confusing.

- **Read from bottom to top and/or from right to left**. This lets you view each word as a separate entity and helps you find errors.

- **Scan the letter to see that the formatting is correct.** Are there 1- to 1½-inch margins all around? Are the sentences limited to 25 words or less and the paragraphs to 5 to 7 lines or less? Did you mix letter formats (full block and modified block, for example)?

What were they thinking?

Here are some lulus that writers may have avoided by reviewing their text carefully. The following are excerpts of actual letters written by doctors. (This isn't meant to single out the medical profession; every profession has its share of written goof-ups.)

✔ James has chest pain if he lies on his side for over a year.

✔ Prior to the patient's birth, she was told that her pregnancy was a normal one.

✔ On the first day his knee was better and on the third day it had completely disappeared.

✔ Margaret Smith was given a genealogical exam at the hospital.

✔ The patient's leg became numb at times and he walked it off.

These beauties are from students' exam papers. (It just *shows to go you* that students aren't being prepared for the business world.)

✔ Charles Darwin was a naturalist who wrote the Organ of the Spices.

✔ It is a well-known fact that a deceased body warps the mind.

✔ To collect sulphur, hold a deacon over a flame in a test tube.

✔ Three kinds of blood vessels are arteries, veins, and caterpillars.

✔ The thermometer is an instrument for raising temperance.

✔ Heredity means that if your grandfather didn't have children, then your father probably didn't have any. So you probably won't have any.

✔ Algebra was the wife of Euclid.

✔ To be a nurse, you must be absolutely sterile.

✔ Artificial insemination is when the farmer does it to the cow, not the bull.

These were taken from reports that policyholders were asked to fill out after automobile accidents:

✔ The pedestrian had no idea which direction to go, so I ran over him.

✔ Coming home, I drove into the wrong house and collided with a tree I didn't have.

✔ The accident happened when the right front door of a car came around the corner without giving a signal.

✔ The telephone pole was approaching fast. I was attempting to swerve out of its path when it struck my front end.

✔ I was on the way to the doctor's with rear end trouble when my universal joint gave way causing me to have an accident.

✔ The guy was all over the road. I had to swerve a couple of times before I hit him.

Striving to be letter perfect

Take a look at Example 5-5 and see what blunders you notice. Then look at Example 5-6, with the answers changed and called out. If you find all the goofs, rip this chapter out of the book and give it to a deserving colleague. You know . . . the one who sends letters with errors as obvious as ketchup stains on a bridal gown. Check out the Appendixes for any trouble spots of punctuation, grammar, abbreviations, or spelling.

| Letterhead |

Febuary 30, XXXX

Mr. and Mrs. Harry Lorenz
14 Ivy Lane
Atlanta, Georgia 30303

Welcome to Atlanta!

Dear Mr. and Mrs. Lorenz

It's a pleasure to welcome you and your family to Atlanta — the Peachtree State. To help you get to know this wonderful area, we've enclosed a map of the recreational and cultural facilities in and around the city. Here are some of the highlights.

1. Georgia State Capital
2. Peachtree Center
3. Tullie Smith House
4. Martin Luther King, Jr., Historic District

And while you're getting to now the city, stop by the Georgia State Bank so I may welcome you personally and share many of the wonderful experiences you can have banking with us. Georgia State Bank is celebrating their 15th anniversary and is sending you as a $10 gift certificate to start a savings account to help us celebrate.

Sincerely Yours,

Leah Zimmerman,
Branch Manager

P.S. Looking forward to seeing you!

Example 5-5:
What's
wrong with
this picture?

Letterhead

February 28, XXXX   February was misspelled. It has 28 days and in a leap year, 29.

Mr. and Mrs. Harry Lorenz
14 Ivy Lane
Atlanta, GA 30303   Use the 2-letter state abbreviation.

Dear Mr. and Mrs. Lorenz: Use a colon after a salutation.

Welcome to Atlanta!   Subject line follows salutation.

It's a pleasure to welcome you and your family to Atlanta — the Peachtree State. To help you get to know this wonderful area, we've enclosed a map of the recreational and cultural facilities in and around the city. Here are some of the highlights: Colon introduces a list.

• Georgia State Capitol   A Capitol is a building.
• Peachtree Center
• Tullie Smith House
• Martin Luther King, Jr., Historic District   Use a bulleted list when there's no priority.

And while you're getting to know the city, stop by the Georgia State Bank so I may welcome you personally and share many of the wonderful experiences you can have banking with us. Georgia State Bank is celebrating its 15th anniversary and is sending you remove "as" a $10 gift certificate to start a savings account to help us celebrate.

Sincerely yours,   The date and complimentary closing are aligned. "Yours" isn't capitalized.

No comma when job title is on a line below the name.

Leah Zimmerman
Branch Manager

P.S. Looking forward to seeing you!

Example 5-6: What's right with this picture?

Remember how important it is to treat e-mail messages as serious business tools. *Proofread* your e-mail messages just as carefully as you proofread letters and memos.

Using the Letter-Perfect Checklist

The Letter-Perfect Checklist appears on the Cheat Sheet in the front of this book. Go through it thoroughly before you send a letter, memo, or e-mail message. It can save you from some of life's embarrassing moments. (There are enough of them we can't avoid.)

❏ My subject line and headlines are informative to spark my reader's interest.

❏ My message is sequenced for the needs of my reader.

❏ My letter has visual impact, including

    ❏ 1- to 1½-inch margins on the top, bottom, and sides.

    ❏ Sentences limited to 25 words.

    ❏ Paragraphs limited to 5 to 7 lines.

    ❏ Bulleted and numbered lists, when appropriate.

❏ My tone reflects my personality on paper.

❏ Spelling, grammar, and punctuation are correct.

❏ I didn't lay my cup down and leave coffee stains on the paper.

Do you get an F in proofreading?

Test your proofreading skills. Read the following **once** and count the F's in the box. Turn the book upside down to read the answer.

FINISHED FILES ARE THE RESULT OF YEARS OF SCIENTIFIC STUDY COMBINED WITH THE EXPERIENCE OF YEARS.

If you counted six, you're right. Most people count three, not paying attention to the word *of* that appears three times.

Part III
The Letter Carrier Cometh

The 5th Wave   By Rich Tennant

"Yes, Mr. Van Gogh, now that I have your
ear, so to speak, let me thank you for
that enticing cover letter."

In this part . . .

When W.H. Auden wrote "Night Mail," he had the vision to know it would make a wonderful lead-in for Part III of *Writing Business Letters for Dummies*. Here's what he wrote:

This is the Night Mail crossing the Border
Bringing the cheque and the postal order.

Letters for the rich, letters for the poor,
The shop at the corner, the girl next door. . .

Letters of thanks, letters from banks,
Letters of joy from girl and boy,
Receipted bills and invitations
To inspect new stock or to visit relations,
And applications for situations,
And timid lovers' declarations,
And gossip, gossip from all the nations.

Chapter 6

Spicy Sales Letters

* *

In This Chapter

▶ Gearing up for a sales campaign

▶ Enticing the reader to open the envelope

▶ Preparing sales letters with pizzazz

▶ Amassing a mailing list

▶ Following up on trade show and site visits

* *

> *It's no trick to be a successful salesman if you have what people want. You ever hear the bootleggers complaining about hard times?*
>
> — Robert C. Edwards, Canadian educator and humorist

Have you ever counted the number of sales letters you receive every week or month? (You probably call them junk mail.) If you stop to count, you realize that your postal carrier is buckling under the weight of all those letters that we often toss out. Why do people flood the mail with unsolicited sales letters? Because sales letters have been and continue to be an effective selling tool. Letters cost much less than media coverage and can be targeted to a specific audience. The bottom line is — well-written sales letters get results!

Establishing a Smiley Tone

SHERYL SAYS When political hopefuls are on the campaign trail, smiling and shaking hands, they're selling themselves. When you make a personal sales call, you too extend your hand and smile. When you write a sales letter, that, too, is a sales call, and you should extend a smile. Friendliness is contagious — when you smile at the reader through your tone, you build an instant rapport. (Check out Chapter 5 to learn more about honing the tone.)

Make your smile one of sincerity that builds the foundation for a successful relationship with the reader. This chapter is chock-full of tips to help you compose letters that radiate warm smiles, not snickers or guffaws. (Smiling doesn't mean grinning all the time; nobody wants to do business with a Cheshire cat.)

Planning Your Sales Letter Campaign

Remember to fill out the Start Up Sheet on the Cheat Sheet in the front of this book. Understanding your audience, purpose, and key issue is crucial. When you understand your customers and know your products and services inside and out, you're ready to start the sales campaign. Here are some tips for getting started:

- **Generate a list of prospects with common characteristics.** For example, if you're promoting a golfing magazine, you must know that your prospects are golfers. If you're writing to members of a networking group, you know they're generally business owners.

- **Understand the demographics.** Know the sex, age, occupation, geographic location, and financial situation of your target audience. You won't get too far trying to sell snow blowers to urban apartment dwellers.

- **View from the eyes of your reader.** In sales letters, emotion sells. Use Number 3 on your Start Up Sheet, "What's in it for my reader?" to appeal to your reader's emotions. We're not talking about logic; emotions stir buyers. The guy in the cubicle next to you doesn't get a new car every two years because he needs reliable transportation. He gets a new car because he "needs" the status that goes with having a late-model car. Understand the benefits that make your products or services attractive to the reader — comfort, convenience, enjoyment, improved health, loyalty, or prestige.

- **Determine the key selling point.** The key selling point may be ease of use, appearance, durability, price, comfort, education, or anything else. Then go one step further. Imagine how you'd feel if you were in your readers's shoes. Being in poor health. Living on a small income. Living in a crowded apartment. Using antiquated software. Having limited education. Paying inflated prices.

- **Plan the sales spiel.** When you write your sales letter, think of AIDA. (This has nothing to do with Verdi's famous opera.)

    Attention: Get the reader's attention

    Interest: Pique his interest

    Desire: Create the desire

    Action: Call for action

✔ **Remember that timing is everything.** Take a peek at question 10 on your Start Up Sheet. When is the best time to deliver the message? When would be too early? When would be too late? For example, if you're announcing a 25 percent discount on all Christmas merchandise, remember that the sales onslaught starts the day after Thanksgiving. That day is considered the heaviest shopping day of the year.

The Envelope, Please

Why do people treat sales and promotion letters as junk mail and place them in the waste basket unread? Because the envelopes don't shout, "OPEN ME!" The envelopes are dull, uninteresting, tedious, boring, mundane, humdrum, and any other adjective you may think of. You get the drift. Following are suggestions for creating captivating envelopes that entice the reader to look inside:

Tempting teasers

Have you ever been lured by a teaser on an envelope? We all have. These are the envelopes that get opened, not tossed in the trash. The key is to get the reader to look inside the envelope — to get his attention. Refer to the "Audience" part of your Start Up Sheet to understand what may appeal to your readers. Here are a few teasers that lured me to look inside envelopes:

> **Pay attention! What's inside is about to change your life.**
>
> **Sample enclosed.**
>
> **Enclosed is the most unusual gift.**

Looking personal

Anything that screams "bulk mailing" is more likely to get tossed than something that seems personal. So, when you're preparing your envelope, try to add a personal touch. Here are a couple of tips for giving your envelope a personal touch and luring the reader to look inside:

✔ Use a first-class *postage stamp,* rather than a postage meter. This gives the envelope the look of a personalized mailing.

✔ Handwrite the name and address of the addressee and don't include a return address. Anonymity arouses the reader's curiosity. (Some companies hire temps to handwrite envelopes just for this reason.)

Here are three sure-fire ways to make your envelope shout junk mail: send it *bulk rate*, *pre-sorted*, or use a *mailing label*. No matter how alluring your envelope is, these markings signal a mass mailing. Following is what bulk rate and presorted demons look like:

Following is an envelope that caught my eye at a quick glance because it looked very official. It took only a moment, however, to realize it was junk mail because of the bulk rate marking. If the sender had put a first-class stamp on the envelope, I probably would have opened it. (For more information on first-class mail and other postal services, check out Chapter 19.)

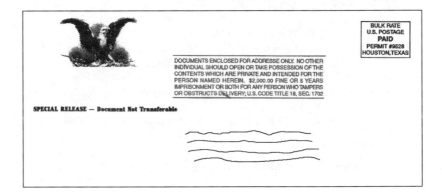

I received an envelope that looked like junk mail and threw it in the trash unopened. As my husband was emptying the trash, the envelope fell on the floor. Something compelled him to open it. He scratched his head and blurted out, "Are you so rich that you're throwing money away?" It was a royalty check for one of my books — quite a substantial one. The publisher had been acquired by another publishing company, and I didn't recognize the return address. So I tossed it. Since then, I never throw anything away until I've opened it. There may be a real treasure inside!

You're on a Roll

When your envelope gets the reader's attention, you want to keep the momentum racing full speed ahead. Here are a few tips for doing just that:

- **Attach or send something:** Attach or include a simple object appropriate for your industry. (I once received a letter from a hotel in Hawaii and found a package of sand stapled to a letter. I thought it was clever and kept the letter and the sand. I stayed at the hotel a year later.)

- **Offer a freebie:** If the gesture is appropriate, offer something for free. Perhaps a coupon or free demonstration. Maybe there's something of interest on your Web site you can let the potential customer know about. People love to get something for nothing.

- **Open with a question, anecdote, parable, or story:** You need a powerful opening. This is good old-fashioned psychology. Novelists call it a hook, journalists call it a lead, and writers call it an opening line. Whatever you call your opening, it makes all the difference. When you ask a question, it gets the reader involved because he's (mentally) inclined to answer it. Anecdotes and parables also involve the reader. Here's an example:

  > As a manager, you probably spend your time attending to the professional development of those who work for you. When was the last time you focused on YOUR professional development?

- **Start with an emotionally compelling headline.** That's where the power is. If you receive a sales letter that starts with the statement, "This Information May Add Years to Your Life," wouldn't you read on?

Adding Pizzazz to Your Sales Letters

After you capture the reader's attention, you can add a lot of pizzazz to your sales letters by using words with panache. Table 6-1 shows words and phrases for a variety of sales situations:

Table 6-1	Expressions with Pizzazz
Situation	*Words with Panache*
Appeal for contributions	Together we can . . . Whatever you send will mean so much. With your help, we'll be able to . . . You'll be able to say with great pride, "I've made a difference!"

(continued)

Table 6-1 (continued)

Situation	Words with Panache
Appeal to senses	A pleasure to behold A rushing brook Emerging from their long winter dormancy The wind in the trees
Authenticity	Has withstood the test of time . . . Often imitated but never equaled The original . . . There's simply no substitute for the real thing!
Classic	A nostalgic glimpse of . . . In the rich tradition of . . . . . . lets you relive . . . The glory of . . . endures the test of time.
Company image	A commitment to excellence Here are just a few of our clients: Our total commitment We had the foresight to . . .
Convenient	Eliminates the need for . . . Located in the heart of . . . Now you can order direct. You'll never again have to . . .
Decision time	Don't take our word for it. Experience it yourself. *You* decide. You have absolutely nothing to lose. You'll just have to experience it for yourself.
Experienced	Listen to what the experts say! We beat the competition hands down. We have vision. We're thoroughly familiar with . . .
Flattery	Discriminating people . . . Men and women of distinction You've been highly recommended by . . . Your . . . set(s) you apart from the general public.
Help	. . . guides you every step of the way. Our job is to make your job easier. You can turn to us with confidence. Your . . . will receive our top priority.

Situation	Words with Panache
Money saving	A fraction of its original cost. Designer quality at affordable prices. Finally, a . . . you can afford. Why pay more for . . .
Salutations	Dear Customer: Dear Patron of the Arts: Greetings! Welcome to . . .
Satisfaction	Sit back and enjoy . . . . . . to your heart's content. Try a little self-indulgence. Your passport to . . .
Status	Among the most exclusive . . . Until now only a select few have . . . Where today's movers and shakers gather. You'll be a member of an elite group.
Superior	A sterling example of . . . America's leading Often imitated but never equaled There's just no substitute for the best.
Transitions	Before I say any more . . . For these and other reasons . . . Now, for the first time . . . With your permission, I'd like to . . .
Unusual	. . . is uniquely suited to . . . Unprecedented You can leave the mainstream behind. You can search far and wide and still never find . . .

Stress benefits, not features

Take a look once again at Question 3 on your Start Up Sheet, "What's in it for my reader?" Talk about benefits (which are about the reader), rather than features (which are about the product or service). For example, the *feature* of new Internet access may be bandwidth. The *benefit* is access to information in a fraction of the time. That's what's in it for your reader.

E-sales promotion

Want free publicity? Tack your name, e-mail address, phone number, and a one-or-two line promotional blurb to the bottom of each e-mail message you send. This isn't spamming (unsolicited advertising). It's marketing, and it's a great way to advertise without spending additional money. Check with your e-mail service provider or the Help screen in your e-mail program to find out how.

Deal with price tactfully. If the strength of your product is that its price is the lowest in its category, you may want to state that up front. If not, why bring up price? Perhaps it's better to wow the reader with the benefits, and leave price for a later discussion.

The long and short of it

Experts (whoever they are) differ on how long a sales letter should be. One group says that you should definitely, absolutely, positively limit a sales letter to one page. Another group says that if the first page grabs the reader's attention, the third or fourth page will clinch the deal. My only suggestion is to follow the guidelines of good letter writing and use good judgment. Stop when you've said enough.

Calling for action

Always end by letting the reader know the next step — what you want him to do. You may want him to fill out an order blank, call you, attend a seminar, or so on. It's helpful to the reader if you pump up the call for action with a headline such as you see below:

Next step

Please fill out the enclosed reply card and put it in the self-addressed, stamped envelope. Our sales representative will call you within one week.

or

Action requested

Join the best of chemical engineers — several thousand to be exact — for this once-a-year event where you can share ideas. Send us your registration forms today.

Using a postscript

Consider ending your letter with a postscript. Studies show that sales letters with postscripts get better results. Use a postscript to reiterate a special offer, restate a deadline, emphasize the call to action, or send regards from the person who referred you. Use the postscript to your advantage!

Sending a self-addressed, stamped envelope (SASE)

The jury's out on this one. Some experts feel that a SASE makes it easier for the reader to reply, so you'll get a larger number of responses. Others feel that volume isn't the key — serious buyers are. Therefore, if the reader uses his own envelope and stamp, he's a more serious prospect or buyer. (So much for the experts.) Let your decision rest with the product or service you sell. Try sample mailings with and without a SASE to see for yourself which yields better results.

Collect your junk mail for a week or two. Look at it. . . study it. . . critique it. . . rewrite it. . . play with it. . . turn it into paper airplanes. Try to incorporate what excited you about each letter and envelope into your written sales spiels. If you do that, your letters will be winners!

Sales letter taboos

The preceding section talks about things that add pizzazz to your sales letters. Here are some taboos that make letters pizzazz-less:

- ✔ **Being too chummy with the reader.** He'll get irritated and think you're insincere.
- ✔ **Being too cutesy.** It's inappropriate in most industries.
- ✔ **Making idle statements.** Comments such as, "You'll be sorry if you miss this opportunity!" don't really tell the reader anything.
- ✔ **Making too many points in one letter.** Concentrate on your strongest selling point — the key benefit and emotional appeal.
- ✔ **Bad-mouthing the competition or making unwarranted claims.** Let your product sell itself.

> ✔ **Making claims such as "revolutionary," "incredible," and "astounding."** These statements and other claims like them sound exaggerated.
>
> ✔ **Letting a brochure speak for you.** The actual sale will come from the letter, not a brochure. You may include a brochure to reinforce the sales letter, not replace it.

Seeing Is Believing!

Following are two examples of sales letters that worked for my clients. Example 6-1 is a cold-call letter to a prospect. It eliminates the date, inside address, and salutation and starts with a thought-provoking quote. It also breaks out the call for action with graphics. Example 6-2 is a letter to a prospect based on a recommendation. Notice how the letter uses the postscript to make the referral source stand out.

Letterhead

Starting with a powerful quote

"If a small to midsize company were to increase its customer retention rate by 5 percent, its profits would double in about 10 years."

—Bain & Company, Boston-based consulting firm

Has one of your customers ever flown into the arms of your competitor because of poor customer service or an ill-timed sales call? If so, it could be costing you millions of dollars in lost revenue! Why does this happen? Because everyone in the organization has disparate databases — no one has the big picture.

The Parnassus CIS Solution
If you're serious about increasing your profitability by fostering customer loyalty, I'd like to share with you the **Parnassus** Customer Interaction Software (CIS) solution. It will give your sales, marketing, and service groups a common database, so they'll speak to customers in "one voice." Here are just some of the reasons **Parnassus** is unmatched by any other CIS solution:

- Increase profitability through customer loyalty.
- Analyze and respond to business trends immediately.
- Empower employees with integrated customer information at their fingertips in a centralized and distributed work environment.

*"With **Parnassus**, our sales force has real-time access to the common customer database. This gives them full knowledge of any questions/problems a customer may have BEFORE they make a personal visit. This has resulted in extreme customer loyalty."*

— Dee Lighted

 Please call me at **(800) 584-1234, extension 35.**

-or-

 Visit our Web site: **www.sample.com.**

Sincerely,

Sammy Sales
Sammy Sales
Sales Representative

Example 6-1:
Cold-call
letter to a
prospective
customer.

Letterhead

January 20, XXXX

PERSONAL

Mr. Don Farber, Vice President
Vermont Technicals
200 Karen Court
Underhill, VT 05489

Dear Mr. Farber:

Our mutual friend, Joe Grayson, suggested that I contact you. My company has helped hundreds of companies bring loyal customers into the fold and maximize their ROI. Because Joe has been so pleased with our product and service, he felt that you too may be interested.

For the past fifteen years, we've been hearing about critical issues such as the ones you may have:

> *"Disparate databases keep us from being one voice to customers."*
> *"We don't have the tools to analyze trends and maximize sales opportunities."*
> *"We don't have round-the-clock access to our network."*

Next step | Punch out next step |
I'll call you next week to see how we may help you solve your critical issues.

Sincerely,

Tony Martinez
Tony Martinez

P.S. Warm regards from Joe.
| Highlight the person who referred you |

Example 6-2:
Joe sent
me!

Compiling a Mailing List

Mailing lists can help you reach a target audience. You can purchase mailing lists or solicit names from satisfied customers/clients. Check out these resources:

- ✔ **Directories and publications:** City and state directories, educational directories, mercantile directories, newspapers (columns or special articles), *Standard and Poor's Register of Corporations, Thomas Register of American Manufacturers,* and trade directories. These publications are available at most local libraries.

- ✔ **Bureaus and organizations:** City and state licensing bureaus, clubs and professional organizations, commercial agencies that specialize in selling mailing lists, conventions, trade shows, and conferences.

Take advantage of trade shows

Another way to compile or beef up your mailing list is to take advantage of trade show leads. When you have a booth at a trade show, have a depository where people leave business cards. Everyone who leaves a card is a potential customer. Every now and then you get a hot prospect who shows keen interest. Give this prospect personal attention. Following is an example of a follow-up letter to a hot prospect:

Dear

I enjoyed meeting you at the Kosherfest in Secaucus, New Jersey, last November and thank you for your interest in our products.

I'm attaching our new flyer which explains why Freeda Vitamins has such a marketable product line. Please note that we are certified kosher and have New Square Kosher Certification. Our vitamins are endorsed and accepted by everyone interested in kosher products.

Next step

I look forward to helping you meet the needs of your customers and will call you next week to see how I may help you.

Sincerely,

Following up on a visit to a customer site

In this heavily competitive world, people do business with people they like. Many products offer similar features and benefits, but the contract often goes to the company that's the nicest to work with.

Show that you're the nicest by thanking a company for its hospitality after you make an onsite visit. This is an opportunity to thank as well as sell, sell, and re-sell. Check out the example below for a thank you letter that may earn you the "Mr. Niceguy Award" and keep the customer coming back for more.

Dear _____ | Show your gratitude and pay a compliment |

I want to thank you and Jim for your hospitality in allowing me to demonstrate the latest version of our software to your MIS team. The response from your team was most gratifying, and the questions were meaningful.

Addressing your concerns | Restate the customer's problems |

During the meeting, the team expressed that their critical issue is. . . They said they need access to. . .

The MIS team agreed to take a look at [product]. If we succeed in proving that we can solve many of your problems, you'll introduce us to Ms. Jackson, your company president. I'm confident that [product] will allow your MIS team to meet its goals.

Next step

I'll call you in two weeks to see if I can be of further help.

Most sincerely,

Don't forget to use the Letter-Perfect Checklist featured on the Cheat Sheet in the front of this book. You don't want to be so embarrassed by an error that you have to change your identity, leave town, and give up your sales position to take up a life of service doing community work.

Chapter 7

In the Course of Your Employment

In This Chapter

▶ Creating application and broadcast letters that set you apart from the pack

▶ Making a good impression with a follow-up letter

▶ Fielding an offer or declining diplomatically

▶ Writing a glowing letter of recommendation

▶ Welcoming and introducing a new employee

▶ Movin' on up — the farewell letter

The only place where "success" comes before "work" is in the dictionary.

— Vidal Sassoon

During the course of your career, you have occasion to write a wide array of letters that relate to employment. The lust-to-dust mentality, where you get out of school, join a company, and forty years later retire from that same company, no longer exists. Statistics show that Americans now change jobs periodically and can have two or three careers within a lifetime. Employment letters aren't limited to finding a job, however. They run the gamut from welcoming a new employee to saying goodbye to fellow employees.

Separating the Gold from the Dross

If your dream job appeared in the classified ads tomorrow, would you be ready?

WANTED: LION TAMER

No experience needed. Must be able to use a whip, run fast, and love cats. Great medical coverage, but no death benefits. (The premiums would kill us.)

If interested, call Leo Lyons at 800-555-LION.

Perhaps this isn't your dream job, but sooner or later you'll see one that is. Make sure you have an application letter ready so you'll be the "mane" candidate.

When an application letter (also called a *cover letter*) is part of your repertoire, you're always prepared for the golden opportunity. *You must send an application letter with each resume,* so it's one of the most important letters you'll ever write. It's the application letter that separates the gold from the dross.

Don't forget to fill out the Start Up Sheet. Your professional future depends on identifying your audience, purpose, and key issue. And don't make the mistake of inventing your purpose and key issue merely to get a job. When you spend almost one-third of your waking hours at your place of employment, it's not just a job. Your career is a social outlet, a place to get kudos, a venue to implement your talents, and much more.

Writing an application letter takes a fair amount of thought and planning, but the time you invest is well worth the effort. As you may have guessed, an application letter isn't written just to thicken the envelope. This is what a well-written application letter can do for you:

- ✔ Inspire the recipient to read your resume.
- ✔ Launch an interview.
- ✔ Determine the course of your career.

Putting your personality on paper

Your friend got an exciting job, and she suggests that you use her application letter. Don't! No matter how wonderful and successful her letter was, it doesn't represent *your* personality on paper. Wouldn't an employer be surprised to meet you and find you're a B-type personality, rather than an A-type? Or that your personality is more informal than formal? Let your application letter reflect *your* words, *your* personality, and *your* attitude.

The following sections explain what compelling application letters should and shouldn't contain.

Letter do's

When you search for a job, let family, friends, and former coworkers know you're on the prowl. Check out the newspapers and professional/trade magazines. Call executive recruiters and employment agencies. You never know who knows someone who knows someone. After you search under every rock and gather leads, write an application letter that incorporates these do's:

- ✔ **Use the reader's name and title.** Never address the reader as *Gentlemen* or *Dear Sir or Madam*. (Check out Chapter 3 for tips on writing salutations.) The company's Web page may have the information you need; the company's receptionist can give you the names and titles; and your local library has reference books you can use.

- ✔ **Include highlights of your career that best sell you.** You don't want to include all the goodies from your resume, but you do want to stress some highlights. For example, list projects you managed, money you saved the company, or anything else that makes you shine. If you're a recent graduate with no experience in the field, talk about relevant courses or volunteer work.

- ✔ **Focus on what you have to offer the company.** Although Chapter 5 talks about placing your focus on the reader, writing the application letter is one of the few times you can get away with using "I" several times. Cast your letter in terms of how your expertise can help the company you're targeting.

- ✔ **Be humble.** Know the difference between being proud of your accomplishments and showing unbearable arrogance.

Save stock phrases and paragraphs in a template so you can pick and choose to create original letters without reinventing the wheel. These phrases are known as *boilerplates*. Check your software's user manual to learn how to save and reuse templates.

Keep the reader in clear focus. A catchy letter may be appropriate in the advertising industry, but it wouldn't be appropriate in the financial world. If in doubt, show your letter to someone in your target industry and get her reaction.

Letter taboos

Here are a few things to avoid when writing an application letter:

- ✔ **Shun conceited and corny remarks such as, "I'm dependable and have a good personality."** Who'd say, "I'm a scatterbrain and agonizingly boring"?

- ✔ **Don't repeat too much of the information in your resume.** Merely put your best foot forward with the highlights and qualifications that make you valuable. Following is an example of how one writer consolidated a half page of her resume into one sentence in her application letter:

   > In my 20 years of experience as a Communication Expert, I've earned numerous awards and gained national recognition. My wealth of experience spans Marketing Communications, Instructional Design, Seminars, Video Productions, and Corporate Training.

- ✔ **Don't write pages and pages.** Limit yourself to one page of three paragraphs. See the section "Hittin' them with all you have in three paragraphs" for details on what these paragraphs should contain.

Pumping up your professional image with letterhead

You can pump up your professional image by sending your application letters on letterhead. You don't have to invest big bucks or get fancy. See Chapter 2 for tips on how to prepare simple letterhead on your computer and what to include. Save the letterhead as a template and use it each time you send out an application letter.

Never use letterhead from your present place of employment. Even if your current employer knows you're looking for another job, that's in very bad taste.

Hittin' them with all you have in three paragraphs

Keep the letter fairly short — generally three paragraphs. The first paragraph relates your source, the second stresses why they should consider you to be the best candidate, and the third asks for an interview. To tweak the words of John F. Kennedy's inaugural address, "Ask not what the employer can do for you; ask what you can do for the employer." Example 7-1 at the end of this section shows an application letter that hits the mark.

Grabbing the reader's attention

Use the opening paragraph to identify your source and grab the reader's attention. This is your chance to make an initial great impression — give it your best shot. Here are a few examples:

- **Advertisement:** Your advertisement for a Chemical Engineer in *The New York Times* is of great interest to me. I have an M.B.A. from Northeastern University and a B.S. in Chemical Engineering from Georgia Tech.

- **Referral:** Frank N. Stein, your Marketing Manager, told me of your need for a Marketing Assistant. Mr. Stein is confident that my background would let me hit the ground running and make an immediate contribution to Petra, Inc.

- **Solicitation:** As a recent graduate of Berkeley College with a major in engineering, I'd like the opportunity to make a contribution to the growth efforts of Sine & Tangent, Incorporated.

Never pass up answering an ad just because you don't have all the stated requirements. Ads always describe the ideal candidate, and companies rarely get all the attributes they look for. As long as you have even one of the requirements, you should go for it. And don't apologize or mention the requirements you don't have. Focus on the strengths you do have.

Mail merging

When you launch a job-search campaign, use the merge feature on your word processor. The merge feature lets you create a letter once and send as many personalized copies as you want. Each copy can have a personalized name, address, salutation, and whatever other variable data you designate. You can also generate an envelope for each letter without typing in the address. Check the user manual of your word processing program to get the scoop.

Putting meat in the middle

The middle paragraph is where you expand on your qualifications. Let the reader know you can do an incredible job for the company because of your past experiences. You can select a few highlights from your resume and present them with bullets. (There's a discussion of preparing bullets in Chapter 5.)

> I have more than ten years' experience in video productions. I'm adept in scripting, filming, and editing. My video on "Productive Unemployment" won me an honorable mention award at the New England Video & Film Festival.

or

> As you can see from my resume, I have five years of experience with UnderHill Company. Here are some of my career highlights that can be of benefit to you:
>
> - Creating and providing comprehensive product terminology to reflect current construction trends and technology
>
> - Monitoring computer programs and recommending system changes and enhancements for three databases
>
> - Reviewing and revising mechanical boards and negatives forwarded to meet printing schedules

If you're answering an ad, your middle paragraph may show an informal table comparing their requirements with your skills:

Your requirements:	*My skills:*
5+ years' experience	Ten years' experience in materials science
Work independently and with others	Self-motivated and team player
Travel a must	Enjoy traveling to new locations and meeting interesting people

Try to avoid dealing with salary requirements in the application letter. Save that discussion for the interview. If you answer one of those nasty ads that demands a number, here are a few options: Ignore it, mention a range, state your current salary, or say that you expect a salary commensurate with your experience. It's really a personal choice.

Ending memorably

End with the request for an interview, and if you haven't already done so, mention that you're enclosing your resume.

> Please give me a chance to meet with you so you can evaluate how my skills will benefit Smith & Co. Please call me at (781) 555-1234 so we may arrange for an interview. (Phone number not on letterhead.)

or

> I've attached a copy of my resume. Please call me so we can arrange for a personal interview. I look forward to meeting with you and showing you my portfolio. (Phone number on letterhead.)

If you don't already have one — invest in an answering machine. Once you go through the trouble of mounting a job-hunting campaign, prospective employers must be able to reach you when it's convenient for them.

The best time to send

Some experts say you should send your letter and resume immediately after the ad appears because the "early bird gets the worm." Others say you should wait at least a week so you're not one of the pack. There's no right or wrong answer. I've done both, and both have worked. Do whichever makes you comfortable. In the meantime, check out Example 7-1 for an application letter that demands to be considered.

Make your English teacher proud

Be aware of the impact of your words, and cast them in a positive light. Check out Chapter 5 for tips on honing the tone of your letter. Following are a few examples of how to give those seeming negatives a positive spin:

You're unemployed:

Positive: "I'm looking for new opportunities."

Negative: "I'm unemployed." (That's akin to telling your date she has dragon breath.)

You're right out of school:

Positive: "I'm exploring two different career paths."

Negative: "I'm looking for my first job."

DONNA RANDALL
2 Jason Terrace, San Francisco, CA 94110   (415) 826-1565

October 30, XXXX   Computer-generated letterhead.

Mr. James Haskell
Haskell Enterprises
3 Ipswich Street
Chicago, IL 60657

Dear Mr. Haskell:

Subject: Candidate for Director of Financial Planning

Jeremy McCoy, Vice President of Finance, told me of your need for
an innovative Director of Financial Planning. I worked with Mr.
McCoy at a former company, and he feels that my background is just
what you're looking for.

Career Highlights   Bullets for key accomplishments.
Following are some of the highlights of my ten-year career as a
financial planner that can benefit Haskell Enterprises:

- Coordinating and consolidating all data for annual profit
  plan and five-year profit plan.
- Preparing capital investment analysis and making
  recommendations for whether or not to buy.
- Making statistical and time sharing models.

The enclosed resume is merely a piece of paper. It doesn't reflect my
enthusiasm, sense of humor, and team spirit. When can we get
together?

                    An interesting closing paragraph.

Very truly yours,

Donna Randall
Enc.

Example 7-1:
Application
letter that
says,
"I'm worth
meeting."

Sending electronically

E-mail messages and faxes are quite popular ways of sending application letters and resumes. These electronic alternatives have a distinct advantage of going directly to the reader.

Just the fax, ma'am

Faxes are a great way to send your application letter and resume because they're typically put in the reader's in-box or on her desk. They're not screened as letters from the post office often are.

Write the application letter for a fax just as you would for sending it snail mail (that is, regular mail). The bonus is that you don't have to use good stationery for the letter or resume because you keep the original. When you send your application letter and resume via fax, consider the following:

✔ Prepare a cover page, which is typically a separate sheet of paper that has the names, phone numbers, fax numbers of the sender and recipient, current date, and number of pages you're faxing. As an option, adhere a Post-It Fax Note that you stick to a blank part of your letter.

✔ If you're launching a big job search and will be sending multiple faxes, fax during off-peak hours for better rates.

Easy does it with e-mail

Many employers accept (and welcome) e-mail submissions. When you send your resume via e-mail, send your resume as an attachment. Use the body of the e-mail message as your application letter.

E-mail messages have the distinct advantage of popping up on the reader's screen. With a great subject line, you can make your application letter and resume shout "READ ME!" (although *Read Me* should never be your subject line). A great subject line for a referral may be "Jack Mason suggested that we get together." For more information on crafting great subject lines, check out Chapter 4.

Don't forget to start your e-mail with a salutation and end with a complimentary closing. For more information on salutations and complimentary closings, check out Chapter 3.

Broadcasting Yourself

A broadcast letter is a networking option for seasoned professionals looking for new job opportunities. It's an application letter and resume rolled into one, so it should contain all the information you want the reader to know about you. (Broadcast letters aren't for people looking for their first jobs or those looking to switch fields.)

Don't limit a broadcast letter to one page if it means excluding information that makes you shine. Broadcast letters are becoming increasingly popular as the job market becomes more competitive and people want to stand out.

I'm not suggesting that seasoned professionals send a broadcast letter instead of an application letter and resume. I'm just letting you know there are options.

Quantifying your accomplishments

As with an application letter, a broadcast letter has an opening paragraph to hook the reader or give the source, one or two middle paragraphs that best "sell" your professional strengths and accomplishments, and a final paragraph that calls for action.

A broadcast letter must contain a lot of the meat you'd ordinarily put in a resume. Prepare at least three bulleted items or headlines that best "sell" your professional strengths and accomplishments in one of the middle paragraphs. Here are a few examples:

- Reduced accounts receivable by $140,000 with improved credit and collection policies.

- Sold more than $800,000 in residential real estate in each of the past five years.

- Increased volume 15 percent by diversifying business from one line to several lines.

- Saved $250,000 on a $3 million expense budget developed for increased schedule. This improved quality by 18 percent.

Action words with pizzazz

The following action words show leadership qualities or special skills you may want to include in your broadcast letter. If you're sending an application letter, these words would most likely be on your resume. For great resumes, you may want to check out *Resumes For Dummies* by Joyce Lain Kennedy (IDG Books Worldwide, Inc.).

Administered	Analyzed	Automated	Budgeted
Chaired	Completed	Conducted	Consolidated
Coordinated	Created	Decreased	Designed
Developed	Directed	Engineered	Facilitated

Formulated	Founded	Implemented	Improved
Increased	Initiated	Innovated	Introduced
Launched	Managed	Marketed	Motivated
Operated	Organized	Presented	Programmed
Published	Reduced	Saved	Solved
Started	Supervised	Trained	Upgraded

The following broadcast letter shows how this all ties together. Notice that this isn't dramatically different from an application letter, but it does stand alone without an attached resume.

Dear

Are your expenses proving too costly or are you in need of a new approach in your accounting department? If so, perhaps you'll be interested in how I reduced annual recurring expenses at Arbee Chemical Company by $450,000 through work simplification, control procedures, and staff reduction.

Career Highlights Bulleting career highlights.

Here are some highlights of my career that may be of value to you:

- Designed and administered the financial reporting system as the company grew from one to four companies.

- Successfully liquidated property appraised at $300,000 for $400,000.

- Recommended the consolidation of three accounting departments after cost-study analysis.

When can we get together?

With this background and history of successful cost reduction, I can help reduce your overall spending. I'll be glad to discuss further details of my experience at a personal interview. I'll call you next week to arrange a time we may get together.

Ends with call to action.

Sincerely,

Thanks for the Interview

Okay . . . your application letter or broadcast letter made the cut, and you've been granted an interview. Don't stop there. Immediately after the interview, take the time to write a thank-you letter. If you have nice handwriting, handwrite the letter. If you have handwriting like mine, use your computer.

Here are some tidbits you may include in the thank-you letter:

- ✔ Mention how much you enjoyed the interview.
- ✔ Express your enthusiasm for working for the company.
- ✔ Use this opportunity to relate something you didn't get a chance to tell the interviewer.
- ✔ Reiterate one of your accomplishments that impressed the interviewer the most.

A friend of mine recently got a job in a very competitive industry. Her supervisor told her that it was between her and another candidate. What tipped the scales in her favor was that she wrote a thank-you letter after the interview and the other person didn't. The follow-up letter gave the supervisor a clear sign that my friend had enthusiasm for the position and the company. Following is a copy of the letter she wrote:

Dear

It was a pleasure meeting with you yesterday morning to discuss the opportunity as Manager of your MIS department. The chance to support this department at Atkinson & Sons is especially intriguing because of the diversity of your technology. I'm sure that my ten-year background in MIS will let me hit the ground running and make an immediate contribution.

Next step   Expressing enthusiasm for company.

I'm eager to share my talents with Atkinson & Sons and look forward to returning for a second interview.

Sincerely,

Yes, We Got Your Resume

SHERYL SAYS

Once you're hired, you may view the application process from the other side of the fence.

With the hectic demands made on people, there's often no time to respond to each applicant with a personal letter. It's polite, however, to acknowledge that you received the resume. Many companies send out form letters or postcards for this purpose. Following is a postcard that acknowledges a resume:

> Dear Candidate:
>
> This is to acknowledge that we received your resume for the position in Process Engineering and Material Science. We've had an overwhelming response to our advertisement, but you can be assured that we'll give your resume careful consideration.
>
> Once this process has been completed, we'll contact each candidate whose background matches our needs. Thank you for considering the Franklin Company.
>
> *Richard Godin*

Sometimes, you have to say "Thanks, but no thanks." Even when you aren't considering a candidate, thank her for applying. You always want to maintain good will. (Who knows, the applicant may be your boss one day.) Following is a postcard letting the candidate down gently. Check out Chapter 4 for ways to tactfully be the bearer of disappointing news.

> Dear Candidate:
>
> Thank you for your recent application to Franklin Company. Although your resume is very impressive, we've received resumes from people whose backgrounds match our needs more closely. We will, however, keep your resume on file in the event that a suitable position should become available.
>
> Good luck in your job search.
>
> *Richard Godin*

The Job Is Yours

It's always a good idea to extend a formal job offer in writing so there won't be any misunderstanding about the terms and conditions. Following is a list of what to include:

- ✔ Starting salary, bonuses, or any other financial considerations
- ✔ Number of vacation and personal-leave days
- ✔ Relocation benefits, if applicable
- ✔ What to expect in insurance benefits
- ✔ Starting date

When you write the offer letter, prepare a section on the bottom where the applicant can sign to indicate her acceptance of the terms. In the following letter, notice how the headlines tell the story.

Dear

Good news opening.

Congratulations: You're our choice for Engineering Manager

It's with great pleasure that we offer you the position of Engineering Manager, reporting to Fran Carlo, Vice President. We offer you the starting salary of $7,000 per month plus a $5,000 sign-on bonus after you've been with us for three months.

Enclosed is a benefits packet

The benefits' packet that's enclosed outlines the health, dental, life, and disability benefits you can expect. We also offer eleven paid holidays, five personal days, and ten vacation days.

We look forward to having you join us

Please let us know you accept this offer by signing your name and date on the bottom of this letter. Return one copy to me by March 1, and keep the second copy for your records. Please call me at extension 334 if you have any questions.

Sincerely,

I accept the above offer:

_____   _____
Name   Date

Don't Shoot the Messenger

No one likes to be the bearer of bad news, especially when someone's career hangs in the balance. When you must deliver such news, check out Chapter 4 for ways to cushion the blow. Here are some things to keep in mind while letting a candidate down gently:

- ✔ Praise her credentials or say something positive.
- ✔ Express your regrets and offer a brief explanation.
- ✔ Offer sincere wishes for her future.

| Eliminating a subject line and headlines makes the bad news less obvious |

Dear

We very much enjoyed meeting with you during your two visits to MRM Corporation when you interviewed for the position of Senior Analyst. Your background is impressive, and you certainly have what it takes to do the job. This was a difficult choice.

| Cushioning the bad news |

There was another candidate, however, with many years' experience in the semiconductor industry, and we feel that she can begin to make an immediate contribution with little or no ramp-up time. We've, therefore, selected her. We wish you success in finding a new position and will keep your name on file for the future.

Sincerely,

Don't reject other qualified candidates until your first choice accepts the offer. There's always a chance that your first choice may decline, and you want to keep the door open for the also-rans. Otherwise, you may be up that well-known creek without a paddle.

If you get a rejection letter, keep in mind that the ideal job is just a phone call or letter away. If you get desperate, the lion tamer's position is still available. You can make a few bucks and get health insurance while you continue to search for the ideal job.

The Terminator

There may be times when you have to terminate an employee. This is probably one of the toughest letters to write. (Check out Chapter 4 for tips on sequencing a bad-news letter.) Following are a few things to include:

✔ **Start with your regrets.** "We truly regret when we have to let someone go because of poor performance."

✔ **Give the reasons why this was necessary.** "Despite several conversations with you letting you know that customers are complaining about your attitude, customers are still complaining."

✔ **Enumerate warnings that were given, if appropriate.** "We've been more than fair. Jay spoke to you about these complaints on March 1, April 12, and again on June 15."

✔ **Make it clear if this is probationary or permanent.** "We can't let someone with a poor attitude interface with our customers. Therefore, we must terminate your employment."

✔ **End on a note of encouragement or wishes for success.** "We wish you good luck in finding employment with another company."

On a final note . . . Don't send or just hand your letter to the victim. Call her into your office, talk through the situation, and then hand her the letter. At that point, the contents of letter shouldn't be a surprise.

Declining an Offer

Don't accept a job offer unless you're certain it's the job you want. If you're unsure, call the prospective employer and let him know that you'd like a short time to think it over. If you decline, do it in a timely manner because the company must find another candidate. You obviously made a strong impression and don't want to burn any bridges. Here are some tips for declining an offer:

✔ State your sincere thanks for the opportunity.

✔ Offer a brief explanation as to why you're not accepting.

- You accepted another position that has greater growth potential.

- You decided you don't want to relocate.

✔ Extend wishes for finding a suitable person to fill the position.

> Dear | *Graciously declining.* |
>
> Thank you so much for offering me the position as Manager of Northeastern Sales. Although it would be a wonderful opportunity, I had to reconsider the travel aspect. It would be difficult for my family if I were traveling to such a great extent. If another opportunity comes along that involves less travel, please consider me.
>
> I would enjoy building my career at Belco Co. and have a lot to contribute.
>
> Sincerely,

Welcoming a New Employee

I joined a company many years ago and for the first week went virtually unnoticed. I have red curly hair and kidded someone that I could have put an Annie doll in my chair and people wouldn't have noticed my absence. Finally, I went around and introduced myself. Make sure this doesn't happen to your new employees.

Say "hello" personally

Always make someone new feel welcome. My husband joined a company recently. Two days before he was to start, his manager sent him the following delightful e-mail message that made my husband feel welcome before he even walked in the door:

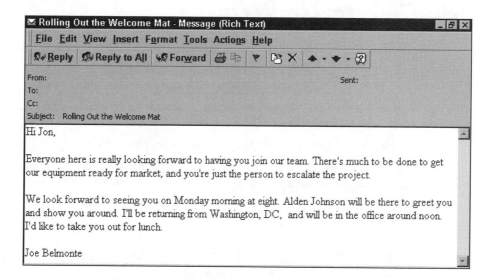

Spread the word to others

Make each new employee feel welcome by spreading the word that she joined your company. Include her name, position, a short biography, and the date she starts. You can place a memo on the bulletin board or send an e-mail message. Following is an e-mail message that welcomes Ms. Milo:

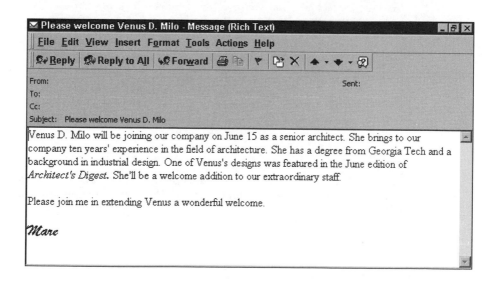

It's Time to Move On

Sooner or later we all move on. (Sometimes it's our choice; sometimes it's not.) If you are asked to resign or choose to depart on your own, remember these guidelines:

- ✔ Simply state that you're leaving. Don't let a farewell letter be a dumping ground for the ills of the company.

- ✔ Let people know the last day you report to work.

- ✔ Wish everyone success. Following is an e-mail message where an employee says "good-bye" because she found another position.

Leaving with lots of goodwill

```
✉ Moving on as of September 1 - Message (Rich Text)                    _ ⎕ ✕

  File  Edit  View  Insert  Format  Tools  Actions  Help

  ✉ Reply   ✉ Reply to All   ✉ Forward   🖨 🗐  ▼  🗋 ✕  ▲ ▾ ▾ ▾ ⚛

 From:                                                      Sent:
 To:
 Cc:
 Subject:  Moving on as of September 1
```

Dear Friends,

After much consideration, I've accepted a teaching position at Berkeley. It offers me a wonderful location, a promotion, and the chance to specialize in advising and teaching graduate students. It's with mixed emotions that I resign my position, effective September 1. I have enjoyed being part of M.I.T. and will always look to my years here with pride, respect, and appreciation for my growth as an educator.

When you leave a place, some of it you take with you and some of yourself you leave behind. I've made many friends in my years here and will always cherish those friendships.

Warmest regards,

Jane

This good-bye e-mail message is from someone who was asked to leave. The reason for leaving is deliberately unclear. However, the ambiguity is handled with great tact.

Short and to the point

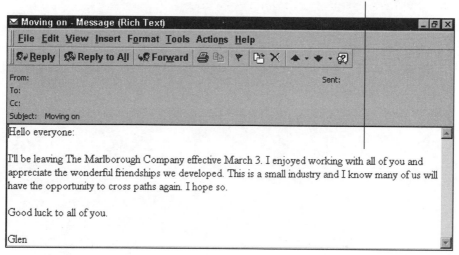

> **Moving on - Message (Rich Text)**
>
> File Edit View Insert Format Tools Actions Help
>
> Reply | Reply to All | Forward
>
> From: Sent:
> To:
> Cc:
> Subject: Moving on
>
> Hello everyone:
>
> I'll be leaving The Marlborough Company effective March 3. I enjoyed working with all of you and appreciate the wonderful friendships we developed. This is a small industry and I know many of us will have the opportunity to cross paths again. I hope so.
>
> Good luck to all of you.
>
> Glen

Don't forget to use your Letter-Perfect Checklist featured on the Cheat Sheet in the front of this book. You wouldn't want to lose a job opportunity as a proofreader because in your application letter you claim to have "Outstanding poofreading skills."

Chapter 8
The Customer Is Always Right

- -

In This Chapter

▶ Staking your claim with a letter

▶ Making prompt and friendly adjustments for your customers

▶ Saying "yes" to the customer

▶ Saying "no" and leaving the customer smiling

- -

We view a customer who is complaining as a real blessing in disguise. He or she is someone we can resell [to].

— Louis Carbone, Vice President National Car Rental

Customers who submit *claims* (a better term than *complaints*) are golden. They take the time to let you know there's a problem because they want to continue doing business with you. For every customer who submits a claim, there are many others having the same problem who simply take their business elsewhere. Therefore, when you receive a claim letter from a customer, view it as something positive — an opportunity to serve him better.

Staking Your Claim

(This section focuses on the person writing the claim letter.) Despite a company's best efforts to do everything right, occasionally something goes awry. The smart company is one that values hearing about mistakes, defects, disappointments, or dissatisfactions with products or services. This gives the company the chance to discover, analyze, and correct these problems — and ultimately serve you better.

Loyal customers are the backbone of every business, and companies *do* want to keep customers happy. Write your letters with this positive attitude in mind.

Learning from the Pro — my Mom

Throughout my childhood, I recall family and friends coming to my mother with complaints about products or services. My mother would sit down at her typewriter and whip out a letter to the offending company. Within a short time, the disgruntled people would report that they'd received an apology, a freebie, or some form of satisfaction. A friend once said, "When Ethel writes a letter, the paper burns." My mother was a great and successful letter writer. This chapter is chock full of what I learned at my mother's knee.

Gathering your information

Before you write a claim letter, fill out the Start Up Sheet to identify your audience, purpose, and key issue. Gather any supporting papers you may have such as receipts, prior correspondence, and anything else that strengthens your claim. Following are some issues to keep in mind that are specific to claim letters:

- ✔ **Audience:** Address your letter to the person in a position to grant your request. That may be the manager, supervisor, or someone else in authority. (Check out Chapter 3 for hints on finding out the names of people in a company.)

- ✔ **Purpose:** Clearly state the action you want — for example, a refund, new product, or nothing.

- ✔ **Key issue:** What exactly is your claim about the product or service? Don't merely say the product isn't working.

Grin, don't grunt

When you write a claim letter, your mantra should be: "Grin, don't grunt." If you grin, the reader is more likely to address your claim. If you grunt, you'll be labeled "just another crank." Assume the company wants to retain your business and will treat you fairly. The following tips can help facilitate fair treatment:

- ✔ **Send your claim letter as soon as the problem arises.** If you wait too long, you weaken your case.

- ✔ **If you're not using letterhead, be sure to include your name, address, and phone number on the letter.** This seems obvious, but it's amazing how many people forget.

✔ **Contact a person in a position to help you.** Get the name of someone in the company who's in a position to act on your claim. You can usually get a person's name (not just job title) by calling the main number or looking on the company's Web site. That person may be the Vice President of Sales or the Director of the Customer Service Department. Here's an opening that works:

> As the Director of Customer Service, I'm certain that you can help me solve the problem I'm having with Foot Fetish, Model No. 2334.

✔ **Start with the assumption that the company is anxious to satisfy you.** Don't be negative, sarcastic, threatening, or hostile. (Check out Chapter 5 for ways to improve the tone of your letter by using words that connote something positive.) The person reading your letter probably isn't the one who caused the problem. He's the one you hope will straighten it out. Following are examples of positive and negative approaches:

> *Positive:* Please send me two purple grape plants (No. 334) to replace the ones that arrived wilted.

> *Positive:* The sign in your door says, "A satisfied customer is our main concern." I believe you.

> *Positive:* Won't you please replace the broken [item]. . .

> *Negative:* Your competitors offer better service. Why should I continue doing business with you?

> *Negative:* Your product (or service) stinks!

✔ **State the facts in logical order.** Include a description of the original transaction and clearly state why you're dissatisfied. Mention names of people you spoke to and dates. Send copies of sales slips, invoices, canceled checks, and such. (You keep the originals.) Following is an example of a headline and opening paragraph:

> **Details of My Dissatisfaction**

> On July 2 I had my car serviced at your shop before leaving on a cross-country trip. After traveling just 150 miles, I had trouble with my right rear wheel. The mechanic told me that the lugnut wasn't tightened sufficiently during the service. I'm enclosing a copy of your invoice and the invoice from the garage that made the repair.

✔ **Ask for a fair adjustment.** If you have a specific adjustment in mind, let the reader know exactly what that is:

> **Action Requested**

> The warranty guarantees material and workmanship for six months. Therefore, I enclose the broken [item] and original sales receipt. Please send me a new [item].

✔ **If you're not sure what's fair, ask the reader to be fair.** Often you get more than you may have asked for.

Next Step

I've been a long-time customer and know you will be fair. Please let me know how we may resolve this.

It's better to send a letter initially rather than make a phone call because a letter creates a paper trail. Consider sending the letter certified mail; doing so engenders a sense of urgency, and your claim may be attended to more quickly. Also, keep copies of all correspondence. If you speak to someone on the phone as a result of your letter, get that person's name and jot down the gist of the conversation.

Following up

If the company doesn't answer your letter, give it the benefit of the doubt and assume your letter got lost in the black hole of postal land. Send another copy and mark or stamp "copy" across the top of the letter. If you don't get a response to your second letter within a week or two, you can assume something about the company's attitude. It's time to take your claim to someone higher up in the company (even the president), contact the Better Business Bureau, or take your business elsewhere. Your follow-up action depends greatly on the extent of your claim and its dollar value.

I'm quick on the draw to let companies know when I'm dissatisfied with a product or service. However, I'm just as quick to let companies know when I'm delighted. Creating a balance is important.

Making Amicable Adjustments

(This section deals with the other side of the fence — a company receiving claims.) A company that views letters of dissatisfaction as *complaints,* rather than *claims*, is missing the mark. The word *complaint* conjures up unpleasant, combative feelings. Many years ago most companies had complaint departments. As companies became more savvy and service oriented, they changed the name of the department to *customer service* or *customer care.* These terms are more positive and conjure up the image of people who want to service and who do care.

When customers aren't happy and don't stake their claims, they fly into the arms of the competition. These dissatisfied customers hurt your bottom line.

What is a customer?

Following are the words of a sign posted at the Freeport, Maine, headquarters of L.L. Bean. This attitude is one of the reasons that L.L. Bean is so successful.

A Customer is the most important person ever in this office . . . in person or by mail.

A Customer is not dependent on us . . . we are dependent on him.

A Customer is not an interruption of our work . . . he is the purpose of it. We are not doing him a favor by serving him . . . he is doing us a favor by giving us the opportunity to do so.

A Customer is not someone to argue or match wits with. Nobody ever won an argument with a Customer.

A Customer is a person who brings us his wants.

It is our job to handle them profitably to him and ourselves.

Responding in a heartbeat

As mentioned earlier, loyal customers are the backbone of every business. To make your customers feel important and to keep them coming back, answer claim letters promptly. Here are a few suggestions for extenuating circumstances:

🖛 Even if you can't help the customer immediately, write to let him know his claim is being addressed. Let him know when he can expect an answer and from whom.

🖛 If you need additional information before you can help the customer, ask for it with a smile, as you see in the example that follows.

Dear

We appreciate your May 4 letter letting us know of [situation]. Because of customers like you who let us know when problems arise, we're able to serve all our customers better. For that we thank you.

Next step

Please send us a copy of the April 20 invoice. As soon as I receive it, I'll turn this matter over to Mr. Charles, Vice President of Customer Service, and you'll be hearing from him directly.

Thank you for giving us the chance to help you.

Sincerely,

When you find yourself responding to the same customer questions or problems repeatedly, you can prepare standard paragraphs or letters (known as boilerplates). Include a personalized statement at the beginning and end.

> *Opening paragraph:* Thank you for letting us address your concern about the recent price increase.

> *Closing paragraph:* As always, you can count on our superior quality. We promise you'll be satisfied or we'll refund your money.

When you get a claim from a customer asking for satisfaction on an item where the warranty has expired, you are in a sticky situation. You do want to maintain goodwill and may consider offering a compromise or goodwill gesture (subject to company policy, of course). Here's a suggestion that may satisfy the customer. "We checked our records and notice that your warranty expired six months ago. However, we want you to be satisfied and offer you a new [item] at a 20 percent discount."

Yes, we can!

When you grant the adjustment the customer asks for, the letter is a good-news letter and, therefore, easy to write. Start by letting the reader know what adjustment you're making. (If you're making special concessions, let that be your little secret. Merely infer that the reader's loyalty is something money can't buy.)

Dear

Subject: We're glad to be of service

I can certainly understand your dissatisfaction even beyond the date the warranty expired. Because you're such a valued customer, we'd like to make amends by [tell what you're going to do].

We value your loyalty and thank you for bringing this to our attention. It's because of customers like you that we're able correct our occasional problems.

Sincerely,

Following are a few things to avoid when granting an adjustment:

- ✔ Don't dwell on the customer's complaint. Merely deal with it.
- ✔ Don't miss a chance to promote future sales such as enclosing a coupon or gift certificate.
- ✔ Never bad-mouth an employee; accept the blame.

Following are two scenarios and how companies responded:

You receive an irate letter from a long-standing customer. The customer states that she's tired of your salesperson who's been rude and keeps presenting a series of unacceptable schemes. Your customer concludes with: "We no longer want [your product] or any further contact with your company." This is the response:

Dear

I'm very sorry to learn of the problem you've had with our salesman, [name]. All our salespeople attend a one-week training program because we expect them to be honest with and courteous to all our customers. Please accept my apology. We've taken corrective action, and you can be assured that [name] will never call on you again.

Won't you let me turn this around?

> Notice the one headline offers to pacify the customer

[Name of customer], your business is important to us, and we're anxious to continue the long-standing relationship we've enjoyed for many years. I'll call you personally next week to see how I can make this up to you.

Very sincerely,

You receive a letter from an irate customer whose order for a five-pound box of chocolate arrived in damaged condition. This response would certainly satisfy me:

Dear

The subject line tells the story

Subject: A new five-pound box of chocolate is on its way

Thank you for taking the time to write about the box of chocolates that arrived damaged. Our guess is that the damage occurred in transit. We mailed you a new five-pound box of chocolates today, and you should have it by the end of the week.

We're proud of our candies and want you to be completely satisfied. Enjoy!

Sincerely,

Don't stop there

After an adjustment is made, continue the dialogue with the customer. Send the customer a follow-up questionnaire letter asking him to rate the quality of your service. This letter can be a boilerplate that you personalize by changing the name and any other variable information. Letter questionnaires, such as the one that follows, provide wonderful feedback for your company. They're a great way to get the customer to seal his loyalty into an envelope.

Dear

Subject: We value your input

Our customer care representative recently spoke to you regarding the inquiry you made. We hope this matter was settled and that you're completely satisfied. Please take a moment to let us know.

CUSTOMER
SATISFACTION
QUESTIONNAIRE

Please take a few moments to fill out the Customer Satisfaction Questionnaire. We're continuously trying to give all our customers the best quality service, and we want to know how we're doing.

| YOUR FEEDBACK | Your feedback is an important part of helping to serve you better. |
| DONATION TO UNITED WAY | To show our appreciation for your time, we'll make a donation to the United Way once you return the questionnaire. |

Sincerely,

Sorry, we can't

Although no one likes to be the bearer of bad news, there are occasions when the customer is wrong and you just have to say "No." Still, your goal is to keep goodwill. (Check out Chapter 3 for ways to sequence your letter when denying an adjustment.) Following is an example of how to say "No" without saying *no*:

Dear

We pride ourselves on our policy not to be undersold. You must be completely satisfied with any merchandise you purchase from us — both for quality and price.

When I looked closely at the advertisement you sent from On-the-Cheap Computers, I noticed that it's for Model 123A. Your receipt is for Model 123B. It's certainly easy to confuse the two.

We do appreciate your bringing this matter to our attention and thank you for your continued support and patronage.

Sincerely,

Example 8-1 is a letter from an irate customer who makes an idle threat. Example 8-2 is the company's courteous reply that ties together the following points:

- ✔ **Acknowledge the customer's point of view.** Either agree with the customer or show your appreciation for his point of view. (Don't be grouchy, even if the customer was.)
- ✔ **Stress what, if anything, you can do.** Never argue with the customer, and avoid expressions such as "your complaint" or "your error."
- ✔ **End on a friendly note.** You want to maintain goodwill and keep the reader as a customer. Remember that he thinks he's right.

Don't forget to use your Letter-Perfect Checklist on the Cheat Sheet in the front of this book. If you inadvertently send a customer a refund check for $212.50 instead of $122.50, you create goodwill. However, if you do that too often you'll be out of business in a New York minute!

June 30, XXXX

CERTIFIED MAIL

Mail-Order Paradise
200 Harmony Road
Cheltenham, PA 19012

To Whom This May Concern: | Cold and impersonal salutation |

On April 25, I ordered a computer from you, and it's a piece of junk. It ran fine for the first two months, then — for no apparent reason — it started crapping out periodically. I put up with it for one week, and now I must insist on a new computer. I'm returning the piece of junk.

This time, send one I can count on. If you don't, I'll contact the Better Business Bureau and tell everyone I know not to buy from your schlock company. | Needless threats |

In this box is the computer and the original paperwork. You'll notice that the warranty guarantees "trouble-free" performance for one year. This computer didn't make it through the first few months. I DEMAND IMMEDIATE ACTION!

Dissatisfied,

A. Crabb
One Surly Corner
Shaft, PA 17975

Example 8-1:
Complaint
from a
grouch.

Mail-Order Paradise
200 Harmony Road, Cheltenham, PA 19012
800-434-3445

July 3, XXXX

A. Crabb | You don't know the writer's sex from the initial |
One Surly Corner
Shaft, PA 17975

Dear A. Crabb:

We agree that a computer that doesn't run reliably is useless. And we do warranty trouble-free performance for one year from the date of purchase. To ensure the highest quality, we thoroughly check all computers before they leave our warehouse. | Agreeing with the customer at some level |

We had your computer thoroughly checked by our service department, and it seems as if it was dropped or met with some untimely accident. The mother board has a slight crack and the outer case has a dent. That's undoubtedly why you started having trouble with it after two months of trouble-free performance.

Here's what we can do
Although this type of damage isn't covered under a standard warranty, we will replace the mother board for $125 and extend the warranty for one year from the repair date. | Stating what you'll do |

Next step
Please let us know if you wish us to make the repairs. If so, we'll repair your computer and promptly return it within one week. It will be as good as new. Thank you for letting us help you.

Sincerely,

Ted Grant
Customer Service Manager

Example 8-2:
Saying "no"
with
panache.

Chapter 9

Cash or Charge?

· ·

In This Chapter

▶ Using credit to lure customers to your business

▶ Sharing the good news of credit approval

▶ Informing customers that their credit application is denied

▶ Crafting collection letters that bring in the bucks

▶ Maintaining customer goodwill, no matter what letter you write

· ·

> *Credit buying is much like being drunk. The buzz happens immediately and gives you a lift. . . The hangover comes the day after.*
>
> — Dr. Joyce Brothers

Ch a a a r g e! That's a common cry in our free-enterprise system. *Plastic* accounts for about 90 percent of all the buying and selling. Some people even suggest that we're on the verge of becoming a cashless society. As a customer, wherever you shop, you can sign up for a credit card and charge purchases on the spot. All you need is a pen, a decent credit history, and an honest face.

As a merchant, you're happy to extend this service because it means more business for you. But it can also mean more headaches — and definitely more letters. Whether you're writing to tell a customer she's been approved or writing to get her to pay an outstanding bill, you need to communicate clearly and with style.

Fill out the Start Up Sheet on the Cheat Sheet in front of this book before you write any credit or collection letter. Money is always a sensitive issue, and you must be attuned to your audience, purpose, and key issue.

Credit is the American Way

The ability to buy now and pay later is alluring — as you see in the quote that opens this chapter. Buying on credit, however, isn't all roses; credit cards do have thorns. As a merchant, for example, you profit from greater sales if you extend credit, but you also have to deal with the following:

- ✔ There are losses from people who don't pay (even though you threaten to take away their firstborn).

- ✔ If you honor major credit cards, your cost of doing business increases because the companies take a percentage of what your customers charge.

Luring new customers

Businesses must constantly market themselves in order to lure new customers. Offering a charge card is one way of getting people hooked on buying from you. But first you must lure them. Check out Chapter 6 for ways to bait the hook for your sales letters. After all, a letter offering credit is a sales letter with a gimmick. Following are suggestions for luring customers by offering charge accounts:

- ✔ Extend credit through a welcoming letter to new families who move into the neighborhood, if that's appropriate for your business.

- ✔ Send out a mailing with coupons or special discounts for charge customers only.

- ✔ Adapt your mailing to a special sale or seasonal celebration for charge customers only.

- ✔ Stress the advantages of buying on credit.

To the consumer: The roses and thorns of buying on credit

As a consumer, if you buy on credit, you don't have to carry large amounts of cash and worry about getting mugged. You can also return or exchange merchandise easily. The downside of credit is that you can easily get caught in the habit of buying more than you can afford and accumulate heavy debts.

Consider the following tips when you send a letter offering credit:

- **Be welcoming and friendly.** Chapter 5 has scads of tips for honing the tone and speaking to the customer from her point of view.

- **Extend an invitation of some sort.** Ask the customer to stop by and browse, contact you, or fill out a credit application and mail it.

  > Please give us a call so we can get together to talk about how our credit arrangements with low interest rates can benefit you.

  > or

  > Please stop by and look around. And while you're here, why not ask about the advantages of saying, "Charge it, please"?

- **Stress information about your merchandise or services.** Highlight the benefits to the customer — superior quality, affordable prices, or whatever. (Chapter 6 has a host of expressions for all sorts of occasions.)

  > We have new and exciting merchandise waiting for you. Please stop by and look around. There's something here for everyone on your Christmas list.

- **Accent the benefits of credit buying.** Be subtle and show the benefits from the customer's point of view.

  > As a Mason cardholder, you'll be notified of special sales that are available only to people with our charge card.

- **Spur action.** Let the reader know what you expect her to do and why.

  > If you return your application before December 1, you'll be eligible for our $100 drawing for merchandise of your choice.

Yes, you're credit worthy

After you run a credit check that shows the customer is credit worthy, the first step in establishing the credit relationship is to send a "good news" letter. Consider including some of these tips:

- **Tell the customer she's been approved.** Say it with a smile.

  > We're delighted to learn of your impeccable credit reputation and welcome you to our family of loyal customers.

- **Mention the terms of credit.** If you explain the terms of credit in the letter, cushion them in the middle because getting down to business takes away from the good news. If you have a pamphlet that explains the terms, mention that it's enclosed. You may mention the latter in a postscript.

> ✔ **Gently urge more buying.** "Gently" is the key word here.
>
>> You'll find several order forms in the center of this catalog that make it easy for you to place your order. Or call us 24 hours a day, seven days a week at (800) 345-5443 to get service with a smile.
>
> ✔ **Thank the customer for her business.** Encourage open communication and discuss company services.
>
>> On behalf of everyone at Jamesons' Discount Store, thank you for putting your trust in us. We look forward to meeting all your needs.

Following is a letter delivering the good news. Notice how the headlines tell the story and how subtly the credit terms are handled in a postscript.

Dear

Welcome to our family of cardholders!

We're delighted to send you your new Brunswick Credit Card; it's your passport to a world of privileges reserved exclusively for our cardholders. Our sales associates will do everything they can to make shopping at Brunswick's a wonderful experience.

Please attend our private showing May 1   Headline provides key information

As a cardholder, you'll receive mailings inviting you to private sales that aren't advertised to the general public. We're having one next Monday, May 1, between 9 and 10 PM and look forward to seeing you there. If you have any special needs or requests, please let us know.

We look forward to seeing you at Brunswick's, where the exciting world of shopping awaits you!

You can count on me,

P.S. The enclosed pamphlet explains the terms of credit and the many benefits of coming to Brunswick's and saying "Charge it."

Better luck next time

If a credit check shows the customer isn't a good risk, you have to be the bearer of the bad news. Your aim is to maintain goodwill and encourage the customer to do business with you on a cash basis. (Check out Chapter 4 for tips on sequencing a bad news letter.) Tell the customer that you're unable to extend credit right now, but give hope for the future. The following tips help you let the customer down lightly:

- ✓ **Thank the customer for her interest in your company.** It will cushion the bad news.

  > We very much appreciate your interest in opening a charge account with PepCo.

- ✓ **Decline with style.** Mention favorable observations if there are any.

  > All your references told us that you're very cooperative and always willing to discuss any details about your financial situation.

- ✓ **Offer alternatives.** Suggest that she reapply at a later date and pay cash in the meantime. If you're a retail store, offer to put merchandise on layaway.

  > In the meantime, we'd be delighted to fill your orders on a cash basis and review your credit request as soon as some of your obligations have been satisfied.

Regardless of the reason you must deny the credit, you want to let customer down gently and preserve the relationship. One way to do this is to cushion the reason for the denial and encourage the customer to pay cash. Notice how that's handled in the following letter:

> Dear
>
> Thank you for your request for credit with Brunswick; it is a genuine compliment to us.
>
> When we checked your credit, however, we weren't able to find any credit information because your business is so new. We know from our own experience that new businesses are wise to watch their expenditures in order to increase cash on hand. We welcome your business on a cash basis and encourage you to reapply in six months. By then your cash position should be much stronger.

(continued)

(continued)

> Cash customers get a 5 percent discount
>
> We're enclosing our March brochure. Please notice that we offer a 5 percent discount to any customer who pays in cash. This should be helpful to you as you begin to grow.
>
> We enjoy serving you.
>
> We look forward to a long and pleasant relationship with you.
>
> Sincerely, ⊞ Positive closing

Absence makes the heart grow fonder

As a merchant, you don't extend credit because you're a good guy. You extend credit because doing so encourages more buying. When customers don't use their accounts for an extended period of time, set your imagination and creativity loose to urge them back (as you see in the example that follows). Here are a few tips:

- ✔ **Think of some gimmicks that would lure you back.** Perhaps notice of a sale or a we-miss-you letter.
- ✔ **Set the right tone**. Never play up "use your credit." Put yourself in the reader's place and ask yourself, "Would that tone lure me back or keep me away?"

Following is a letter that lured me back to a store in my town:

> Dear ⊞ Notice the subtlety of the tone.
>
> It's a pleasure to call you one of our valued customers. We want to continue giving you the kind of service you deserve and let you know we've missed seeing you.
>
> Please stop by to take advantage of the special once-a-year inventory sale offered to our charge customers only during the week of October 15. We're here to help you whenever you visit us.
>
> Sincerely,

Goodwill goes a long way

Never, never, never, never send a bill to a customer assuming he isn't going to pay. It's rude, and the accusation causes ill will. Following is an excerpt from an offensive letter I received from my bank.

Rental is due on your safe deposit box #123 for the period ending March XXXX. To avoid a **late fee** *of $5.00, payment must be received by the last day of the month.*

What's wrong with that picture? The key phrase that jumped out at me was "late fee" in bold print. My first thought was: "Gee, this is the first bill they sent; how can my payment be late?" After I read the letter more carefully, I realized how tacky it was. The folks at the bank assumed that my payment would be late, so they started the letter with a threat.

(This was a form letter, not a suggestion that I don't pay my bills on time. Every safe deposit box customer got the same tasteless letter.)

Pay-Back Time: Collection Letters

If buying is the heart of a business, collection is its lifeblood. People appreciate many collections — paintings, stamps, and pet rocks — but they don't appreciate collection letters. Settling an account quickly benefits everyone. The longer an account remains unpaid, the less likely it is to be paid.

Someone once said that the most tender part of a person's anatomy is her pocket. There are people who go to extremes to avoid honoring their debts. One fellow even placed his own obituary in the newspaper and mailed a copy to all his creditors. These are a few wacky excuses I've read about over the years:

- ✔ It isn't my fault. I've run out of checks and the printer is on strike.

- ✔ I wrote your address and telephone number on my shirt cuff and my wife took it to the laundry.

- ✔ I had your address in my hand and a sudden gust of wind blew the paper into the river. I tried to go after it but nearly drowned.

- ✔ I was on the way to the post office with your check when I slipped on the ice. The envelope got lost in a snow bank, and I'll have to wait until the snow melts in the spring to find it.

Examples 9-1 through 9-4 at the end of this chapter run through the collection series: gentle reminder, strong reminder, request for an explanation, and final call to action. The following outlines how to tactfully write these letters for maximum results. (Notice how the block style is more appropriate than the full block because the placement of the date helps balance the sailboat in the logo. Check out Chapter 5 for more about letter styles.)

Be gentle at first

The first letter should be a gentle reminder because a missed bill is often an oversight on the part of the customer. Perhaps payment and the reminder even cross in the mail. This first reminder may be a letter, pre-printed card, sticker attached to the bill, or note on the bottom of the second bill. You may even use this as an opportunity to promote more buying. The following tells you how to send a first reminder:

✔ **Mention the possible oversight.**

> Have you sent payment for your last invoice? If it's on its way . . . thanks. If not, please sent it out today.

✔ **Use this as a sales opportunity to encourage more buying.**

> The Almanac predicts a blustery hot summer. Have you considered purchasing central air for your home? During the week of May 5, ComfortZone is offering a pre-season sale on our entire inventory of central air units with discounted installation costs.

> Wouldn't it be refreshing to know that you'll keep cool on those sizzling summer days?

✔ **Make payment easy.**

> Please send us your check in the enclosed self-addressed envelope.

Get a little stronger

If the gentle reminder is ignored, get a little stronger in the second letter. However, you still want to maintain goodwill. Consider these suggestions:

✔ **Reaffirm the good relationship you've enjoyed.**

> We look forward to continuing the wonderful relationship we've had over the last several years.

✔ **Stress the customer's financial obligation.** This may be a variation of the first notice.

> This is the second reminder for you to send us your check for [amount]. If it's on its way . . . thanks. If not, please sent it out today.

✔ **Employ sales tactics.**

> When you mail your payment of $345.90 by June 10, why not send in your summer order?

✔ **Make payment easy.**

> Please send us your check in the enclosed self-addressed envelope.

Start a little arm twisting

The customer ignores two attempts to collect what's due you. Perhaps the customer has a good excuse; he's in jail and will pay you back when he gets out. Short of something out of the ordinary, you expect prompt payment and may want to apply some light pressure. The following tips make your position clear:

- **Request an explanation.**

  We're puzzled that you haven't answered our first two letters. Please call us immediately so we can discuss what prevents you from putting your check in the mail.

- **Hint that there may be an error.**

  You've always paid your bills promptly, and we're wondering if there may be a problem. Is there an error in the bill? Were you dissatisfied with the merchandise?

- **Offer viable options.**

  Here are a few options you may consider: Send your check for $1,233.44 today, send us an explanation, or call us about an easy payment plan.

Wage the final campaign

You're running out of patience. The customer ignores your first three letters, so your final attempt takes on a different tone. Give the customer one last chance to pay. Even at this point, you still want to salvage the relationship if that's possible. Here are some things to consider:

- **Give a firm deadline.**

  Don't use as soon as possible (ASAP) as a deadline; it's not a date.

  You must send payment in full by January 31, or we'll have to place this situation in the hands of our attorney. Please don't make such an action necessary.

- **Stress the dangers of a bad credit rating.**

  For three months, you've ignored all our attempts to contact you. We've been fair and have given you every opportunity to settle this bill. As an upstanding member of the business community, your credit reputation is of great value, and you'd be doing yourself a great disservice by blemishing it.

- **Offer one last chance.**

  This is the last time we'll contact you directly. You'll hear from our attorney next. Put your check for $550 in the mail today.

To err is human

No matter how careful you are, you may eventually send someone a collection letter inadvertently. If that happens, apologize without groveling. Be brief, and assure the customer you're taking steps to ensure such a mix-up won't happen again. Hopefully the customer will be divine (forgiving). Perhaps your letter of apology may read like this:

We don't make mistakes often, but this one was a whopper. You're one of our valued customers, and we applaud you for always paying your bills so promptly. I don't know how this happened, but you can be assured it won't happen again.

All I can say is that we goofed and we're truly sorry.

To show you really mean business, consider sending this final letter via certified mail, return receipt requested. Chapter 18 tells you all about postal services and shows examples of forms to fill out.

Don't forget to use your Letter-Perfect Checklist featured on the Cheat Sheet in the front of this book. Imagine telling a customer "you can no*t* buy on credit" instead of "you can no*w* buy on credit." Just one typo like that can cause a customer to fly into the arms of your competitor.

Captain Jon's Boat Basin

One Commodore Place, Salem, MA 01970
Phone: (978) 555-1235 * Fax: (978) 555-1234
www.captainjon.com

February 1, XXXX

Ms. Dee Linquent
One Alamo Lane
Witch Hazel, OR 97123

Dear Ms. Linquent:

Subject: Account No. 7892

> Assuming an oversight and
> encouraging more buying

Perhaps the first bill for $275 slipped your mind and your check is already in the mail. If so, we thank you and ask that you disregard this letter.

To get more helpful sailing hints such as the ones included in your recent shipment, all you need to do is ask. If there is any other way that Captain Jon's can help to make your boating experiences more pleasurable, please let me know.

Sincerely,

Captain Jon Allen
Store Manager

Example 9-1:
This is the first experience. Be gentle.

Captain Jon's Boat Basin

One Commodore Place, Salem, MA 01970
Phone: (978) 555-1235 * Fax: (978) 555-1234
www.captainjon.com

March 1, XXXX

Ms. Dee Linquent
One Alamo Lane
Witch Hazel, OR 97123   Slightly stronger but still friendly

Dear Ms. Linquent:

Subject: Account No. 7892

This is just a brief reminder that your account is two months past due. If you haven't sent us your check for $275, why not take care of it today? If you already sent it, thanks.

You've always been one of our valued customers, and we look forward to continuing the fine service you've come to expect from us. As a businessperson yourself, you appreciate those who meet their financial obligations in a timely manner. We do, too.

Within the next two weeks you'll receive our catalog displaying our new line of nautical treasures. We look forward to helping you with all your boating needs.

Sincerely,

Captain Jon Allen
Store Manager

Example 9-2:
Come on guys; settle the account.

Captain Jon's Boat Basin

One Commodore Place, Salem, MA 01970
Phone: (978) 555-1235 * Fax: (978) 555-1234
www.captainjon.com

April 1, XXXX

Ms. Dee Linquent
One Alamo Lane
Witch Hazel, OR 97123   Hinting at an error and requesting an explanation

Dear Ms. Linquent:

Subject: Account No. 7892

It's been three months since we sent your bill for $275, and we still haven't received your check or an explanation. You've always paid so promptly that we're wondering if perhaps there are circumstances that prevent you from meeting your obligation or if there is some error in your statement.

Please call me so that we can work together to preserve your fine credit standing. Or place your check for $275 in the enclosed self-addressed, stamped envelope. Thank you.

Sincerely,

Captain Jon Allen
Store Manager

Example 9-3:
Hellooooo.
Are you
ignoring
me?

Captain Jon's Boat Basin

One Commodore Place, Salem, MA 01970
Phone: (978) 555-1235 * Fax: (978) 555-1234
www.captainjon.com

May 1, XXXX

CERTIFIED MAIL, RETURN RECEIPT REQUESTED

Ms. Dee Linquent
One Alamo Lane
Witch Hazel, OR 97123

Dear Ms. Linquent:

Subject: Final attempt to settle Account No. 7892 `Strong subject line`

For four months we've been writing to you in an attempt to clear up
your unpaid balance of $275. You've ignored all our letters. We'd
like to settle this matter between ourselves, and this is the last time
we'll write to you about this matter.

If your check reaches us by May 10, your credit reputation will
remain intact, and we'll be able to continue doing business with you
on a credit basis as we've done for so many years. If not, you leave us
no choice but to turn this matter over for collection. Please mail us
your check for $275 today. `Here's the ultimatum`

Sincerely,

Captain Jon Allen
Store Manager

Example 9-4:
No more
mister nice
guy.

Chapter 10

Ask (Nicely) and Ye Shall Receive

In This Chapter

▶ Asking for what you want

▶ Responding to requests

▶ Turning a down request gently

I understand the Hacienda Hotel will be holding an all-nude slot tournament. Can I get all the information regarding this event? Also, do you have other nude gambling events? It's really the only way to ensure against cheating.

— Ted N. Nancy, *Letters from a Nut*

At some point, we all write letters asking for something. Regardless of what you request, always remember the basics you learned at your mother's knee: Say *please* and *thank you* abundantly. Remember the old adage, "You attract more bees with honey than with vinegar."

When you request something from non-English speaking people (or companies), consider saying *please* and *thank you* in their native tongue. Foreigners don't necessarily expect you to write to them in their native language, but showing you made an effort to learn a few words goes a long way.

	Please	***Thank you***
French	*S'il vous plait*	*Merci*
German	*Bitte*	*Danke schön*
Japanese	*Dozo*	*Arigato*
Spanish	*Por favor*	*De nada*

Asking the "Write" Questions

Inquiries range from routine information about a product or service to requests for a favor or cooperation. Have you ever wondered why some requests get results while others don't? This chapter gives you some insights into why. It looks at requests from both sides — the person making the request and the person responding to it.

When you initiate a request, pay special attention to question 3 on your Start Up Sheet: "What's in it for the reader?" When possible, offer the reader something in return for what you're asking. The offering doesn't have to be money; it may be something as inexpensive as a compliment.

When you write to someone who isn't expecting your request, you must give him all the information he needs to fill your request. Check out Chapter 4 for details on answering who, what, when, why, where, and how. Keep your request warm and courteous so that the reader will want to help you. Here are some morsels to include or omit:

- ✔ **Get to the point immediately.** Be sure to include the name of your source and any other specifics that will facilitate a quick response.

    Please send me answers to the following questions about the GPS unit advertised on page 5 of your *Basically Boating* catalog. (Use a bulleted list so the reader can respond to specific questions.)

- ✔ **Never open or close your letter with an apology.** If you say, "I know you're busy but. . . ," your reader will quietly respond, "You're right. I'm too busy."

- ✔ **Be specific.**

    Specific: Please tell me what features Model No. 235 has that Model No. 234 doesn't.

    Not specific: Please tell me about your Model No. 235.

- ✔ **If you need a response by a certain date, make that clear.**

    Specific: Please send me a confirmation by June 11.

    Not specific: Please send me a confirmation as soon as possible. (As soon as possible isn't a date.)

- ✔ **Highlight what's in it for the reader.** (The following example shows that in the headline.)

    Don't get snowed in!

    The almanac predicts a very cold and snowy winter. Don't get snowed in. Stop by and check out our new line of snow blowers.

> ✔ **Leave an opening for a refusal if you're asking the impossible.** You must let the reader save face. Check out Chapter 4 for ways to say "No" graciously.
>
>> Would it be possible to have the 7,500 newsletters ready by June 6? I realize that we're asking the impossible and would understand if you can't.
>
> ✔ **End with a "thank you."**

Following is a letter to the editor of a magazine requesting permission to use published material. Notice that, in addition to giving all the information, the writer is enclosing a self-addressed, stamped envelope (SASE). Use your judgment as to when that may be appropriate.

Dear

Subject: Permission to Reprint Excerpts of "Getting the Highest ROI"

I'm writing a white paper on return on investment (ROI) for my company's Web site and would like permission to include the first two paragraphs of your article entitled "Getting the Highest ROI," by Simon Murphy, that appeared in your January 15, XXXX, issue.

If you can grant permission to reprint these paragraphs, please fill out the release form that's attached and return it to me in the self-addressed, stamped envelope. I will, of course, give proper credit to your publication and the author. Thank you.

Sincerely,

Following is a request for information. If you incorporate several questions into one letter, number the questions so the reader can respond without reiterating each one.

Dear

Please answer the following questions regarding the Reserve Credit Customer Account you advertised in Sunday's edition of The Morning Sun:

(continued)

(continued)

> 1. Is there an activity fee for each transaction?
>
> 2. Will I have the flexibility to access cash in an emergency?
>
> 3. When does your billing cycle start and end?
>
> Please send me an application blank so I may sign up if this seems to be the right type of account for me. Thank you.
>
> Sincerely,

Goodwill Responses

When you answer an inquiry or request — even if you can't grant the request — you're in a wonderful position to build goodwill, stimulate confidence, and generate sales for your company.

Give every response priority treatment. If you don't, the competition will. Here are some guidelines that may be helpful in keeping your inquirers happy and coming back for more:

✔ **Answer each request punctually.** Even if you can't give the inquirer the information he asked for, let him know when he can expect an answer and from whom. At least he'll know his request hasn't disappeared into a black hole in space.

> Mr. Juan Sanchez, our manager, is better able than I to address your issues. Mr. Sanchez will be out of town for the next two weeks, and he'll call you once he returns.

✔ **Keep the response brief.** Because your response was asked for, you don't need to bore the reader to tears with the nitty-gritty about what led you to write.

✔ **Thank the inquirer for taking the time to write.**

> Thank you for requesting copies of our newsletter. If you find it informative, please share it with your friends.

Saying "Yes" with a smile

Everyone likes to be the bearer of good news, so writing a letter granting a request is easy. Here's some information to include:

- ✔ **Begin with the good news.**

   I'm delighted to send you our latest brochure, "Keeping Customers Coming Back for More," which addresses many of your concerns.

- ✔ **Confirm the details.**

   I'll be happy to meet with you at your office on July 16 at 2:00.

- ✔ **Try to spur a sale.** Do this tactfully and without pressure.

   I've enclosed a sample of *Sharks and Scuba* magazine. If you find the magazine enjoyable and enlightening, perhaps you'd like to receive a copy each month. Just use the handy order blank, and you'll be up on all the latest in the scuba diving world. If not, just enjoy this complimentary copy!

The following example responds to a request for a catalog and price list. Rather than just putting the catalog and price list in an envelope, the writer took the time to include a warm letter. (Check out Chapter 6 for more about writing spicy sales letters.)

Dear Mr. Gorman:

It's a great pleasure to send you our latest catalog and price list. We guarantee your 100 percent satisfaction, whether your order is for $25, $250, or $2500. We look forward to serving you and welcome you to our growing family of satisfied customers.

Sincerely,

Following is an e-mail message that responds to a request to meet for a business lunch:

Subject line tells the story

```
┌──────────────────────────────────────────────────────────────────┐
│ ✉ Lunch on May 1 is fine - Message (Rich Text)        _ ⯊ ✕        │
├──────────────────────────────────────────────────────────────────┤
│  File  Edit  View  Insert  Format  Tools  Actions  Help            │
├──────────────────────────────────────────────────────────────────┤
│  ℛ Reply   ℛ Reply to All   ℛ Forward   🖨 🖺  ▼  🗗 ✕  ▲ · ▼ · 🗐   │
├──────────────────────────────────────────────────────────────────┤
│ From:                                              Sent:           │
│ To:                                                                │
│ Cc:                                                                │
│ Subject:   Lunch on May 1 is fine                                  │
├──────────────────────────────────────────────────────────────────┤
│ Sarah,                                                          ▲  │
│                                                                    │
│ Yes, I'll be available for lunch on May 1 to discuss the details   │
│ of the Salinger Vs. Salinger case. Let's                           │
│ plan to meet at the Continental Cafe at noon. I'll make the        │
│ reservations.                                                      │
│                                                                    │
│ Bob                                                             ▼  │
└──────────────────────────────────────────────────────────────────┘
```

At the end of this chapter you see two response letters. In Example 10-1, Ms. Wolf accepts an invitation to speak at the Aching Feet Hiker's Club. In Example 10-2, she declines with panache. Following are suggestions for doing just that.

Saying a friendly "No"

Most requests are reasonable, and you can grant them. However, you do receive requests that aren't reasonable, and you must be the bearer of that news. Once you understand how to sequence a letter for bad news, you can say "No" and still keep customers coming back. (See Chapter 4 for more information about sequencing a bad news letter.) Here are some suggestions specific to this sort of letter:

✔ **Open with something friendly.** It may be as simple as thanking the person for making the request.

> I'm flattered to be asked to speak before your group to discuss my new book, *Funny Laws & Other Zany Stuff.*

✔ **Detail the reasons you can't grant the request.**

> There are several candidates who've thrown their hats in the ring. Before I decide which one to publicly endorse, I need to learn more about each one.

✔ **Offer a substitute or compromise, if appropriate.**

Although we have a policy of no returns on custom orders, please accept the enclosed gift certificate which you may apply to your next order.

✔ **Close with something positive.**

We wish you continued success and thank you for thinking of us.

Don't forget to use your Letter-Perfect Checklist featured on the Cheat Sheet in the front of this book. Additionally, if your letter says that you're enclosing something in the envelope, make sure you enclose it. Otherwise, your forgetfulness may be construed as carelessness. No one likes to do business with careless people.

June 16, XXXX

Mr. Robert Littlehale
5 Gardner St.
Salem, NH 03079

Dear Mr. Littlehale:

Acceptance is obvious from the headline.

Subject: I accept your wonderful invitation

I'm flattered that you asked me to speak at the annual meeting of the Aching Feet Hiker's Club at 9 PM, on Friday, August 14, XXXX. At the end of July I'll be returning from three weeks of backpacking in Mount Washington, so this will give me an audience to "bore" with the details of my adventure. By then I'll surely have aching feet, so my talk will be timely.

Thanks for offering to make arrangements for me to stay at the Himalayan Lodge for Thursday and Friday evenings. Judging from the brochure you enclosed, I'm sure to enjoy the visit. I'll probably arrive late Tuesday evening and stay through the weekend. I expect to pay for the additional evenings.

Next step

I'll call you when I get back from Mount Washington to firm up the details. I'd like to bring slides of my trip, so I'd appreciate your arranging for a 35 mm slide projector if that's possible. Have a wonderful aching-feet-free summer.

Fondly,

Beth Wolf

Example 10-1:
I'd be delighted to share my aching feet stories.

June 16, XXXX

Mr. Robert Littlehale
5 Gardner Street
Salem, NH 03079

Dear Mr. Littlehale:

Subject: I appreciate your kind invitation   The headline tells the story

Being asked to speak at the annual meeting of the Aching Feet
Hiker's Club on Friday, August 14, XXXX is a real honor. I'll be
backpacking in Mount Washington from August 1 through 28, so I
must regretfully decline.

Please give me a chance to say "Yes" another time

I'd love to share some of my stories with your group at another
meeting. Perhaps one of your monthly meetings would be
appropriate.

Fondly,

Beth Wolf

P.S. I'll surely have aching feet while your annual meeting is taking
place. So, I'll be thinking of you.   The postscript adds a warm touch.

Example 10-2:
Sorry, I have
to rearrange
my sock
drawer.

Chapter 11

May I Have Your Order, Please?

In This Chapter

▶ Including all necessary information when placing an order

▶ Attempting to fill your customers' orders

▶ Asking for more details to fill an incomplete order

▶ Knowing when to send a reply

In our factory we make lipstick. In our advertising, we sell hope.

— Charles Revson, one time Chairman of Revlon, Inc.

While juggling jobs, errands, and families, people no longer have the time to stroll through malls and leisurely shop. Therefore, mail order has become big business. It offers convenience, detailed information, excellent guarantees and return policies, and generally good service. This chapter provides insights from placing an order to responding to the order.

Make sure to fill out the Start Up Sheet on the Cheat Sheet when you're placing or acknowledging an order.

Ordering with Smarts

As a customer, you'll probably complete and mail an order form, phone the company, or order directly from its Web site. However, there may be instances when those avenues aren't available, and you need to send a letter. When you order anything by letter, make sure that you cover all your bases. Following are tips on what information to include so the company can fill your order promptly and accurately:

- **Open with a courteous request.** When you start the letter with a "smile," you get results.

  - Please send me the following. . . .

  - I'd like to order. . . .

- **Mention the source.** If there's a date or number on the catalog you're ordering from, mention that.

- **Send a complete description of the merchandise.** Prepare a grid that includes whichever of the following are appropriate: quantity, page number, color, grade, size, weight, model, price, extended price, or other special distinctions. Include local tax, insurance, and shipping and handling, if applicable.

- **State the method of payment.** If you enclose a check, mention the date and check number. If you use a credit card, state the account number and expiration date. Never send cash through the mail.

- **Indicate the shipping address.** If your mailing address differs from the address on your letterhead (or if you're not using letterhead), be sure to include it.

- **Specify the method of shipment.** If you need the order in a hurry, specify that you're willing to pay additional postage for one of the express services. If not, the company will select the method of shipment.

The people filling your order aren't interested in how you enjoy working with their company or how you plan to use their merchandise once it arrives. So spare them the details. KISS your letter — keep it short and simple. Check out Chapter 5 for great tips on doing just that.

It's metric to me!

The United States is one of the few countries that doesn't use the metric system. When you order something from another country, always include the metric equivalents for weight, length, and so on. Look in any good reference book or the back of a dictionary to find metric equivalents for what you're ordering.

We're Pleased to Fill Your Order

An order processor's job is never easy — especially during crunch times (such as the final hours of the Christmas rush). Can you imaging trying to fill the order for the customer in the following example at the beginning of April when the folks in Northern climates are coming out of winter hibernation and getting into gardening mode?

> Dear
>
> Several years ago I ordered five plants from you, and I'd now like to order five more. I can't remember the name of the plants, but they have big green leaves, small pink flowers, and bloom in July. I can't seem to find the catalog either. Please send me five more of the plants I just described and send me a bill. Thank you.
>
> Very truly yours,
>
> Clueless in Coconut Grove

What's missing? Just about everything the order processor needs to fill the order. If you think letters like this one are uncommon, think again. These kinds of letters arrive more often than you can imagine. Ask any prematurely gray-haired order processor that you know.

Brimming with customer service

Public-relations minded companies acknowledge all orders they can't ship immediately. Following is a simple acknowledgment card that makes customers feel cared about. Company employees fill in the blanks by hand for an added personal touch.

> We at Smith Company are delighted to fill
> your order for _____, which will
> ship on _____.
> Serving you is our pleasure and we
> hope you will give us that privilege again soon.
> *Name*

When you order from the Web, many companies send standard acknowledgments via e-mail. This lets you know that they did, in fact, receive your order. For those of you who are worried about hackers getting your credit card number, here's welcome reassurance: Many companies encrypt card numbers to help prevent such thefts.

Gimme details

Letters that omit critical information are so common that many order processors reply by using form letters or cards that list all the possible reasons why they can't process an order. The processors merely place a check mark next to the applicable reason(s). Include some of the tips below to keep the customer happy and ensure that your order processors return from lunch or don't quit after the first day on the job:

- ✔ **Start with an upbeat opening.** You'll have your order in time for Christmas, just as you expect.

- ✔ **Tell the customer the exact information you need.** However, before we can ship your order, you must let us know. . . .

- ✔ **Make replying easy for the customer.** Please jot down the [what's missing] on the enclosed card and return it to us. Then we'll ship your [merchandise] immediately. Have a wonderful holiday!

The letter or card is intended to get the information you need without making the customer feel stupid. Following is a post card that makes responding easy for the customer. The company places a check mark next to the information it needs to fill the order and leaves a space for the customer to fill in the missing details by hand. Because the postage is usually pre-paid, customers should quickly return the card.

The *hydrangeas* you ordered are among our best buys of the season. Please give us the information checked below, and we'll ship your plants immediately.

    ☐ Catalog number _____
    ☐ Quantity _____
    ☑ Color _____

We hope you'll get many years of pleasure from the plants you order from us. Remember our one-year money-back guarantee.

Garden of Eden Delights

Other times to get in touch

A number of other circumstances may surface which require you to touch base with a customer. When one of these reasons applies, send the customer a letter or card immediately:

- **You can only fill part of the order.** Let the customer know what she will receive and when. Give the customer any options that are appropriate, and apologize for any inconvenience.

- **You need to substitute one item for another.** Always notify the customer when you must substitute one item for another — even if the substitution is minor.

  Explain the reason for the substitution.

  Tell what you'd like to substitute.

  Give her the option of refusing.

- **You can't fill the order immediately.** Write to the customer promptly, citing the reason for the delay. A customer will understand the logical reason for a delay, but won't tolerate long, silent waiting periods.

Don't forget to use your Letter-Perfect Checklist featured on the Cheat Sheet in the front of this book. Here's a story of where transposed letters resulted in lost business. John Powers, a columnist for *The Boston Globe Magazine*, stopped to look at a menu posted in the window of a restaurant. It listed Ceasar salad (the *a* should be before the *e*). Mr. Powers' walked past the restaurant and commented: "I won't eat in a restaurant that can't spell its own food . . . If an eatery doesn't know Ceasar from Caesar, can it be trusted with raw eggs? Botulism, after all, can ruin your whole day."

Chapter 12

Getting Personal in Business

- -

In This Chapter

▶ Composing letters from the heart

▶ Offering words of encouragement

▶ Asking a favor

▶ Exchanging gifts

▶ Extending congratulations

▶ Apologizing with dignity

▶ Letting holiday spirits soar

- -

The hardest thing to learn in life is which bridge to cross and which to burn.

— David L. Russell, American educator

*P*ersonal business letters build bridges; therefore, every business person should write them. Personal business letters aren't the same as personal letters. You write personal letters to your grandmother letting her know the kids are off to summer camp. You write personal business letters to professional associates to let them know you care.

If you ever wanted to thank a staff member for a favor or a job well done, express regrets to a coworker who's been let go, offer condolences to a bereaved colleague, or give encouragement to a coworker who's going through difficult times, you've had the opportunity to share a little of what's in your heart. Personal business letters build and cement relationships and create goodwill — the key to all successful business relationships.

Exposing Your Human Side: General Guidelines

Personal business letters take a number of forms. They may be typewritten, handwritten, or typewritten with a handwritten note at the bottom. They may even be e-mail messages. Regardless of the form, be prompt, thoughtful, and honest. Personal business letters follow these guidelines:

- ✔ **Don't use letterhead.** Using company letterhead detracts from the warmth of your message. Use plain white paper, your personal note paper, or send an e-mail message.

- ✔ **Be brief.** Even a single sentence or short paragraph may be appropriate.

    I'm delighted for you, Nancy.

    or

    I enjoyed seeing you at the trade show last week. I was particularly glad to hear that you left your former job and are now with the law firm of Smith & Smith. What a wonderful opportunity!

- ✔ **Don't exaggerate.** For example, "I'd venture to say that. . ." is more appropriate than "I'll bet you a million bucks that. . . ."

Where Seldom Is Heard, an Encouraging Word

There's nothing more comforting to people in distress than the care and concern of others. A personal note to a colleague expresses your concern very clearly. Sometimes that's all people need to put a smile on their faces.

Finding words for a colleague in distress

A few years ago I noticed that a fellow I worked with seemed rather down for several days on end. I didn't want to intrude, but I wanted to show him that I cared. I sent him the following handwritten note, and I can't tell you how much he appreciated my concern:

Dear

I can't help but notice that you haven't been yourself lately. I'm not trying to pry — just want to let you know I care. If there's anything I can do, please let me know.

Sincerely,

Offering condolences

If you've ever lost a loved one, you know how devastating the loss can be. Notes of sympathy tell you that — even though an important part of your life is gone — there are people who care about you. These notes are often read again and again and provide comfort to bereaved families. Something as simple as "The news of your wife's death saddened us all. Please accept our sympathy at this difficult time" is appreciated.

Writing the condolence letter

Condolence letters are difficult to write because people generally don't know what to say. Feelings of confusion are perfectly normal, but don't let them stand in the way of helping to ease someone's pain. Here are a few pointers that may help:

✔ **Don't sugar coat the experience.** Using the words *die*, *death*, or *dead* is okay. That is what happened.

> Those we love never truly die; they live forever in our hearts. May the love you and Minerva shared be of comfort to you and your family.

✔ **Describe an experience you shared with the deceased or special qualities you remember.**

> Over the years, we always looked forward to Jack's visits. He was a gentleman in every sense of the word. There aren't many people in the industry who had his depth of knowledge or such a warm regard for others. We'll truly miss him.

✔ **If you didn't know the deceased person well, focus on the sympathy for your coworker's loss.**

> I don't know what to say, except that my heart is breaking for you. Although I didn't known Casey well, I've always heard of her devotion to you and the family and of all the wonderful work she did for charity. Everyone will certainly miss her.

The most important thing about a note of sympathy is to send it — even if you can't find the right words. Your words are less important than the expression of your feelings.

Responding to condolences

Many people respond to expressions of sympathy. Some people send pre-printed cards; others personalize the message. Which is more appropriate is a matter of choice. You may consider sending a boilerplate reply to a pre-printed sympathy card and a personalized note to a personalized expression. Check out this one:

> The memories you shared about my wife were a great source of joy to me and the children. Thanks so much for sharing them and for being so thoughtful. Messages such as yours mean a great deal to me.

Wishing a speedy recovery

When an employee is out for an extended period of time, warm wishes from coworkers help to heal the soul. Wishing coworkers well and letting them know they're important is an ultimate gesture of humanity in a sometimes impersonal workplace environment.

Following is a little get well wish I've used time and again. People who are recovering from surgery have always enjoyed the (attempt at) humor.

> Dear
>
> Hope you get better nice and quick.
>
> Cause someone like you should never be sick.
>
> (I know you're not sick, but I couldn't think of anything that rhymes with operation.)
>
> Fondly,

When people take the time to extend get-well wishes, let them know how much you appreciate the effort. Following is an e-mail message thanking coworkers for get-well wishes:

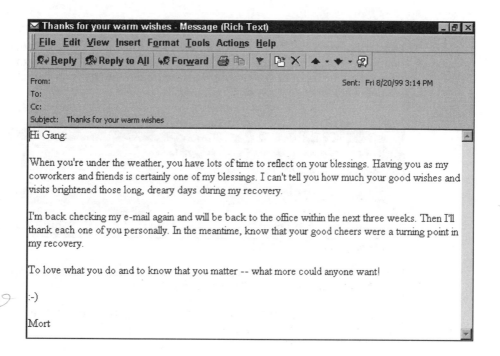

Hi Gang:

When you're under the weather, you have lots of time to reflect on your blessings. Having you as my coworkers and friends is certainly one of my blessings. I can't tell you how much your good wishes and visits brightened those long, dreary days during my recovery.

I'm back checking my e-mail again and will be back to the office within the next three weeks. Then I'll thank each one of you personally. In the meantime, know that your good cheers were a turning point in my recovery.

To love what you do and to know that you matter -- what more could anyone want!

:-)

Mort

Bidding farewell

There are many occasions on which you have to say "goodbye" to coworkers. Some of those occasions are pleasant; others aren't. This section offers suggestions for both.

The dreaded pink slip

If you've ever been let go from a job — no matter what the reason — you know how devastating that can be. To add fuel to the fire, people often avoid you because they don't know what to say. (Perhaps they're reminded: "It could've been me.") The key thing to remember is to *be supportive without prying.* Following are a few expressions of support:

> I just heard. I know what a terrible blow this is; it happened to me two years ago. The only advice I can offer is to focus on your many years of experience and know how marketable you are. The job market is red hot, and you'll be scooped up in no time!

> or

> If there's anything I can do to help, please call on me. I'd be happy to review your resume, run you through a mock interview, or help with just about anything else.

Oh, those golden years

Even though people may look forward to retiring, doing so constitutes a major life-style change and can cause a lot of angst. Kind words remind the retiree that he hasn't been put out to pasture. Following is an e-mail message sent to a coworker who's retiring:

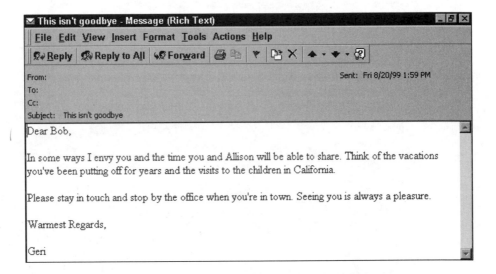

Dear Bob,

In some ways I envy you and the time you and Allison will be able to share. Think of the vacations you've been putting off for years and the visits to the children in California.

Please stay in touch and stop by the office when you're in town. Seeing you is always a pleasure.

Warmest Regards,

Geri

Don't forget to use a salutation and complimentary closing in an e-mail message. Chapter 19 has lots of good tips on using e-mail effectively.

Just One Favor, Please

When you need to ask someone for a favor and there's a chance he may not be able to grant it, write a letter or send an e-mail message, rather than talk to the person face to face. Asking in print gives him a chance to say "No" without giving you the evil eye.

This section is different from Chapter 10, which deals with business requests. This section relates to requests of a personal nature.

Making a request

Notice how the following e-mail message incorporates these issues to consider when asking for a personal favor:

- ✔ Open with a personal message.
- ✔ Provide details about your request.
- ✔ Give the person a chance to refuse.

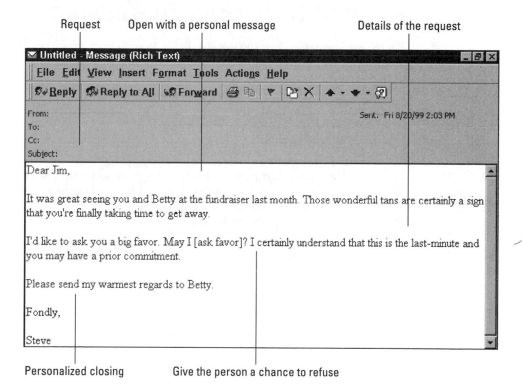

Request   Open with a personal message   Details of the request

Untitled - Message (Rich Text)

File Edit View Insert Format Tools Actions Help

Reply   Reply to All   Forward

From: Sent: Fri 8/20/99 2:03 PM
To:
Cc:
Subject:

Dear Jim,

It was great seeing you and Betty at the fundraiser last month. Those wonderful tans are certainly a sign that you're finally taking time to get away.

I'd like to ask you a big favor. May I [ask favor]? I certainly understand that this is the last-minute and you may have a prior commitment.

Please send my warmest regards to Betty.

Fondly,

Steve

Personalized closing   Give the person a chance to refuse

Refusing a request

Granting a request is easy — Sure! Love to! But if you're the one refusing, open with an expression of regret, give a short explanation, and close with the hope of being able to help in the future. Or consider offering an option.

Polite refusal: It's not easy saying "No" to someone who's been such a help to me. However, I [reason]. I hope that the next time you need me, I'll be there for you.

Offering an option: I called Max Benjamin to see if he could pitch in, but he's no longer living in Boston. Perhaps Susan Peterson may be able to help you. Give her a call at 617-253-4455, and mention my name. Good luck!

It's Better to Give than to Receive

Giving gifts is part of our business culture. People give gifts to say thank you, I'm sorry, congratulations, and more. When you give a gift or want to acknowledge receiving one, write a personal note.

Offering a gift

A gift isn't always money — it can be a turkey at the holiday season, a gift certificate to a great restaurant, or tickets to the see the New York Yankees. (You can tell I'm a New Yorker at heart and which team I cheer for!) When you give a gift, be certain that you *give it in the right spirit and expect nothing in return*, such as in the example that follows:

Dear

InterSoft is proud of people such as you whose contributions are responsible for the company's success the past year. Without your efforts, we wouldn't be providing high-quality services to our customers. Thank you for your hard work and great accomplishments.

Please accept this cash bonus as a token of my appreciation for helping InterSoft meet its corporate objectives.

Congratulations!

Acknowledging an appropriate gift

You learned at your mother's knee to say *thank you* when someone gives you something. Little did you realize how well your mother was preparing you for the business world. The following illustrates how you may thank a coworker for a birthday surprise. Consider writing the note by hand; the gesture adds a touch of warmth.

> Dear
>
> When you put the beautifully wrapped gift on my desk a few days before my birthday, I must admit it was a struggle to wait until the day of my birthday to open it.
>
> Thank you so much for the wonderful book *Gifts from the Sea*. I started reading it over the weekend and will always treasure it. What a great choice!
>
> Fondly,

Acknowledge every gift, even if it's not for you personally. Following is a thank you for a donation sent to a non-profit hospital.

> Dear
>
> It's with great pleasure that I acknowledge your generous contribution to the Good Samaritan Hospital. We'll be pleased to mention your name as a "Friend of the Hospital" in our next bulletin. Our best wishes to you.
>
> Thanks so much!

Acknowledging an inappropriate gift

When you're given an inappropriate gift or one you think is in bad taste, you may still acknowledge the gesture. Your acknowledgment, however, lacks the warmth and enthusiasm of one that's appropriate. For example, notice the difference between the following thank you and the ones for appropriate gifts:

> The book you gave me was a pleasant surprise. I appreciate the thought. Thank you.

Some gifts between business colleagues should never be given or accepted. If you receive an inappropriate gift and don't know what to do, consult your company's policy manual or seek guidance from a knowledgeable adviser. Inappropriate gifts may be ones that are extravagant, racy, or constitute sexual harassment. In the latter case, contact your Human Resources department.

Refusing a gift

Some companies and government branches have strong policies against employees accepting gifts because such an act creates the illusion of impropriety. At the least, this action suggests favoritism; at worst, bribery. If you must return or refuse a gift, be tactful but also clear about your employer's policies so the gesture isn't repeated. Following is a note that tactfully declines such a gift:

> Dear
>
> How kind of you to remember me. I appreciate your consideration and generosity and know that a great deal of thought went into selecting the beautiful scarf. However, it's against company policy to accept gifts from clients. Therefore, I return the scarf to you with regret.
>
> I wish you an enjoyable holiday and success in the new year.
>
> Warmest regards,

Mazel Tov!

Take advantage of opportunities to congratulate people; these opportunities are innumerable. The following tips represent all the situations in this section:

- ✔ Be enthusiastic.
- ✔ Show sincerity, not envy.
- ✔ Stick to the person's achievement, not one of your own.

When someone gets a promotion (even if you think the job should've been yours) show your support. Always keep people as allies. Following is an expression of support sent via an e-mail message:

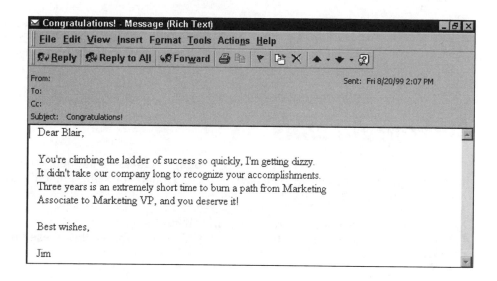

When someone accepts a position outside your company, the new job gives you another opportunity to offer congratulations. Here are two ways to present such a sentiment:

> It's time to bid you fare-thee-well. Although everyone in the organization will miss you greatly, I know this is an important career move. The Ozawa Company is lucky to have you join its ranks. Please know that we'll miss you and will be cheering for you.

> or

> I read in the latest bulletin that you've just been appointed CEO of the Seasonnaire Foundation. I'm sure you're excited about the challenges that await you. Lots of success and happiness.

Expressing kudos

People who give 110 percent effort deserve to be acknowledged by those at the top as well as by their peers. Following are two ways of expressing kudos:

> **From the top:** The MIS project wouldn't have been completed on time without your gallant efforts. You and your entire team showed excellence. Congratulations! We certainly appreciate your dedication.

From peers: Everyone at Merit Financial Services congratulates you on being awarded Employee of the Quarter. You've been an inspiration to all of us and are always ready to lend a hand. We can't think of anyone more deserving of this award than you.

Making Amends

However hard you try do the right thing, blunders do happen. When you inadvertently make a mistake, own up to it and apologize immediately. And don't make a lame excuse.

If the person you offended is nearby, have the guts to apologize in person, rather than send a note. If you're not able to do that, follow these tips for sending a written apology:

- Send a handwritten note.
- Be sincere.
- Make amends if you can.
- Promise to avoid such behavior in the future.

> Dear
>
> I can't believe that I missed your meeting this morning. I have no excuse other than it just slipped my mind. I forgot to write it on the calendar, and I guess my memory isn't what it used to be. This is my cue to start writing everything down.
>
> I'll call you tomorrow to get the details of what I missed and promise this will never happen again.
>
> Sincerely,

Getting in the Holiday Spirit

Holidays represent wonderful opportunities to connect with vendors, clients, or customers. Remember, however, that Christmas and Hanukah aren't the only holidays. Why not schmooze on the Fourth of July, Labor Day, or Thanksgiving?

A real estate agent I dealt with sends out Thanksgiving greetings each year. Her messages make her stand out from the pack because she's the one who sends me a Thanksgiving greeting. (I get a gazillion Christmas and Season's Greetings and can hardly remember who sent them — this one I remember.) Following is the greeting I received most recently:

Dear Friends,

During the Thanksgiving season my thoughts turn warmly and gratefully to those who help make my real estate business such a pleasure. I truly give thanks for your trust, loyalty, and friendship.

Happy Thanksgiving!

Grace Holmes
Holmes Realty

Don't forget to use your Letter-Perfect Checklist featured on the Cheat Sheet in the front of this book. Sending someone a letter of congratulations and spelling his name wrong is not only embarrassing, it kills the essence of your message.

Chapter 13

You Are Cordially Invited

In This Chapter

▶ Inviting people to company parties, open houses, and more

▶ Including all necessary information on an invitation

▶ Deciding among formal, semi-formal, and informal invitation styles

▶ Responding to invitations

President Coolidge invited some Vermont friends to dine at the White House. They were worried about their table manners and decided to do everything President Coolidge did. The meal passed smoothly until coffee was served. Coolidge poured his coffee into a saucer. The guests followed suit. He added sugar and cream, and the visitors did likewise. Then, Coolidge leaned over and gave his [saucer] to the cat.

— *Curmudgeon's Corner*, as reported in Ann Landers' column

*I*n business, you have several opportunities to extend invitations to colleagues, associates, customers, and others. Whether you invite them to a black-tie affair, seminar, or country hoe-down, you want your invitation to be *inviting*. This chapter gives you guidelines and suggestions for inviting business associates to a variety of events you may host — formal, semi-formal, and informal.

Come One — Come All!

The invitation is the first impression that your intended guests receive about your event; it should make them look forward to coming. The invitation establishes the tone for the celebration and generates excitement for the event. The color, size, design, and texture of the invitation must all work together to reflect the image of the sender and the nature of the function.

Invitations come in all shapes and sizes — anything from the $5.00 packet you buy at a stationery store to the formal engraved invitation. I even received an unusual invitation that looked like a computer terminal and another that was a jig-saw puzzle I had to put together. Of course, both related to the business of the company and were very creative.

You may ask yourself whether you should be conventional or dare to be different. That's like asking whether Max Factor is better than Mary Kay. The question is strictly cosmetic and often a matter of personal preference and cost. The main thing to keep in mind is that the invitation is a statement about you and the type of event you're hosting.

No matter what kind of function you host or what kind of invitation you send, there are certain things you should include.

- ✔ **Name of host(s).** If appropriate, you may want to also include the hosts' company name and/or company logo.

- ✔ **Inviting phrase.** Here are a few inviting phrases to include in semi-formal or formal invitations:
    - requests the pleasure of your company
    - cordially invites you to
    - would like to have you join us
    - please celebrate with us
    - stop by for wine and cheese

- ✔ **Guest of honor or purpose.** Why are you hosting this event?
    - to introduce, meet, or honor
    - it's the holiday season
    - it's picnic time
    - to mark a special anniversary
    - moving to a new location
    - customer appreciation

- ✔ **Date.** The formality of the date depends on the decorum of the event.

    Formal: Friday, the eighth of April, Nineteen hundred ninety-nine (year written out)

    Semi-formal and informal: Friday, April 8, XXXX

✔ **Time.** The time follows the date.

> **Formal:** at eight o'clock
>
> **Semi-formal:** at 8 o'clock
>
> **Informal:** at 8 PM

✔ **Address.** Put the city and state on a line below the street address.

✔ **Refreshments.** If you plan to serve refreshments, mention generally what they are. You may be serving cocktails, lunch, dinner, wine and cheese, buffet, and so on. If you ignore the issue, the reader should assume you're not planning to serve anything. (You may see people showing up with coolers and flasks.)

✔ **Dress.** (This isn't a yes or no, unless you run a nudist colony.) If you're planning a formal affair, you may say "Black tie optional." For an after-hours office function, you may say "Business dress." For a pool party, you may say, "Please bring bathing suits." If you don't mention dress, the reader will use her own discretion.

✔ **Cost.** If the reader is expected to incur a cost, be sure to mention what it is. No one likes last-minute surprises; they create ill will. If you expect attendees to pay for their own booze, for example, you may say something like, "Soft drinks will be provided, and a cash bar will be available."

✔ **Response.** Let people know how to respond — for example, by phone, e-mail, or response card (for formal events).

> *Note*: RSVP is French for "répondez s'il vous plaît."

Some hosts ask for *Regrets Only,* instead of RSVP. Regrets only means that the host wants to hear only from those who don't plan to attend. The disadvantage is that people tend to be forgetful and don't respond even though they won't be attending. If you want a reasonably accurate head count, ask people to respond either way. After all, you wouldn't want to have too many monkey-brain canapés left over because there weren't enough victims to eat them.

Informal invitations

Informal invitations can be in letter format and follow the same guidelines as any business letter you write. *Make sure, however, that people can easily recognize the letter as an invitation.* Don't make the mistake of assuming that everyone reads your pearls of prose thoroughly. Following is how you may word a letter to customers inviting them to a buffet to show appreciation for their loyalty. This would be on company letterhead.

Dear

> The subject line may even be in a contrasting color.
> With color printers, it's simple to generate color.

Join us for a buffet dinner so we can thank you for your loyalty!

You've played an important role in the success of our company, and we want to thank you personally. Please join us for a buffet dinner. Dress casually and bring a big appetite.

Where: Commodore Hotel

When: August 12 at 8 PM

Please call me by August 5 to let me know whether you'll be joining us. We look forward to welcoming you.

Most cordially,

Informal invitations, such as those sent to employees, may be sent via e-mail. Following is an example of how an employer may show appreciation for all the hard work employees have been doing:

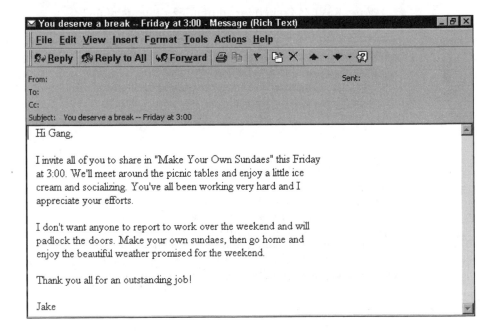

Semi-formal invitations

Semi-formal invitations can be computer-generated and printed on your laser or ink-jet printer. You may choose solid color paper, letterhead, or paper with a design appropriate for the occasion. Check the large stationery chains; they have a wide assortment of paper appropriate for semi-formal invitations. Example 13-1 is an invitation to a holiday party printed on paper just for the occasion.

When you center or right-justify the text or present it in a format different from a letter, it takes on the look of an invitation.

Mayberry Associates cordially invites

you and a guest to its

Annual Holiday Party

at the

Renaissance-Century Hotel

Nyack, New York

Saturday, December 12, XXXX

at 8 o'clock

RSVP by calling Todd Sweeney at ext. 456

by December 5

Example 13-1: Computer-generated invitation to join the holiday festivities.

Semi-formal invitations span a large array of business events. For example, companies and schools often host open-house-type events to lure people into their facilities. (Financial planners host investment seminars as a hook to sell their services. Large real estate companies offer free dinners to lure customers to buy time-sharing units. The opportunities go on and on.) Example 13-2 is a semi-formal invitation to a seminar that hooks the reader with a prominent guest speaker. The school prepared the invitation on letterhead; it unmistakably looks like an invitation.

Anytime you host an open-house-type event, offer a hook that doesn't sound like a commercial. After all, no one is coming to hear you jabber about your wonderful company, school, or whatever. Remember question 3 on your Start Up Sheet: "What's in it for the reader?"

Formal, printed invitations

Formal invitations are usually done by a professional printer. They're generally printed or engraved in black on white or ecru paper. Formal invitations are often accompanied by response cards and envelopes. Example13-2 is a formal invitation from a board of directors inviting selected guests to celebrate the opening of new offices.

If you want to get really snazzy and add a very elegant touch, consider hiring a calligrapher to hand write the envelopes. If you don't want the additional expense, find someone with nice handwriting to address them. Don't run envelopes for formal invitations through your printer.

Timing is everything

Whether you plan a business meeting, seminar, dinner party, potato sack race, or office party, timing is of the essence. Give people as much notice as you can because they have busy schedules and their calendars fill up quickly. Also, if people are coming from out of town, they may need to make travel arrangements. In the next column are guidelines for how far in advance to send invitations:

If you have formal invitations done by a professional printer, factor in the time for the print process, which can be several weeks or more. Check with your printer.

Function	Lead time
Company Picnic	4-6 weeks
Evening Reception	4-6 weeks
Cocktail Party	2-4 weeks
Holiday Party	Around Thanksgiving
Seminar	As soon as it's scheduled

Radison School
45 Smith Road, Larose, LA 70873

(777) 454-3435
www.radisonschool.edu

AUTHOR DR. BARD WILLIAMS SHARES THE EXCITEMENT OF THE WEB

Radison School hosts Dr. Bard Williams, author of *Web Publishing for Teachers*, part of the Dummies Series by IDG Books Worldwide. Dr. Williams is a "technology evangelist" who has been sharing the excitement of classroom technology for educators for years. Join us for this FREE seminar!

Date: September 16, XXXX
Time: 2:00 PM
Place: Larose campus

Benefit from Dr. Williams' Keen Industry Insights

If you're like most educators, you are anxious to explore the brave new world of the Internet. He'll strip away all the "technobabble" and teach you how you can harness the power of the Internet in your classroom. Here are some of the topics that Dr. Williams will cover:

- Explore Web page production and find out how to use powerful Web page creation tools.
- Build your own strategies for teaching and learning with the Web.
- Uncover tips on marketing your Web pages.
- Find out about Java and JavaScript and how they can liven up your Web pages.

At the seminar, you'll learn about the exciting new programs offered at Radison school, and you'll have a chance to meet many of the faculty members.

How to Reserve Your Seat

If you haven't already done so, please make your reservation now. Seating is limited. Register on the Web at **www.radisonschool.com** or call us at **1-800-RADISON, ext. 476.**

Example 13-2:
Seminar invitation with a hook.

Canceling that all-important event

If you have to cancel an event, notify each guest personally. If time is short, phone each guest or send a Mailgram. (Check out Chapter 18.) If time permits, write a personal letter. Following is an example of how a cancellation letter may read:

It's with deep regret that I must cancel the open house scheduled for Friday evening, May 15. My mother is ill, and I'll be flying back to Columbia this evening. I'll reschedule this event when I return.

Responding to the Invitation

It's a sad commentary on today's society that people need to ask for our responses when they send invitations. We should respond to any invitation without being asked. But we're all human, and — even with the best intentions — we're often hopelessly remiss when it comes to responding to invitations.

Following are some tips for responding to invitations — the most important one is to *do it*:

- ✔ Respond to the invitation immediately by doing what you're asked — phone, e-mail, fill out a formal response card, or whatever. If you don't respond while it's fresh in your mind, you may become one more of those remiss folks. (If you happen to meet your host on the street and say, "I just received your invitation and I'll be there," that doesn't constitute a response.)

- ✔ If you're responding on a formal response card and won't be attending, don't merely check "will not attend." You show class if you add a little note on the back giving a reason. *Will not attend because we'll be out of town. I'll call you next week.*

- ✔ Whenever you refuse an invitation, give a brief reason (with *brief* being the key word). A long-winded explanation sounds like an excuse, rather than a reason. (An *excuse* may be that you have to rearrange your sock drawer; a *reason* may be that you have a previous engagement.)

On a final note. . . . You aren't expected to respond "No" to an invitation where you're asked to pay money in the form of tickets or anything else.

Don't forget to use your Letter-Perfect Checklist featured on the Cheat Sheet in the front of this book when you prepare invitations. Wouldn't you be embarrassed if you sent out invitations for Sunday, January 25, and January 25 is a Saturday? You may have guests showing up on Saturday as you stand there in your underwear.

The Board of Directors

of

Marric Consulting Corp.

cordially invites you to a cocktail reception

on the occasion of the opening of its new

offices.

Friday, the eighth of April,

[year written out]

at eight o'clock

24 Besen Parkway

New Holland, PA 17557

(Black tie optional)

RSVP by March 15, XXXX

Example 13-3:
Put on your
best bib and
tucker.

Chapter 14

Professional Potpourri

- -

In This Chapter

▶ Including transmittal letters with correspondences

▶ Dealing with absences

▶ Turning down requests

▶ Keeping people informed during a merger

▶ Asking for membership renewals

▶ Announcing yourself to the world

▶ Soliciting funds and donations

▶ Sending praise

▶ Presenting winning proposals

▶ Asking to use published material

- -

The volume of paper expands to fill the available briefcase.

— Jerry Brown, former Governor of California

Companies send out gazillions of letters that don't fall into a specific category. This chapter gives you a sampling of the orphan letters, memos, and e-mail messages that you're bound to write at one time or another. Remember to use all the letter-writing guidelines in this book in the following letters — including the Start Up Sheet.

Beam Me Up, Scotty!

You must send a letter of transmittal (also known as a *transmittal letter* or *cover letter*) anytime you mail a check, report, form, legal document, policy, manuscript, survey, or just about anything else you stuff in the envelope. Here are some guidelines:

- ✔ Keep the letter brief.
- ✔ Identify what's included in the envelope.
- ✔ Mention the reader's action item, if any.

Dear

Subject: *(A few details about the contract)*

I'm enclosing two copies of the contract. Please sign and return both copies to me in the self-addressed, stamped envelope.

Next Step

Then I'll sign both and return one to you, so we'll each have a copy.

Sincerely,

Enclosure

When you send a file as an e-mail attachment, the body of your e-mail message is a letter of transmittal that tells the reader what the attachment is about.

Who's Minding the Store?

When a manager is gone from the office for an extended period of time, someone must mind the store. Promptly answering incoming mail is important to the company's image of caring about customers. The administrative assistant (or the person designated to do so) should acknowledge mail in a timely manner in the manager's absence. Here are a few pointers:

- ✔ Explain why you're writing, and not the manager. Sign your name.
- ✔ Be careful about making commitments you're not authorized to make.
- ✔ Don't divulge personal reasons for the manager's absence (golf tournament or implants for baldness).
- ✔ Be gracious and willing to help.

Dear

I'd like to acknowledge that we received your May 15 letter. Mr. DeMarco will be away from the office until June 1, and I'll bring this to his attention as soon as he returns.

If there's anything I can do for you in his absence, please let me know.

Sincerely,

Name
Administrative Assistant

Blame It on the Rain

Perhaps we all joke about the "yesman" because it's easier to say "Yes" than it is to say "No." No one wants to be the bearer of bad news; however, turning down requests is part of life, especially in business. As a skilled letter writer, you can say "No" and still maintain the goodwill of the reader. Check out Chapter 5 for ways to refuse with style and still get the results you want and Chapter 10 for additional tips on turning down requests with grace.

Here are some broad-brush tips for helping the reader save face when you must refuse a request:

- Be honest with your reason and timely with your reply.
- Compliment the reader for something, if appropriate.
- Detail why you're disappointing him. Be honest, but tactful.
- Cushion the bad news between a pleasant opening and closing.
- Offer a compromise or hope for future dealings.

No, I can't accept your proposal

When people work hard to put together a proposal but they're not the ones selected, they deserve a telephone call the day the decision is made. Follow the call with a letter and reiterate the items in the preceding bulleted list. After all, these folks invested a lot of time in trying to win your favor (rounds of telephone calls, meetings, and presentations — not to mention the stress of waiting to find out whether they get a thumbs-up). The following tactfully notifies an also-ran that he wasn't selected for a project:

Dear

> By omitting the subject line, you lessen the negative impact

Calling you this morning was quite difficult. You and your colleagues made an excellent presentation and would have done a superb job for us. The decision boiled down to the fact that Kraft Unlimited, the company we selected, has a lot more experience in setting up large enterprise systems.

We Look Forward to Working with You in the Future

The next time we have a project that fits your specialty more closely, we'll be in touch. Please thank your entire team and commend them on a job well done.

> Notice the continued praise

With personal regards,

Denying a request for an interview

A precarious situation can result when friends or colleagues ask for your help in getting an interview with your company. If you think the person is a viable candidate, there's no problem. If you don't think he's suited for the position, that can place you in an awkward position. The following note shows you how to decline graciously:

Dear

Your friendship is very important to me, and I hope you won't be too disappointed that I can't arrange for you to come in to meet Mr. Johnson. I believe you would have done a wonderful job for us. However, Mr. Johnson felt that your qualifications are better suited to a more junior position.

In the meantime, don't stand still! You have great qualifications and need to get your resume out there. I'll continue to keep my eyes open for a position at my company that may be right for you.

Warmest personal regards,

SHERYL SAYS

For a wealth of tips on other job-related letters, take a look at Chapter 7.

Mixing, Matching, and Merging

Companies are involved in mergers all the time. They merge with each other; they merge departments; and they merge work groups. Whenever a merger is imminent (and rumors have a way of preceding formal announcements), people go into a tizzy. Whether rumors are true or false, they invariably take on a life of their own and get distorted.

SHERYL SAYS

Can you recall the game of telephone you played as a kid? The message at the end of the line bore no resemblance to the original message. The same thing happens in business, and the results can be catastrophic. Here are two messages that stave off rumors and manage the process of merging — the first is a memo from a CEO to his managers to implement a merger; the second is an e-mail message from the CEO to the staff announcing the benefits of a merger. (Notice that the gating word is *benefits*.)

> ### Letterhead
>
> Date: April 10, XXXX
>
> To: All VPs, Directors, and Managers
>
> From: Corey Dalton, CEO
>
> Re: Merger with ITB, Ltd.
>
> So far we've been able to keep the plans of this merger at the top levels, but I'll be announcing it to the entire staff in an e-mail message next week. Here are some things we must be thinking about to minimize the shock and maximize productivity during the transition:
>
> - Prepare for a highly charged emotional response. Mergers are stressful times.
>
> - Make employees feel valued so they'll remain loyal and productive.
>
> - Re-recruit our good people. When some start to leave, others think it's the right thing to do. This can drain us of wonderful resources.
>
> - Make whatever changes you need to as soon as possible. When the merger is announced, people sit around waiting for the axe to fall.
>
> In the final analysis. . . . Let people know that change is an opportunity to grow and get out of old routines and ways of doing things.
>
> Thanks for your support.
>
> *Corey*

Example 14-1:
Memo to managers to put a plan in place for a merger.

Notice how the announcement is cast as a benefit

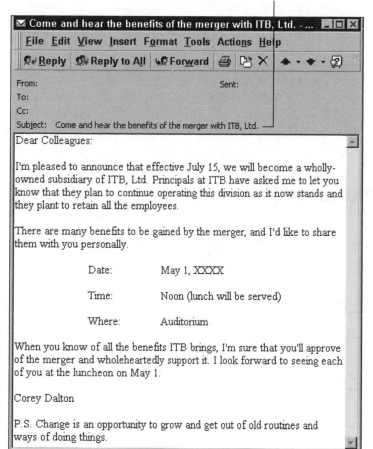

Example 14-2:
E-mail message to the troops announcing the benefits of a merger.

> ✉ Come and hear the benefits of the merger with ITB, Ltd. - ... _ □ ✕
>
> **File Edit View Insert Format Tools Actions Help**
>
> **Reply**   **Reply to All**   **Forward**   🖨 ⬚ ✕   ▲ ▾ ▾ ▾ 📄 »
>
> From: Sent:
> To:
> Cc:
> Subject: Come and hear the benefits of the merger with ITB, Ltd.
>
> Dear Colleagues:
>
> I'm pleased to announce that effective July 15, we will become a wholly-owned subsidiary of ITB, Ltd. Principals at ITB have asked me to let you know that they plan to continue operating this division as it now stands and they plant to retain all the employees.
>
> There are many benefits to be gained by the merger, and I'd like to share them with you personally.
>
>   Date: May 1, XXXX
>
>   Time: Noon (lunch will be served)
>
>   Where: Auditorium
>
> When you know of all the benefits ITB brings, I'm sure that you'll approve of the merger and wholeheartedly support it. I look forward to seeing each of you at the luncheon on May 1.
>
> Corey Dalton
>
> P.S. Change is an opportunity to grow and get out of old routines and ways of doing things.

We Want You Back

People let memberships lapse for a variety of reasons. Sometimes they just forget and need a reminder, such as the one that follows. Consider giving your reader motivation to renew by offering a discount, coupon, or other incentive.

> Dear Member:
>
> We miss you as a member of the spa and look forward to welcoming you back. We've purchased many new pieces of equipment and added many more classes and instructors.

(continued)

(continued)

We'll be increasing rates on January 1. However, if you join now, you can take advantage of the lower rates and apply this $15 coupon towards our already low price.

Offering an incentive

Here's to your health,

Enclosure

Welcome to my World

New businesses must always make themselves known. Following is an actual announcement used by "my son, the chiropractor" to announce to members of the Chamber of Commerce that he was opening his office. Here are a few guidelines to consider when you write an announcement:

✔ Explain what's in it for the reader (Question 3 on the Start Up Sheet).

✔ Use this as an opportunity to get your readers on your side. In the example, Dr. Lindsell wants to find out more about the reader so the reader may be one of his resources.

✔ Don't put pressure on the recipient. Notice how Dr. Lindsell asks the reader to call.

Essential Family Chiropractic
comes to the Village of Owen Brown on May 10, 1999

Dear Chamber Member:

I'm proud to become part of the Chamber Community and would like to share my enthusiasm for "Optimal Health Through Chiropractic" by offering a *free* health care demonstration to your employees. It will enable me to make a contribution to the optimal health of the men, women, and children of our community.

Also, I plan to compile a list of resources for myself and my patients and would like to learn more about you, your business, and the things in the community that are important to you. Please call me at (410) 312-7790 so we may arrange a time to get together. I look forward to meeting you.

Yours in health,

Dr. Eric L. Lindsell

I Gave at the Office

Asking for money is never easy, especially when the reader isn't getting anything tangible in return (such as a free meal). We all have our favorite charities, yet the postal carrier needs a weight-lifting belt from toting the stacks of solicitation letters he delivers each day. How do you appeal for funds and set yourself apart from all the others tapping into the same pool of people?

- ✔ Identify the charity.
- ✔ Convince the reader that a donation is worthwhile.
- ✔ Stress the satisfaction the donor will get from making a contribution.
- ✔ Talk about the progress you've made because of donations.

Take a look at the solicitation letters you receive. Notice what moves you to make a contribution or what prompts you to throw the letter in the trash. Pay attention to teasers on the envelope and special words or phrases in the letter that tug at your heartstrings. (See Chapter 6 for spicy sales letters.) Here are a few openings and closings you may consider:

Openings:

- ✔ When we see a very sick child stricken with a fatal disease, it tugs at our emotions. Each one of us is someone's child with the need for love and emotional support. Sometimes we also need financial support.
- ✔ Each year the Golden Club sends letters to our friends asking for help for our revered seniors. So far, your donations have [list successful projects donations have funded].
- ✔ Won't you join us helping to build a much-needed wing on our hospital.

Closings:

- ✔ We need you because we can't do it alone.
- ✔ We thank you, and the animals you save thank you.
- ✔ With friends like you, no one needs to fight [disease] alone.
- ✔ Please write your tax-deductible donation to [fund] and place it in the self-addressed envelope. Thank you so much for your continued support.

Singing Your Praises!

So many of us are quick to complain when things don't go well. However, praising others when things do go well is just as (if not more) important. Words of appreciation are worth the effort because they generate lasting goodwill. We all need a little pat on the back once in a while and don't get encouragement often enough. (When we pat ourselves on the back, we often wind up with a sore arm.) Following are some things to ponder:

- ✔ Be specific about why you're praising the person.

- ✔ Be gracious, but don't gush with compliments. You want to sound sincere.

Openings:

- ✔ Last month we held our annual banquet meeting at your hotel. I want to compliment your staff on the excellent service and luscious food. To show our appreciation, we want to reserve your Banquet Room for October 1 for next year's annual banquet.

- ✔ People often complain about poor service but don't take the time to comment on outstanding service. That's just what I'd like to do.

- ✔ I want to commend the flight crew aboard Flight 345 from San Francisco to Boston on June 2. Despite a two-hour delay on the runway and many cranky passengers, they demonstrated wonderful humor and kept smiling. I, for one, appreciated their efforts.

Closings:

- ✔ Because I can't possibly thank all the wonderful people personally, please share this letter of appreciation with them.

- ✔ A lot of the credit goes to you for setting such a great example!

E-mail is a terrific, effective, and easy way to send words of appreciation to a person or group. Send the message while the thought is fresh in your mind; it's quick and easy. Chapter 19 is chock-full of e-mail tips.

On Bended Knee

People often send one- to three-page sales proposals in the form of a letter and use the memo format for internal proposals. Sales proposals try to entice prospects to buy your product or service. Internal proposals range from suggesting ways to change a procedure to recommending that funds be appropriated for a large purchase.

Following is an excerpt from a letter proposal I wrote to one of my clients. I got the assignment to write the brochure.

Dear _____ | Notice how headlines punch out the key areas. |

Subject: Proposal for your capabilities brochure, RFP No. 234

Thank you for considering me to write your capabilities brochure. Following is a detailed outline of the project from start to finish:

Project Description:

- Writing text for 6-page (3-panel) brochure

- Page size: 8½ by 11 inches

Process: | Notice the process is a numbered list. |

1. Schedule initial 1 to 1½ hour meeting with key people to brainstorm and complete Start Up Sheet. (We need to clearly identify the audience, purpose, and key customer benefits.) Will schedule a second meeting if needed.

2. Prepare first draft and submit for review.

3. Make appropriate changes and schedule meeting if necessary.

4. Submit second draft and send for review.

5. Make final changes.

Deliverable:

Hard copy and floppy disk with text layout prepared in MS Word.

Assumptions:

- Acme will supply all the capabilities to be included.

- Acme will supply visuals and be responsible for printing.

- There will be two rounds of moderate revisions.

(continued)

(continued)

> *Cost:*
>
> Cost will be $3,450. (Added scope or changes thereafter will be billed at the hourly rate of $65 and discussed prior to proceeding.) Payment will be divided into thirds:
>
> - ⅓ when we agree to proceed.
> - ⅓ when the first draft is submitted.
> - ⅓ when the disk is delivered.
>
> *Schedule:*
>
> To meet a Labor Day deadline, we'll need to schedule our first meeting early in the week of June 20. (Bottlenecks generally happen during the revision process, and we're getting into vacation season.)
>
> *Next Step:*
>
> I look forward to working with you to produce a brochure that will help increase Acme's bottom line. I'll give you a call next Monday so we may take the next step.
>
> *Sincerely,*

To learn more about writing winning proposals, check out *Business Writing For Dummies* (IDG Books Worldwide, Inc.), which I also wrote. It contains an entire chapter devoted to writing sales proposals, internal proposals, and fund-raising proposals.

Just Love What You Wrote

If you want to use material that's been published (illustrations, photographs, speeches, articles, charts, and the like), you must get permission from the publication or author.

Following are some tips on what you may include:

✔ Be specific about what you want to use. Include the publication name, date, page number, and anything else that will help identify what you want permission for.

✔ Tell the reader exactly how you're planning to use the material.

✔ Offer to send the publisher or author a copy of how you use their material.

I always type a release form at the bottom of such a letter to make it easy for the person to reply. I also include a self-addressed, stamped envelope. Following shows what a release portion of the letter may look like:

I grant permission for [insert your name] to use the material requested above.

_____   _____
Name   Date

Don't forget to use your Letter-Perfect Checklist featured on the Cheat Sheet in the front of this book for all your business letters. If you thank someone for a $150 donation when they sent $1,500, next year you may be $1,350 short. They may only send $150.

Part IV
The Part of Tens

The 5th Wave — By Rich Tennant

Now take your time and see if you can identify the person who attacked you on e-mail.

In this part . . .

No ...*For Dummies* book is complete without this section. This part enhances the essence of the book with short chapters that offer a medley of timely tips such as: energizing your e-mail messages, submitting an article to a magazine, understanding postal services, cleaning up your paper piles, and other good stuff.

Chapter 15

Ten Hints for Writing Memorable Memos

In This Chapter

▶ Starting at the top

▶ Applying good management skills

▶ Using memos for informal reports

▶ Inking your "John Hancock"

How you write memos provides a clue to your style of management as well as your personality.

— Letitia Baldridge, *Complete Guide to Executive Manners*

E-mail messages have replaced many of the interoffice memos that used to buzz around the office, but memos are still a viable way to send internal messages within your office, division, or company. Although a lot of office communication is verbal, putting certain things in writing is preferable: praising a person or team for a job well done; transmitting ideas, decisions, and suggestions; referencing facts or figures; and (as Jerry Seinfeld says) yada, yada, yada! In this chapter, I share some of my favorite tips for writing effective memos.

Know the Rules of the Road

A memo is a letter without an inside address, salutation, complimentary closing, or formal place for a signature line. Here are a few other things to keep in mind:

- The primary difference between a letter and a memo is form and method of delivery. (An air mail memo would be folding the paper into an airplane and flying it across the room.)

- Limit each memo to a single subject. If you need to cover two or more subjects, send two or more memos.

- Be as polite as you would be if the memo were a letter to a customer or client. Always include "good-manners" phrases such as, "Thank you very much," "I'm sorry that I couldn't. . . ," and "I'd really appreciate it if. . . ." Courtesy goes a long way.

- You can use jargon, acronyms, initialisms, and other stuff your colleague(s) will recognize.

Check out Part II for help getting your memo into high gear and adding spit and polish. Make sure you use your Start Up Sheet on the Cheat Sheet in the front of this book.

Use a Header

If your organization uses memos frequently, it probably has pre-printed forms. If not, consider any of these headers:

To:	TO:	Date
From:	FROM:	To:
Date:	DATE:	From:
Subject:	SUBJECT:	Subject:

After *To:* in the heading, follow the written and unwritten lines of protocol. List people in order of ranking, from high to low. For example, if you're writing a memo to the higher ups in the company, the order may be CEO, President, Vice President, Director, Manager, and so forth down the line.

Don't Use Memos to Share Bad News

Some managers don't deal well with people and hide behind memos. Use good judgment. For example, if your company is merging and people will be laid off, don't write a memo for goodness' sake. Hold a meeting and tell folks what's going on. Although sharing bad news face to face is often difficult, doing so is more humane than putting it in writing.

Display a Sense of Humor

Bill Cosby said, "You can turn painful situations around through laughter. If you can find humor in something, you can survive it." You may use humor more liberally in a memo than in a letter because you're probably acquainted with the reader(s). If you have a sense of humor (and you probably do), lighten up and let it show. Use a sense of humor to take the edge off a stressful situation, not to detract from the situation. You may start with something as simple as, "The good news is. . . ."

Complain Constructively

Don't use memos as a dumping ground. If you need to put a complaint in a memo, be constructive. My mother always taught me, "If you can't offer a way to do something better, don't complain."

> *Constructive:* Let's discuss several ways to help you focus on details more effectively.

> *Critical:* One of your faults is poor attention to details.

Use Proper Form When You Write a Memorandum Report

Interoffice memos are often used to generate informal reports within a company. Because the memo is for internal readers, you may assume that the reader is familiar with the jargon of your industry. Here are some things to include in a memo report. Check out Chapter 4 for ways to make your subject line and headlines specific and to sequence for the reaction of your reader(s).

- ✔ Subject: Title of the report
- ✔ Introduction
- ✔ Issues
- ✔ Conclusions or recommendations

If your memo report runs longer than one page, use the same second-page heading as you would in a letter, as shown in Chapter 5.

Sign on the Dotted Line

On a memo, there's no formal place for a signature. However, signing your name or initials on the *From:* line or on the bottom of the memo is a good idea so that no unscrupulous person can send a memo in your name. After people get used to seeing your John Hancock, they may raise an eyebrow or two if they get an unsigned memo from you.

Proofread and Edit Your Memo

Be sure to use the Letter-Perfect Checklist featured on the Cheat Sheet in the front of this book. You don't want to be remembered as the person who dated her memo February 30.

Chapter 16

Ten Tips for Querying a Magazine

- -

In This Chapter

▶ Who's hot and who's not

▶ Write it and they will print

▶ Avoiding the last writes

- -

Publish or perish.

— Popular expression in the academic world

At some point in your career, you may have "pearls of information" to share. The way to reach your target audience is by writing an article for publication in print or on the Internet. There are thousands of publications, from focused industry newsletters to national magazines and newspapers to electronic journals. Getting your name in print isn't that difficult. Here's what it takes:

- ✔ A good idea
- ✔ Target publication(s)
- ✔ A dynamite query letter — one that will whet the editor's appetite
- ✔ Lots of determination

Don't underestimate the value of determination. Before my first article was published, I must have sent it to every publisher in the universe. I received so many rejection letters, I could have wallpapered the Taj Mahal. However, I never gave up and am now a professional writer with a slew of articles and 15 books to my credit!

Don't Procrastinate; Just Do It!

If you're worried that your writing isn't good enough to be published or that no one is interested in your work, don't be! Most editors thrive on articles from outside contributors. If you ever wrote a newsletter, you know how difficult it can be to find authors who will write and submit interesting articles. Magazine editors have the same problem.

Know What's in It for You

People who publish, either in the academic realm or the business world, are part of an elite group. And the more prestigious the publication, the greater the value! When you publish an article, you add prestige to your reputation and your company's. Not all publications pay for articles or offer honoraria; the payoff is in getting published. You can order reprints of articles to include in sales packets and proposals. And the best part is that you're not marketing yourself or your product — the publication is doing that for you!

A reprint of an article you write is a great promotional piece to attach to your resume. Once you have something appear in print, you're thought of as an expert — even if the article is about a hobby or special interest.

Hook Up with the Right Publication

You're a professional. You know what publications you and your colleagues read. If you're unsure of where to submit your topic, contact professional organizations and ask for suggestions. Or contact the publication and ask for demographic information about readers.

Test the Waters

No one wants to burn the midnight oil for naught. So, before you labor over writing a lengthy article, find a publication that may be interested. Some publications readily accept unsolicited manuscripts; others "tell you" they rely on staff writers. (I put *tell you* in quotes for a reason.) Every publication worth its salt knows that input from a broad range of contributors strengthens its publication.

Don't Take "No" for an Answer

Even if the editor tells you he doesn't accept unsolicited material, don't let that dissuade you from sending a query. You'll be hard to ignore if your topic is impressive and presented exquisitely.

The famous photos of John F. Kennedy's assassination were submitted by an amateur photographer — a photographer who had never been published. The photos and the photographer received worldwide acclaim.

Read the Masthead

The masthead is the page at the front of the publication that lists publishers, editors, phone numbers of branch offices, board of reviewing editors, member societies, and other good stuff. The only people who read mastheads are the mothers of the people mentioned and wannabe writers (who read them insatiably). Here's how to slice and dice the masthead:

- At first glance, you notice that nearly everyone listed is an editor of some sort. Trying to decipher who does what is the real challenge. The best way to find the editor who accepts unsolicited manuscripts is to call the publication or check the *Writer's Market* — an annual publication that gives you the inside scoop. (There's more about it later in this chapter.)

- Here are a few phrases you may see:

   "Publisher assumes no responsibility for care and return of unsolicited manuscripts."

   "Unsolicited manuscripts, photographs, artwork, and materials should include ample postage and a self-addressed, stamped envelope (SASE); otherwise they will not be returned."

Gee whiz — doesn't that contradict what I just said and sound like publications want to discourage freelance submissions? Absolutely not! They depend on submissions to keep their publications afloat. What they want to discourage is the amateur who hasn't taken the time to learn the ropes.

Send Simultaneous Submissions

It's perfectly acceptable to send queries to several publications simultaneously. *But don't send your **manuscript** to more than one publication at a time.*

Publications frown on the "spaghetti approach." (You know the old theory of throwing spaghetti against the wall to see what sticks.) If you get more than one positive response, decide which publication you most want your work to appear in and send your manuscript to it only. This publication may retain the publishing rights. If it doesn't bar you from publishing the same material elsewhere, you're then free to submit it to other journals.

If your topic is very revolutionary or controversial, there may be some obstacles to getting it published. Editors aren't necessarily crusaders. Crusaders in the publishing industry either receive journalism awards or get fired.

Become Intimate with the Journal You're Targeting

Before you write a query, read at least a half dozen back issues of the journal you're targeting. Reading the magazine will give you a good idea of what sort of articles the journal looks for, what style and tone to use, how long articles are, and lots of other useful information.

Know What Editors Look for in a Query Letter

Here are some specific things editors look for in a query:

- ✔ What's the article about?
- ✔ Does it present anything new or insightful?
- ✔ What percentage of readers will the article interest?
- ✔ Does it overlap with other articles?
- ✔ Does the author make his point logically?
- ✔ Is the author's writing clear?

Following is a query letter I sent to a magazine for an article I wrote. The letter is short, to the point, and incorporates the elements of writing a solid query letter. The proof is in the pudding; the article was published.

Dear

Proposed Article: "Cutting Information Overload in the Electronic World"

I'd like to submit for publication a chapter from my new book, *Business Writing For Dummies*, that I turned into an article. "Cutting Information Overload in the Electronic World" is one of the hottest topics in the business world today.

Electronic communications is a relatively new medium and people are struggling with its do's and taboos. This is such a popular subject that I expanded the workshops I deliver to include this much-sought-after information. I know this topic will be of great interest to all your readers.

Next Step

Please let me know if you'd like to include this article in an upcoming issue. Thank you.

Sincerely,

Get a Copy of the Latest Writer's Market

Writer's Market is an annual publication that's a writer's bible. You can find it in bookstores, libraries, or on the Web. It discusses how to get published, how to write for a publication, and what the markets are. Many of the big-name magazine and book publishers tell you what they look for and whom to contact.

Here are a few things in *Writer's Market* you shouldn't take as gospel:

- ✔ *Reports promptly.* Yes, they may report the rejections promptly. They pass around queries that are being considered.
- ✔ *Reports in two to four weeks.* Two to four months may be more like it.
- ✔ *Pays five to ten cents a word.* You can bet you'll get five.

Don't Hold Back Information

Writers often are concerned that a publication might steal their article ideas. When you're dealing with a reputable publication, you *can* trust the editor to act honorably. He won't allow staffers to report your idea or assign your topic to another writer. Therefore, provide whatever information adds strength to your proposal.

Good luck!

Chapter 17

Ten Things to Remember About Proper Forms of Address

In This Chapter

▶ General business addresses

▶ In the military

▶ Government officials

▶ Members of the clergy

▶ College or university heads

People care more than perhaps you realize how they are written to. . . . Whether an outside person is overly sensitive on the subject or whether your office is overly casual about this subject, someone should care enough to do something about it.

— Letitia Baldridge, *Complete Guide to Executive Manners*

Yes, I know this part of the book is called the Part of Tens. So then why does this chapter contain only five sections? Because these five sections contain double the information, that's why! Besides, using the proper form of address is essential to making a positive impression on your reader, so the subject deserves its own chapter, and this seemed like the perfect part.

 If you offend the reader by addressing him incorrectly, you risk nullifying the reason you're writing. The proper forms of address include the inside address (which is carried over to the envelope) and the salutation. Check out Chapter 3 for details.

Following are a couple of general guidelines:

- ✔ Never write *To Whom This May Concern* or *Dear Sir or Madam*. These addresses sound cold and impersonal. Instead, try to find the name or job title of the person you're writing to. You can often find such information by calling the company and talking to the receptionist.

- ✔ Once a person has achieved the title of *Honorable*, she retains the title throughout her lifetime.

In some cases, forms of address are affected by the relationship between the reader and the writer; therefore, the following tables offer guidelines, not rules. For example, if the CEO of a company knows the governor of her state personally, she'd address the governor by her first name.

General Salutations: Formal and Informal

When you address people formally, follow the salutation with a colon. When you address them informally, use a comma. Table 17-1 shows how to address people for formal and informal salutations:

Table 17-1	Formal and Informal Salutations	
Inside Address	*Formal*	*Informal*
Mr. Ted Bially	Dear Mr. Bially:	Dear Ted,
Ms. Phyllis Bially	Dear Ms. Bially:	Dear Phyllis,
Mr. and Mrs. Ted Bially	Dear Mr. and Mrs. Bially:	Dear Ted and Phyllis,
Mr. James Haskell and Ms. Donna Randall	Dear Mr. Haskell and Ms. Randall:	Dear Jim and Donna,
Messrs. Steve and Josh Bottazzi	Dear Messrs. Bottazzi:	Dear Steve and Josh,
Mmes. Tammy and Nicole Brossi	Dear Mmes. Brossi:	Dear Tammy and Nicole,
Messrs. Samuel Fleming and Robert Jones	Dear Messrs. Fleming and Jones:	Dear Sam and Bob,
Mmes. Jane Seiffert and Nubia Aurandt	Dear Mmes. Seiffert and Aurandt:	Dear Jane and Nubia,

Inside Address	Formal	Informal
Doctor Brad Louca, or Brad Louca, M.D.	Dear Doctor Louca:	Dear Brad,
Dr. Charlotte Maye and Mr. Samuel Maye	Dear Dr. and Mr. Maye:	Dear Charlotte and Sam,

Keep the following in mind:

✔ **When the doctor isn't a medical doctor (M.D.), address the doctor as you see in Table 17-1**. However, substitute the correct designation. Here are a few popular ones:

Abbreviation	Full Title
D.C.	Doctor of Chiropractic
D.M.V.	Doctor of Veterinary Medicine
D.D.S.	Doctor of Dental Surgery

✔ **An attorney in the United States is referred to as *Esquire* or *Esq.* The** inside address is *Larry Lawyer, Attorney at Law; Larry Lawyer, Esquire*; or *Larry Lawyer, Esq*. The formal salutation is *Dear Mr. Lawyer:*, and the informal salutation is *Dear Larry,*. Two or more attorneys are *Esquires* or *Esqs.*

Military Might

Military folks are more formal than folks in the private sector. For example, military people address each other by their rank and surname, rather than by first names. Table 17-2 reflects the U.S. Armed Forces (except the U.S. Navy, which follows), and Table 17-3 reflects the U.S. Navy. Both are in descending order, from high ranking to low.

Table 17-2	U.S. Armed Services	
Rank	**Inside Address**	**Salutation**
General	General James Triollo	Dear General Triollo:
Major General	Major General Seth Thomason	Dear General Thomason:
Colonel	Colonel Harry Pape	Dear Colonel Pape:
Lieutenant Colonel	Lieutenant Colonel Harvey Morse	Dear Colonel Morse:

(continued)

Table 17-2 *(continued)*

Rank	Inside Address	Salutation
Captain	Captain Glenda Mason	Dear Captain Mason:
Second Lieutenant	Second Lieutenant Randy Vaughn	Dear Lieutenant Vaughn:
Warrant Officer	Warrant Officer Catherine Sabatini	Dear Ms. Sabatini:
Sergeant Major	Sergeant Major George Abramowitz	Dear Sergeant Major Abramowitz:
Master Sergeant	Master Sergeant Hillary Glenn	Dear Sergeant Glenn:
Corporal	Corporal Matthew Kalin	Dear Corporal Kalin:
Private First Class (or Private)	Private First Class (or Private) Sara Hanson	Dear Private Hanson:
Airman First Class (or Airman)	Airman First Class (or Airman) Kenneth Clark	Dear Airman Clark:

Table 17-3 **The U.S. Navy**

Rank	Inside Address	Salutation
Admiral	Admiral Edward Dunne	Dear Admiral Dunne:
Rear Admiral	Rear Admiral Kathleen Sullivan	Dear Admiral Sullivan:
Captain	Captain Paul Estey	Dear Captain Estey:
Lieutenant Commander	Lieutenant Commander John Mann	Dear Commander Mann:
Lieutenant	Lieutenant Brian Rogers	Dear Mr. Rogers:
Ensign	Ensign Don Farver	Dear Mr. Farver:
Warrant Officer (all grades)	Warrant Officer James Freund	Dear Mr. Freund:
Enlisted Personnel (all grades)	(Rank) Nancy Nowarth	Dear Ms. Nowarth:

A typical complimentary closing in military correspondence may be "Respectfully yours," for high-ranking officials, and "Yours truly," for low-ranking officials.

Government Gurus

Table 17-4 offers tips when writing to U.S. Governmental officials. Even if you're sending your representative an e-mail message, you should still use the proper form of address.

Table 17-4	U.S. Governmental Officials	
Official	*Inside Address*	*Salutation*
President	The President, The White House	Dear Mr. (Madam) President:
Vice President	The Vice President, United States Senate	Dear Madam (Mr.) Vice President Groening:
Chief Justice	The Chief Justice of the United States Supreme Court	Dear Mr. (Madam) Chief Justice:
Senator	Honorable Clint Liveoak	Dear Senator Liveoak:
Representative	Honorable Nicole Haaning	Dear Ms. (Mr.) Haaning:
Cabinet Member	Honorable Colin Leary	Dear Mr. (Madam) Secretary:
Ambassador	Honorable April Maschmeier	Dear Madam (Mr.) Ambassador:
Governor	Honorable Jason Roscoe	Dear Governor Roscoe:
Mayor	Honorable Nancy Powers	Dear Mayor Powers:
Judge	Honorable David Feldman	Dear Judge Feldman:

The standard complimentary closing is "Respectfully yours," for high-ranking officials, such as the ones in Table 17-4.

The Religious Realm

When writing to members of the religious community, refer to Table 17-5 for the proper forms of address.

Table 17-5	Church and Synagogue Officials	
Official	*Inside Address*	*Formal Salutation*
The Pope	His Holiness the Pope	Your Holiness:
Cardinal in the U.S.	His Eminence, Bryland Sutton	Your Eminence:
Archbishop in the U.S.	The Most Reverend Jon Sauder	Your Excellency:
Bishop in the U.S.	The Most Reverend Keith Nightenhelser	Your Excellency:
Monsignor	The Right (or Very) Reverend Gregory Sanders	Right Reverend:
Priest	The Reverend Shan Bell	Dear Father Bell:
Sister	Sister Mary Elizabeth Husted	Dear Sister Mary Elizabeth Husted:
Protestant Minister	The Reverend Amber Bowers	Dear Ms. (Mr. or Dr.) Bowers:
Rabbi	Rabbi Pat Williams	Dear Rabbi Williams:

Use "Respectfully," or "Respectfully yours," as the complimentary closing when writing to high-ranking clergy and "Very truly yours," for low-ranking clergy.

Campus Companions

The term *Professor* is generally reserved for those who have doctorate degrees. However, if you want to earn points (literally), call all your instructors "Professor." Flattery will get you everywhere! Table 17-6 gives you hints for addressing college and university officials.

Table 17-6	College and University Officials	
Office	*Inside Address*	*Salutation*
President of College or University	Dr. (Mr. or Ms.) Jacqueline Wiles	Dear Dr. (Mr. or Ms.) Wiles:
Dean or Assistant Dean	Dean (Dr.) Benjamin Rogers	Dear Dean Rogers:
Professor	Professor (Dr.) Rebecca Travis	Dear Professor (Dr.) Travis:

People generally start business letters with *Dear Somebody*. Are these people really *dear* to you? When I write *Dear Aunt Raye* or *Dear Susan*, I use *dear* sincerely because my friends and relatives truly are dear to me. However, when I write to Mr. Smith to complain about poor service, he isn't dear to me. Why use the term? Because proper forms of address dictate it. (If any of you know how this practice started, I'd enjoy hearing about it.)

Neither message had anything to do with the original message Tom had sent, yet neither person changed the subject line for the reply. The subject line should always reflect the message.

Use Another Program to Compose Long Messages

When your message is longer than two screens, prepare the document in your word processor, spreadsheet, or graphics software. Then you can send the message in any of the following ways:

Send as attachments

If you've used another program to compose a lengthy document, attach the file to your e-mail message. Most e-mail software lets you attach multiple files to one message. Here are a few tips for attaching a file:

- ✔ **Be sure your reader can receive the file.** Not all e-mail systems handle files in the same way. If you're not sure that your intended recipient can actually receive your file, send a test file to the reader to check for compatibility.

- ✔ **Let the reader know what file format you're sending.** Even if you and your recipient use the same software, you each may have different versions of it, and files aren't necessarily *downwardly compatible* (able to be read by a previous version of the software).

- ✔ **If an attached file is long, compress it.** Files compressed in programs such as WinZip, StuffIt, Expander, and Zipit can speed delivery and cut down on network traffic. Let the reader know what program you used to compress the document so she can uncompress the file on her end.

If your message can't get through for any reason, it will bounce back with a notation, *Daemon* (which is a Greek word meaning "spirit"). Mailer daemons are good spirits because they can tell you what the problem is in sending.

Post to your intranet

If a message is of interest to a wide range of people within your company, post it to your company's intranet. Then send an e-mail message letting people know the message is there. This is a great way to share the details of the company picnic and other issues of interest to your colleagues.

Chapter 18

Ten Things to Know about Using the U.S. Postal Service

In This Chapter

▶ All you ever wanted to know about postal services here and abroad

▶ Stamping out needless costs

> *And he wrote in the king Ahasuerus' name and sealed it with the king's ring, and sent letters by posts on horseback, and riders on mules, camel, and young dromedaries.*
>
> — *Book of Ester 8:10*

*T*his quote from the Bible is one of the earliest references to any form of postal service. Closer to home (and to a period in our own history), mail to early American colonists crossed the Atlantic Ocean in ships from England to the colonies. Letters were delivered to reputable taverns or coffee houses where the addressees would pick them up. This process kept English colonists in America connected to friends and kinfolk in the mother country.

In this chapter, I include many services offered by the U.S. Postal Service (USPS). This list is far from complete, but I tried to capture the most popular services. I don't include rates, because rates have a way of hiking up. Always check with your local post office for current rate schedules and any questions you have on these or any other services.

Domestic Mail Services: In and Around the USA

Domestic mail includes everything between the United States, its territories and possessions, the United Nations, Army and Air Force Area Post Offices

(APOs), and Navy Fleet Post Offices (FPOs). Here are some standards that domestic mail must adhere to:

- ✔ **Weight:** Less than 70 pounds. (No problem with a letter unless it's chiseled in stone.)

- ✔ **Length and girth:** Less than 108 inches, except parcel post, which maxes out at 130 inches.

- ✔ **Thickness:** A minimum of 0.07 inches thick. Pieces that are ¼ inch thick or more, must measure at least 3½ by 5 inches. (I don't know what happens to smaller pieces; perhaps they just get lost.)

First class

First class is the post office's fastest delivery except for Priority or Express. It applies to sealed letters, postal cards (sold by the post office), postcards (from Grandma on her trip to Florida), business reply cards, and greeting cards. A single rate — usually the current cost of a first-class stamp — applies to all items of up to one ounce. The envelope can be stamped or metered. If the correct postage isn't used, your letter will be returned to you — eventually.

My next door neighbor had a mild heart attack and was home from the hospital in a few days. At the local post office, I mailed a card to his home stuffed with funny clippings. Inadvertently, I didn't put enough postage on the envelope. Eighteen months later it was returned to me. So, I walked the card over to his home — a year and a half later. At least he knew I thought of him, even if it was way after the fact.

Don't use bulk mail postage for letters — even for mass mailings — because bulk mail postage shrieks "junk mail." Mail all business letters first class. After you put in the effort of writing, sealing, and stamping, you at least want the addressee to open the envelope.

Certificate of Mailing

Many people don't know that a certificate of mailing exists. Instead they use certified mail, which is three to four times more expensive. If you merely want proof that you sent a letter to the addressee on a certain date, get a certificate of mailing. This service is great when you mail your tax return at the stroke of midnight on April 15 and want proof that you made it under the wire. Here's what a certificate of mailing looks like:

U.S. POSTAL SERVICE **CERTIFICATE OF MAILING**

MAY BE USED FOR DOMESTIC AND INTERNATIONAL MAIL, DOES NOT PROVIDE FOR INSURANCE — POSTMASTER

Received From:

_____

_____

One piece of ordinary mail addressed to:

_____

_____

_____

Affix fee here in stamps or meter postage and post mark. Inquire of Postmaster for current fees.

PS Form 3817, Mar. 1989

Certified Mail

Send a letter certified mail when you need proof that it reached its destination. You can indicate restricted delivery so that no one other than the addressee can sign for the letter, or you can indicate that anyone at the address can sign for it. The receipt for certified mail card is returned to you for your records. Following are two certified mail forms: a receipt for certified mail and a domestic return receipt, both sides.

Z 486 210 735

US Postal Service
Receipt for Certified Mail
No Insurance Coverage Provided.
Do not use for International Mail (See reverse)

Sent to

Street & Number

Post Office, State, & ZIP Code

Postage $

Certified Fee

Special Delivery Fee

Restricted Delivery Fee

Return Receipt Showing to Whom & Date Delivered

Return Receipt Showing to Whom, Date, & Addressee's Address

TOTAL Postage & Fees $

Postmark or Date

PS Form 3800, April 1995

Fold at line over top of envelope to the right of the return address

CERTIFIED

Z 486 210 735

MAIL

SENDER:
- Complete items 1 and/or 2 for additional services.
- Complete items 3, 4a, and 4b.
- Print your name and address on the reverse of this form so that we can return this card to you.
- Attach this form to the front of the mailpiece, or on the back if space does not permit.
- Write "Return Receipt Requested" on the mailpiece below the article number.
- The Return Receipt will show to whom the article was delivered and the date delivered.

I also wish to receive the following services (for an extra fee):
1. ☐ Addressee's Address
2. ☐ Restricted Delivery

Consult postmaster for fee.

Is your RETURN ADDRESS completed on the reverse side?

Thank you for using Return Receipt Service.

3. Article Addressed to:

4a. Article Number

4b. Service Type
☐ Registered   ☐ Certified
☐ Express Mail   ☐ Insured
☐ Return Receipt for Merchandise   ☐ COD

7. Date of Delivery

5. Received By: *(Print Name)*

8. Addressee's Address *(Only if requested and fee is paid)*

6. Signature: *(Addressee or Agent)*
X

PS Form **3811,** December 1994   102595-96-B-0229   Domestic Return Receipt

---

UNITED STATES POSTAL SERVICE

First-Class Mail
Postage & Fees Paid
USPS
Permit No. G-10

• Print your name, address, and ZIP Code in this box •

TO EXPOSE ADHESIVE REMOVE LINER

Certified letters can't be insured, so don't use certified mail when anything of monetary value is in the envelope. Use registered mail instead.

Registered mail

Registered mail gives you maximum protection and security when you mail anything of monetary value (such as bearer bonds). Registered mail may be combined with restricted delivery, return receipt, or cash on delivery (C.O.D.) mailings. If the registered item gets lost, you can receive compensation for the actual paid and insured value of the item up to $25,000.

Priority Mail

Priority Mail is defined as first class mail that's supposed to reach its destination within 2–3 days. This time frame, however, isn't a guarantee. The benefit of Priority Mail over regular first class mail is that Priority Mail looks important and is more difficult to lose. For a fee, the post office will pick up Priority Mail at your home or office.

Express Mail

Express Mail is a premium service guaranteed for next-day or second-day delivery — whichever you choose. Insurance of up to $500 is included in the fee, and you can purchase additional insurance of up to $5,000. For an additional fee, the post office will pick up Express Mail at your home or office.

Mailgrams

A Mailgram is a mail-via-satellite service offered by Western Union in conjunction with the USPS. If you want to send a Mailgram, contact Western Union and input your message by fax, telephone, computer terminal, or Telex. Western Union transmits the message to the addressee's post office. The post office prints the message, puts it in a window envelope, and delivers the message as first class mail. The envelope has a blue stripe across the front, suggesting something of importance inside. A Mailgram gives you high impact at a relatively low cost. Here are some specifics:

- There's a basic charge for the first 100 words (not counting name, address, and signature).

- Messages received before 7 p.m. at the destination time are made the next day. Messages received after 7 p.m. are delivered the second day.

- Large volumes of Mailgrams can be delivered by putting mailing lists on a computer tape, which holds 10,000 addresses.

International Mail

Anytime you send a letter overseas, there's no alternative to airmail — unless you put your letter on a "slow boat to China." If you mark AIRMAIL or PAR AVION on the envelope, it's easily recognizable as an overseas letter. Here are some vital statistics to keep in mind:

- Minimum length and height: 5½ by 3½ inches
- Maximum thickness: 0.007 inches
- Maximum length: 24 inches
- Maximum length + height + thickness: 36 inches

Special services

Registered mail is available to all countries except Cambodia and the Democratic People's Republic of Korea (North Korea). Return receipts for registered mail and insured parcels are also available. Certified mail and C.O.D. aren't available for international mail.

Addressing the envelope

When you send a letter to an international address, always type it in English. (Of course, you don't translate into English the name of the street or town.) Type the name of the country in all capital letters on the last line of the address block.

The post office requests that envelopes be typed in all uppercase (domestic and international) with no punctuation. However, the public "fish" haven't taken the bait. In other words, people don't use the all caps and no punctuation format too often. Here's what may appear on an envelope to England in all uppercase with no punctuation:

MS KATHY BLYTHE
4563 PALACE ROAD
LONDON WIP 6HQ
ENGLAND

Other Carriers

There are mail carriers other than the USPS. The most common two are Federal Express (FedEx) and United Parcel Service (UPS). In addition to calling these carriers directly, you can mail from Mail Boxes, Etc. or Kinko's, or look for drop boxes outside professional buildings or shopping centers.

Check the Yellow Pages of your phone directory under "Delivery Service," "Messenger Service," or "Courier Service" to find out about mail carrier services and the applicable rates. (My local directory intersperses limousine and taxi services with mail delivery services. Many taxi and limousine companies also provide messenger services.)

Cost-Cutting Tips

Following are a few ways to keep postal costs down:

- ✔ Keep your mailing lists up to date.
- ✔ Don't use special services unless you need to.
- ✔ Have current postal rates on hand.
- ✔ Have postal scales checked regularly for accuracy.

Following are a few things to keep in mind when you use a postage meter instead of stamps:

- ✔ Change the date each day.
- ✔ Be certain the amount of postage is correct. If the envelope is borderline, err on the side of additional postage.
- ✔ Check to see that the imprint is clear. (Postage meter ink is known as "hot" ink.)
- ✔ Make sure all the envelopes face in the same direction when you run them through the meter. If you don't, your postage imprint may be on the back of the envelope or on top of your return address.

Print postage at your computer (legally)

Take advantage of PC Postage to print domestic first class, Priority, and Express Mail envelopes right at your desktop. You can quickly and easily add an indicia (meter stamp), bar code, return address, image, or promotional copy. To learn about the companies that offer this USPS-approved service, do an Internet search on **PC Postage**. You pay these companies a monthly fee plus usage rates.

Chapter 19

Ten Tips for Cutting E-M@il Overload

In This Chapter

▶ Cool, calm, and collected

▶ While we're on the subject

▶ Delivering the message

▶ Tone it down

▶ What's the urgency?

▶ Who's peeking?

▶ Breaking the chain

E-mail technology is marching forward too fast for social rules to keep up, leaving correspondents to police themselves and sometimes commit gaffes that would make Miss Manners wince.

— Jeffrey Bair, columnist

E-mail is the main stop on the information superhighway; it's one of the primary tenants in cyberspace real estate. E-mail is the new medium for traditional hard copy letters, memos, and other documents business people write. However, the ease of sending and receiving e-mail messages may cause inherent problems. People often compose on the fly without re-reading their messages, and disconnected messages often go back and forth.

I peppered this book with little tidbits for energizing your e-mail — everything from saying "hello" and "goodbye" to your reader to using the proper tone both here and abroad. This chapter is devoted to the big tidbits of e-mail, but I suggest that you look for the e-mail icon as you read through the rest of this book for other handy tips.

Don't Use E-Mail as a Shotgun

People have a tendency to prepare e-mail messages on the fly and fire them off to everyone in the universe. As I repeat many times throughout this book, e-mail is a serious business tool. Be certain to fill out the Start Up Sheet and read through Part II when you're sending anything more than a "let's-do-lunch" message to someone you know well.

I'm part of a team of 20 people working on a large project. We live and work in different parts of the United States and keep in touch by e-mail, intranet, and meetings, when appropriate.

Ten team members were at a meeting. During the meeting, one team member got the sad news that his father died. Certainly all the team members needed to be told of the tragedy. The nine team members at the meeting each sent e-mail messages to the ten of us who weren't there. Yes, 90 messages were sent out, each absent member receiving the sad news nine times. That's over-load at its finest hour.

Before e-mail messages became so easy to shotgun, one person would have volunteered to either make phone calls or send notes to each of the ten team members who needed this information.

Make the Subject Line Reflect the Message

You must be sensitive to the subject line when you reply to, forward, or initi-ate an e-mail message. Chapter 4 talks about how important it is to create a seductive subject line whenever you send an e-mail message. Remember that the subject line is the reader's only clue as to what your message is about. If the subject line isn't compelling, your message may not be read.

When you reply to someone's message, change the subject line if you change the theme of the message. Here's a real incident: Tom came to work on a foggy morning and noticed that someone's headlights were on. Tom sent a message to everyone in the company with the following subject line: *White Honda, license plate 123 ABC left lights on*.

People realized that Tom was at his desk, and responses came back immedi-ately. Following is the text from just two of the messages that used Tom's subject line *White Honda, license plate 123 ABC left lights on*:

Message 1: "Tom, I'd like to attend Wednesday's class. What time?"

Message 2: "What are you doing for lunch today?"

Post it on your Web site

If the message is of interest to a wide range of people outside your company, post it on your Web site. This is a great way to post press releases, price changes, and other such information.

There's a difference between an intranet, and a Web site. Access to an intranet is generally restricted to the people within the organization. A Web site is available to the public — unless the site is for paid subscribers only.

Tone It Down

In every form of business writing, your tone is your personality on paper. E-mail messages often go to masses of people you have never met, so accurately conveying the tone of your voice is critical. Following are suggestions at a glance for getting your tone across. (Check out Chapter 5 for details on honing the tone domestically and internationally.)

- ✔ KISS the message; keep it short and simple.
- ✔ Use the active voice.
- ✔ Select positive words, not negative ones.
- ✔ Be courteous and direct.
- ✔ Don't use all capital letters; writing in all caps is too much like shouting.

Don't Send Rambograms

In the world of cyberspace, you can easily forget that a human being is reading your e-mail message. Don't send out angry messages — known on the Web as *flames*. Each e-mail message is a permanent record of what you say. Even if you receive a flame, extinguish it and give yourself time to cool off. Remember this axiom: Send in haste, repent at leisure.

Following are some cooling off tips:

1. Compose your reply and include all the spicy, nasty insults you really want to say.

2. *Don't send the message.* Instead, save it to a file.

3. After you cool off — even hours or days later — revisit what you wrote and ask yourself: "Would I say this to the person's face?" If you wouldn't say it, don't send it!

Save "Urgent" for Situations That Are

There are people who designate "urgent" as the priority to all their messages. I can recall instances when I didn't respond to an "urgent" message because the sender was the "little boy who cried wolf." Perhaps you, too, have had that experience. Following are two pieces of advice for wolf-criers:

✔ Unless a message is urgent, don't tag it as such.

✔ If something is truly urgent and you must get the message through as quickly as possible, consider phoning rather than risking that the recipient won't see the message in time. People are more likely to listen to phone messages than read e-mail messages. (One example of when to phone instead of sending an e-mail would be when you need to schedule or cancel a meeting at the last minute.)

On the flip side, if a message is merely informational, consider starting the subject line with *FYI*. People will begin to recognize that notation as a clue to read the message at their leisure.

Create an Electronic Filing Cabinet

Saving copies of important messages you send and receive is prudent. Your diligent record keeping may come in handy for business, legal, or historical reasons. Many people print out messages of value, but the following tips help keep the trees from wincing:

✔ Create a file structure in your e-mail system, much like you would with a paper-based filing system.

✔ Save important messages in your word processing files.

✔ If the message is something to share with your colleagues, post it on your company's intranet and send an e-mail with a link to the message.

Notify Others When Your Address Changes

The comedian Rodney Dangerfield did a spiel that went something like this: When he was a young boy, his parents sent him off to school one morning. When he arrived home, the house was empty; the furniture and people were gone. His parents had moved and left no forwarding address.

In the e-mail world, people too disappear without a trace. Whenever you change your e-mail address (whether you changed companies or service providers), let those you correspond with know your new address. After all, when you move your office or change your phone number, don't you let people know? The number of mailer daemons reporting missing people is amazing.

Be Careful What You Write

The Electronic Communication Privacy Act (ECPA) upheld a company's right to monitor the e-mail messages of its employees. *The company foots the bill; it can peek at will.* So, don't send anything through cyberspace you wouldn't want your mother to read. Following are two stories of people who thought e-mail was safe:

- ✔ In a small New Jersey town, the police seized the e-mail of a murder suspect in order to further the investigation of the homicide case. On the strength of the evidence, which included incriminating e-mail messages, the man was charged with the murder.

- ✔ A noted New York columnist was shocked by an e-mail invasion. When he received a bluntly critical e-mail message from a young ethnic female colleague, he responded with a barrage of sexual and racial epithets that got him suspended for two weeks.

Break the Chain

Chain letters and scams are rampant in the electronic world; they contribute dramatically to information overload. Bill Gates isn't experimenting with an e-mail tracing program and asking for your help; National Public Radio and the Public Broadcasting Service aren't gathering support to defend funding; Mrs. Fields isn't selling her cookie recipe; and the sky isn't falling. Even if there were a rocket disaster that contained plutonium and it spread over the entire Northern Hemisphere, do you really think such important information would reach the public in a chain e-mail letter?

If you're absolutely, positively, and emphatically compelled to forward that 15th-generation message you get, at least have the decency to trim the 25 miles of headers showing everyone else who's received the message in the last several years. And it's a good idea to get rid of all the > symbols that begin each line letting everyone know the message has been around the e-world a gazillion times.

Tips for Dr. E-mail and her patients

Some doctors are using e-mail as a vehicle to communicate with patients. Like everything else, e-mail use by doctors has pluses and minuses. Following are some e-medical tips for doctors and patients:

As a patient:

✔ Never use e-mail for emergency situations. If you have an emergency, phone your doctor or call 911.

✔ Know that your e-mail may be read by others. At home, your little brother may read your message and blab information that you don't want the family to know. At the office, your employer is legally entitled to peek.

✔ Assume that whatever you send may wind up as part of your permanent medical records.

✔ If you get a second opinion or medical advice, be wary of advice from someone you don't know or know about.

As a doctor:

✔ Let your patients know what information is appropriate for e-mail — making appointments, requesting prescription renewals, and the like.

✔ Be sensitive to the fact that messages you send may be read by someone other than the patient. Be especially careful with subject lines. For example, don't use: *Positive results of pregnancy test.* (This is an exception to creating a direct subject line.)

✔ Remind patients that their e-mail messages may be read by nurses and receptionist. Let them know if you routinely include e-mail messages in their permanent files.

✔ Never forward a patient's e-mail message without the patient's electronic or written consent.

Proofread and Edit Your Message

Don't forget to use your Letter-Perfect Checklist featured on the Cheat Sheet in the front of this book. Don't be like the woman who sent an e-mail message to hundreds of people in the United States, Europe, and Asia. Underneath her name, she wrote her title: *Vice President of Pubic Relations* (notice that she left the "l" out of *public*).

Chapter 20

Ten Ways to Jettison Paper Piles

· ·

In This Chapter

▶ Cleaning up the infobog

▶ Determining whether you're a clutterbug

▶ Starting a recycling program

· ·

Unless you clean up your [office] living space, you can't clear up your head.

— Karen Rubin, professional organizer based in Los Angeles

*O*ffice constipation (also known as paper clutter) comes in all varieties: loose, stapled, white, ivory, embossed, matte, textured, and gloss, to name a few. Papers pile high on our desks; they teeter on top of file cabinets; they bulge from in-boxes, out-boxes, cardboard boxes, and trash baskets. Papers lurk everywhere — in the halls, outside cubicles, in empty cubicles, and anywhere people can find an inch of space.

Why keep unnecessary papers around? Have you ever had to dash to the first aid box, find a Band-Aid, and try to stop the bleeding from a nasty paper cut inflicted by an innocent-looking piece of paper lurking on your desk?

Furthermore, clutter is just sloppy. What would you think if you walked into a bank and each teller's station was strewn with loose bills and coins? Would you have confidence in that bank? Or if you walked into a surgeon's office and his desk was cluttered with body parts? The mess would gross you out. Even if he were tops in his field, you'd take your kidney problem elsewhere. Neatness sends a message. It says, "I'm in control."

Determine Whether You're a Clutterbug

Platoons of people — from the CEO all the way down — are overrun with papers. Are you one of them? Ask yourself these questions and put a check in the appropriate column to find out whether you're a clutterbug.

	Always	Sometimes	Never
Do I look like a klutz wading through piles of paper to find something on my desk that I need in a hurry?			
When I'm not there, can others find what whey need without ransacking my office?			
Have I filed everything that needs to be filed?			
Do valuable letters wind up with coffee stains or other deadly spills?			
Are the file drawers ready to explode?			
Do I keep all the "just-in-case-I'll-need-them" letters for indefinite periods of time?			
Does my in-box pile up faster than cars during rush hour?			
Am I afraid to throw something away just in case I need it later?			

Know What Being a Clutterbug Costs You

"So what if I'm a clutterbug?" you may ask. Experts agree that paper inefficiency can cost you 20 percent of your working life. That takes into account papers that are misplaced or lost in addition to time spent looking for them or re-creating them. Therefore, if you work 40 hours a week and multiply that by 50 weeks (assuming you're one of those poor souls who gets only a two-week vacation) you work 2,000 hours a year. Take 20 percent of that, and you waste 400 hours each year. Gee whiz! That's 10 weeks or 50 days a year. If you work weekends or overtime, the total is even higher.

Clean Up the Burial Ground

If you're buried in paper, here are some sure-fire ways for getting out from under the avalanche. No matter how hopelessly you're buried, don't go through the piles with a machete. There may be (and probably are) valuable things in those piles. Once you throw something out, it's gone forever. Following are some tips for getting your piles (not in the medical sense) under control:

Create paper mountains

Divide your papers into three piles. If you're buried so deeply that the piles will fall over, use boxes.

✔ **Pile 1: I Must Get to This**

Activate everything in Pile 1. Answer the letter, then file it. Route the papers to the appropriate person. Or put the papers in a file folder with other papers that are in the same category. Don't just re-pile the stuff!

✔ **Pile 2: I'm Saving This Just in Case**

This is the hardest pile to deal with because we all need just-in-case assurance. If in doubt, don't throw it out. Put this stuff in a special file and revisit the papers regularly.

✔ **Pile 3: The Paper Has Turned Yellow**

Immediately get rid of everything in Pile 3. If you haven't needed the papers by now, chances are you never will. Even if the yellowed letter informs you that you won the sweepstakes, your opportunity to collect has probably passed.

I worked with a guy who had an immaculate office — just the other extreme of the infobog. Nary a piece of paper was in view or a germ in sight. The only things on his desk were his computer and a jar of candy (which is why I visited him often). He even had a wall (cubicle)-mounted telephone so the phone wouldn't take up room on his desk. This guy never had a wrinkle in his clothes or a hair out of place. Everyone kidded that he spent all his time tidying up and didn't have time for much else. (He wasn't the most productive staff member.) While avoiding the infobog is great, striving for an office with a floor you can dine on can be just as time consuming.

Recycle: What goes around comes around

It's estimated that 70 to 80 percent of all the paper used in offices is waste. Therefore, it's economically and environmentally prudent to recycle. If your office doesn't have a recycling program, shame on it! Learn about recycling bond paper, computer paper, envelopes (without windows and self-sticking labels), uncoated fax paper, newsletters, laser/copy paper, and other paper products by writing to the American Paper Institute, 260 Madison Avenue, New York, NY 10016. You can also call the Institute at 212-340-0600.

You can arrange to have your recycled paper collected by a wastepaper broker or your local municipality.

Identify the Sources of Your Clutter

After you understand where your clutter comes from, you can start to reduce it. For example, if a coworker copies you on things you don't need, talk to him and let him know what is and isn't important to you.

- If you accumulate mail, open your mail near your wastebasket and immediately recycle anything you don't need. Act immediately on what you do need.

- Bundle all papers that relate to a specific project. The bundle may be a file folder, rubber band, or anything else that creates a single unit.

- If you're inundated with junk mail, there are several ways to ebb the flow:

    Write "no" or "not interested" on return cards and ask to be taken off the mailing lists.

    Write to the Direct Marketing Association, Mail Preference Service, Box 3861, Grand Central Station, New York, NY 10163-3861 and ask for its free "mail preference" form. This service often gets you removed from mailing lists.

Ditch Magazines

Look through all the magazines you've been piling up. Clip the articles you want to save, then recycle the magazines! When you get new magazines, look through them as soon as you can so they don't pile up.

Empty Your In-box and Out-box

These boxes have a tendency to take on lives of their own. To avoid letting them get out of hand, set deadlines for emptying them and stick to your deadlines. You may need to empty the boxes daily, weekly (not weakly), or monthly. The longer you let the paper accumulate, the bigger the cleaning job.

I try to spend the first 10–15 minutes of my day going through papers. I'm usually energetic early in the day and find the morning a good time to unclutter. Find a time that works for you.

Toss Out Old Drafts

Even though all the rough drafts you've prepared represent your blood, sweat, and tears, once they're done, do you really need each paper version? If you really do, find an out-of-the-way place to stash them. If the documents are highly confidential, consider shredding them.

Use Electronic Media

Instead of sending interoffice memos, think about sending e-mail messages or posting to an intranet or extranet. For example, if you're notifying colleagues about a meeting, e-mail is a great way to get the information out. If you're giving directions to the company picnic, post the directions on the intranet. Check out Chapter 19 for more information about electronic postings.

When something is in electronic form, you don't need to print it. Using less paper saves your company big bucks. As Bill Gates points out in *Business @ The Speed of Thought* (published by Warner Books), "The U.S. government alone spends $1 billion annually printing documents that are already available on the Web." Imagine how many homeless people that money can feed.

Gates points out many advantages of going digital: "Digital technology can transform your production processes and your business processes. . . . No more stacks of paper in which you can't find what you need. No more pawing through piles of books and reports to find marketing information or sales numbers."

E-mail has its own overload potential and must be treated with respect. Check out Chapter 19, as well as my other book, *Business Writing For Dummies*, published by IDG Books Worldwide, for great tips on dealing with overload in an e-mail environment.

Whatever happened to the paperless office?

When computers first hit the scene, everyone predicted that the 1990s would usher in the era of the *paperless office*. However, the paperless office has been as real as the paperless bathroom. (One example of the waste of office paper is the U.S. government's printed bid requirements for a cargo plane. The document weighs 3½ tons. Yes tons, not pounds.)

Instead of computers cutting paper consumption, they increased it. Just take a look at the file cabinets that line the walls of any office. Following is a small version of a poster-size sign I saw on the filing cabinet of a U.S. government facility. It was attached to a bank of file cabinets that filled a room. Doesn't it make the trees wince?

> If you remove a folder or document from this file, please fill out an AF-614 and follow the directions at the top of the form. These forms can be found in the first folder on the second shelf. Please re-use old forms until all spaces are filled.

Part V
Appendixes

The 5th Wave   By Rich Tennant

"You're able to read the chicken bones just fine. It's the grammar you use when writing with them that needs work."

In this part . . .

This part is chock full of easy-to-apply guidelines for the sticky wickets of punctuation, grammar, abbreviations, and spelling. This isn't like your standard textbook that drones on and on about stuff such as "restrictive clauses." That's for your HMO.

Appendix A

Punctuation Made Easy

• •

I'm glad you came to punctuate my discourse, which I fear has gone on for an hour without any stop at all.

— Samuel Taylor Coleridge, English Poet

Punctuation is one of the most significant tools you can use to create documents in your own voice. When you speak aloud, you constantly punctuate with your voice and body language. You also make a sound in the reader's head when you write. Your "writing voice" can be a dull, sleep-inducing mumble (like a tedious, unformatted document) or it can be a joyful sound, a shy whisper, or a throb of passion. It all depends on the punctuation you use.

General Guidelines

If you omit a mark of punctuation or place it incorrectly, you can dramatically alter the meaning of your sentence. In the following sentences, you can see the differences in meaning.

> Woman without her man is a savage.

> Woman: without her, man is a savage.

I present the punctuation marks in the order in which they're most commonly used and confused.

We're hungry let's eat mom

How would you punctuate the headline sentence it to make its meaning clear? Check out the possibilities below

We're hungry. Let's eat, mom.

We're hungry; let's eat mom.

This stresses the importance of punctuation. I'm sure your mother would agree.

Different (key) strokes for different folks

The following three sentences are worded identically. Yet, the different marks of punctuation give each a unique sound:

Dashes: The Ace Chemical Company — winner of the Service Award — just introduced its new product line. (The emphasis is on what's enclosed in the dashes.)

Parentheses: The Ace Chemical Company (winner of the Service Award) just introduced its new product line. (This construction plays down what's enclosed in the parentheses.)

Commas: The Ace Chemical Company, winner of the Service Award, just introduced its new product line. (What's enclosed in the commas is neutralized.)

Commas

Commas are the most used (and misused) punctuation mark. While a period indicates a *stop* in thought, a comma acts as a *slow sign* — something like a speed bump. Commas let you know which items are grouped together, what's critical to the meaning of the sentence, and more.

✔ Use commas to separate three or more items in a series. A comma before the final *and* or *or* is optional. It can, however, increase the clarity. The choice is yours, but be consistent.

✔ Use a comma before a conjunction *(and, but, or, nor, for, so, yet)* that joins two sentences.

> ***Complete sentences:*** Joe recognized the four delegates, but he can't recall their names.

> ***Second clause not a sentence:*** Joe recognized the four delegates but can't recall their names.

✔ Don't place a comma before *because.*

✔ Use commas to separate items in an address or date. (But don't use any punctuation before a ZIP code.)

> As of Saturday, September 16, 1998, UniData Corporation's address becomes One Adam Street, Marlborough, MA 01752.

✔ Use commas to set off an expression that explains, modifies, or emphasizes the preceding word, name, or phrase.

> Main Street, our town's main thoroughfare, will be closed to traffic tomorrow.

✔ Use commas to set off a word(s) that directly addresses the person to whom you're speaking by name, title, or relationship.

> Please let me know, Senator, if you can add anything to that.

✔ Use a comma after an introductory phrase if it's followed by a complete sentence. This type of clause may include introductory words such as *when*, *if*, *as*, and *although*.

> If we advertise in that magazine, our sales should increase.

✔ Use commas around a phrase that isn't necessary to the meaning of the sentence.

> My older son, the one you met last Monday, is an architect. (He is an architect regardless of when you met him.)

✔ Don't place commas around information that makes the sentence clear.

> The person who meets all our qualifications will never be found.

✔ Use commas to set off expressions that interrupt the natural flow of the sentence. These expressions can include: *as a result, in fact, therefore, however, consequently, for example, in fact,* and *on the contrary.*

> We will, therefore, continue with the project.

✔ Use commas to show contrast.

> The assignment is long, but not difficult.

✔ Use commas to identify a person quoted directly.

> In 1981, Bill Gates said, "640K ought to be enough for anybody."

✔ Use commas to set off designations, titles, and degrees that follow a name.

> Max Lorenz, CPA, will be our guest speaker.

✔ Use a comma to divide a sentence that starts as a statement and ends as a question.

> I can't think of anything further, can you?

✔ Use commas to separate items in reference material.

> You can find an area code map in *The Office Professional's Quick Reference Handbook,* Fourth Edition, by Sheryl Lindsell-Roberts, page 224.

✔ Use a comma to separate words when the word *and* is omitted, and to separate adjectives.

> Please include a stamped, self-addressed envelope.

> It may be a long, long time before we see him again.

Ending Punctuation

Ending punctuation refers to periods, question marks, and exclamation points.

Periods

The period is the stop sign of punctuation. It slows you down and makes you take a breath before you go into the next thought.

- ✔ Use a period after a statement, command, or request.
- ✔ Use a period after words or phrases that logically substitute for a complete sentence.

    Okay.

    No, not at all.

- ✔ As a general rule, use periods when writing abbreviations, acronyms, or initialisms, although a number of dictionaries cite many abbreviations without periods — YMCA, FDIC, and CPA, for example. When in doubt, check it out. For more information about abbreviations, acronyms, or initialisms, see Appendix C.

Question marks

A question mark, like a period, serves as a stop sign — a break in thought — with an added air of mystery. Although you probably use question marks correctly, there are a few tricky situations, which I hope these guidelines can demystify.

- ✔ Use a question mark after a direct question.
- ✔ Use a question mark after a short, direct question that follows a statement.

    You saw the requisition, didn't you?

- ✔ Use a question mark after each item in a series of questions within the same sentence.

    Which of the candidates has the most experience? Mary? Joe? Jeff?

    For this sentence, is the correct punctuation mark a period? A comma? A question mark?

- ✔ Use a question mark enclosed in parentheses to express doubt.

    He said the contract is due on April 8 (?).

One space, not two

In the olden days of typewriters it was sound advice to space twice after a punctuation mark. It was the only way to separate one sentence from another clearly. With computers, there's a clear distinction between sentences because of proportional spacing. Therefore, you should space once — not twice — after a period, colon, exclamation point, question mark, quotation mark, or any other mark of punctuation that ends a sentence.

Exclamation points

Exclamation points are reserved for words or thoughts that show strong emotion.

> Please try to do better!

> The business merger was a success. Congratulations!

Colons and Semicolons

A semicolon is a separator that's stronger than a comma and weaker than a period. A colon directs the reader's attention to what follows. This section shows you how to use both of them correctly.

Colons

A colon is a mark of anticipation. It serves as an introduction and alerts you to a close connection between what comes before and after it.

✔ Use a colon after an introduction that includes or implies *the following* or *as follows*.

✔ Use a colon to introduce a long quotation.

✔ Use a colon to separate hours and minutes.

Semicolons

Consider semicolons a cross between periods and commas. They create more impact than commas, yet less than periods. Following are some rules about when to use them:

✔ Use a semicolon in place of a conjunction *(and, but, or, nor, for, so, yet),* to join complete sentences.

> The raw material is supplied by our Georgia plant; the finished product is made in our Chicago plant.

✔ Use a semicolon before expressions that can be removed without changing the meaning of the sentence, as when a parenthetical word or phrase introduces a separate sentence.

> The project came to a standstill during the strike; however, we did eke out a small profit.

✔ Use a semicolon to separate items in a series when the items themselves have commas.

> The three most important dates in our company's history are January 15, 1937; April 8, 1952; and July 30, 1994.

Dashes and Parentheses

Dashes and parentheses affect how the reader understands information. Dashes highlight the text; parentheses play down the text.

Dashes

Dashes (often considered strong parentheses) are vigorous and versatile, and have several uses. They can stand alone or be used in pairs. Just don't overdo dashes or they lose their impact.

In Microsoft Word you have two ways to form an em dash (—). An em dash gets its name from the capital *M,* which is the same width.

1. Type two hyphens. If you don't space between the second hyphen and the word that follows, the two hyphens magically become an em dash.

2. Click Insert, and highlight Symbols in the drop-down list that appears.

And speaking of spaces — some writers leave one space before and after the em dash, others leave no spaces. It's dealer's choice.

Use the following rules to help you with your dashing dashes.

✔ Use dashes to set off expressions you want to emphasize.

> This brand of software — as unbiased tests have disclosed — is more powerful than what you're currently using.

✔ Use a dash before a word that sums up preceding text as an option to a colon. (Be consistent in your style.)

> The dishwasher, the washing machine, the dryer — items that eventually need repair.

✔ Use a dash to indicate a strong afterthought that disrupts the sentence.

> I know you're looking for — and I hope this helps — a list of qualified people.

✔ Use a dash before the name of an author or work that follows a direct quote.

> *You can turn painful situations around through laughter. If you can find humor in something, you can survive it.*
>
> — Bill Cosby

Parentheses

Parentheses (often considered weak dashes) are like a sideshow; they're used to enclose a word or words that aren't integral to the meaning of the sentence. A parenthetical expression is one that doesn't change the meaning of the sentence (removing the expression doesn't alter the gist).

Some examples of when to use parentheses follow.

✔ Use parentheses around an expression that you want to de-emphasize.

> This brand of software (as unbiased researchers have established) is more powerful than what you're using.

✔ Use parentheses around references to charts, pages, diagrams, authors, and so on.

> Please read the section on fossils (pages 36–52).

✔ Use parentheses to enclose numerals or letters that precede items in a series.

> We are hoping to (a) meet the Mayor, (b) express our views, and (c) submit our petition.

✔ When you enclose a sentence in parentheses, punctuate it as a sentence.

Other Punctuation

Last, but not least, are quotation marks, apostrophes, hyphens, slashes, and brackets.

Quotation marks

Quotation marks are reserved for those occasions when you cite something verbatim.

If you're paraphrasing, don't use quotation marks.

> *Quoting:* Mr. Schultz said, "Please come to the meeting at 2:00."

> *Paraphrasing:* Mr. Schultz asked her to come to the 2:00 meeting.

Follow these general guidelines for using quotation marks.

✔ Place commas and periods inside quotation marks.

> The most desired response is "yes."

✔ Place semicolons and colons outside quotation marks.

> The person being sued is the "defendant"; the person suing is the "plaintiff."

✔ Place question marks and exclamation points inside the quotes only when they apply to the quoted material.

> "What's the circulation of that newspaper?" he asked.

✔ Place question marks and exclamation points outside the quotes when they apply to the entire sentence.

> Did he say, "Our circulation is over a million"?

✔ Use quotation marks to enclose direct quotes.

> "Our industry is vital to the economy," said the CEO.

✔ Use quotation marks to enclose articles from magazines, songs, essays, short stories, one-act plays, sermons, paintings, lectures, and so on.

> *Loony Laws & Silly Statutes,* by Sheryl Lindsell-Roberts, has a chapter entitled, "Sorry, My Dance Card's Full."

✔ Use quotation marks to set off words or phrases introduced by expressions such as *the word, known as, was called, marked, entitled,* and so on. (Italics serve the same purpose; just be consistent.)

> *Quotes:* The phrase "each and every" should always have a singular verb.

> *Italics:* The phrase *each and every* should always have a singular verb.

✔ Use quotation marks to set off words used in an unconventional manner. (Again, you can use italics instead.)

> That clue was a real "red herring."

✔ Use single quotation marks around a quotation within a quotation.

> The consultant said, "You would do well to heed Mr. Smith's advice: 'Give the public what it wants and you will be in business for a long time.'"

Apostrophes

Apostrophes show possession or omissions. They're not flying commas.

Possession

Possession refers to ownership, authorship, brand, kind, or origin. These guidelines demonstrate how to use apostrophes to show possession:

✔ Apostrophes are most commonly used with nouns to show possession.

> The host called the guests names when they arrived.

> The host called the guests' names when they arrived.

> (Which host would you prefer?)

✔ Form the possessive case of a singular noun by adding an apostrophe.

✔ Form the possessive of a regular plural noun (one ending in *s*) by adding an apostrophe after the *s*.

> The companies' headquarters will relocate after the deal closes.

✔ Form the possessive of an irregular plural noun (one not ending in *s*) by adding an apostrophe and *s*.

> The salespeople's territories are being divided.

✔ To show joint ownership, add the apostrophe and *s* after the last noun. To show single ownership, add the apostrophe and *s* to each noun.

> **Joint ownership:** Jim and Pat's cubicle is near the lounge.

> **Individual ownership:** Jim's and Pat's cubicles are near the lounge.

✔ In hyphenated words, put the apostrophe at the end of the possession.

> He worked at his brother-in-law's factory for eight years.

✔ To make an abbreviation possessive, put an apostrophe and *s* after the period. If the abbreviation is plural, place an apostrophe after the *s*.

> The Smith Co.'s sale starts next month.

> Two M.D.s' opinions are needed.

- Express time and measurement in the possessive case.

    We'll have an answer in one week's time.

- Use an apostrophe to show possession of initialisms or acronyms. Some writers eliminate the apostrophe when there's little chance of misreading.

    I used AAA's towing service last week.

The names of companies and publications are often written without apostrophes. When in doubt, check it out.

Omission

Everyday contractions are the most obvious example of apostrophes used in place of a letter or letters. Basic guidelines follow:

If you want to highlight a negative statement, consider a contraction. *Don't* is more noticeable than *do not*.

- Use an apostrophe to show that letters (as in contractions) or numbers (as *the '70s*) are missing.

- Use an apostrophe to form the plural of a number, letter, symbol, or word.

    Sally doesn't always pronounce her r's at the end of a word.

    No if's, and's, or but's.

Some companies frown on using contractions and prefer the more formal style. Defer to the style of the company.

Hyphens

Don't confuse hyphens (-) with em dashes (—). They're different species. Hyphens function primarily as spelling devices.

- Use a hyphen to join a unit of two or more words modifying a noun.

    The bank extended the family a 30-day note.

    The bank extended the note for 30 days. *(Comes after the noun.)*

- Use a hyphen for compound numbers and written-out fractions.

    One-hundred-fifty-two people attended the meeting.

    This is three-fourths the annual revenue.

- Use a hyphen to join *ex-* and *-elect* to a title.

    Did ex-President Carter return to his farm after he left office?

✔ Use a hyphen to add to the clarity of the word.

> I re-sent the message yesterday.

✔ Use a hyphen between a prefix that ends with a vowel and a word beginning with the same vowel. (When in doubt, check it out.)

> The television station pre-empted our production company's program.

> The meeting you missed was only semi-important.

Slashes

These critters go by a variety of names: slant line, virgule, bar, or shilling line. They separate or show an omission, such as in care of (c/o) or without (w/o).

✔ Use slashes in and/or expressions.

> The sales/advertising departments are deciding on the issues.

✔ Use slashes in Internet addresses.

> http://www.dummies.com

Brackets

Brackets aren't substitutes for parentheses. They have their own place in the world, as the following guidelines explain:

✔ Use brackets to enclose words you add to a direct quote.

> He said, "The length of the trial [from early June to late July] was entirely too long."

✔ Use brackets as parentheses within parentheses.

> Your order (including one dozen blue pens [which aren't available], three dozen green pens, and five dozen red pens) will ship on Monday, September 8.

Appendix B
Grammar's Not Grueling

This is the sort of English up with which I will not put.

> — Winston Churchill (A comment against clumsy avoidance of a preposition at the end of a sentence, from *E. Growers Plain Words*)

You may remember when you were a kid, asking your mother, "Mom, can Pat and me go to the movies?" Your mother replied," That's Pat and I," and she didn't give you the money until you corrected your grammar. Although you didn't think so then, your mother was doing you a favor. Poor grammar didn't get you far with your mother, and it doesn't get you far in the business world.

I don't get into the nitty-gritty details of every part of speech because I don't want to bore you to tears. Rather, I touch upon the most troublesome areas in alphabetical order.

Adjectives

An adjective adds pizzazz to a sentence. It's a word, phrase, or clause that modifies, describes, or limits the noun or pronoun it's describing. You can use adjectives to transform an ordinary sentence into a tantalizing one.

> *Ordinary:* The computer stared back at me.

> *Tantalizing:* The softly humming computer — its flat screen glowing with a gentle blue light — invited me to start my letter.

An adjective answers at least one of the following questions: What kind? Which? What color? How many? What size?

Quickie quiz

Take a look at the following sentences and see what errors you notice, if any. (Turn the book upside down for the answers.) If you find all the mistakes, tear this chapter out of the book and share it with a deserving coworker.

And, if you're so grammatically correct, feel free to skip this appendix entirely.

1. A group of 50 people are waiting to see the president.

2. With most of the votes counted, the winner was thought to be her.

3. Everyone in the room, including the president and vice president, is being asked to do their share.

4. What was the name of the speaker we had yesterday?

5. James, who enjoys this type of assignment, would certainly be interested if he was here now.

6. The Jones Company is celebrating their 50th anniversary.

Answers

1. A group of 50 people *is* waiting to see the president. (*Group* is a singular subject and takes a singular verb.)

2. With most of the votes counted, the winner was thought to be *she*. (*She* was thought to be the winner. The nominative case is used when the pronoun is the subject of the sentence or it follows any form of the verb *to be*.)

3. Everyone in the room, including the president and vice president, is being asked to do *his or her* share. (*Everyone* takes a singular verb, even if you throw in specific people. After all, the president and vice president are part of everyone.)

4. What *is* the name of the speaker we had yesterday? (The speaker's name hasn't changed. Why use the past tense?)

5. James, who enjoys this type of assignment, would certainly be interested if he *were* here now. (Not a statement of fact. He isn't here now.)

6. The Jones Company is celebrating *its* 50th anniversary. (The Jones Company is a singular subject and takes a singular verb.)

Forms of adjectives

Adjectives take different forms, depending on the noun or nouns they're modifying.

Use a *positive* adjective when you're not comparing anything.

Business is *slow.*

Use a *comparative* adjective when you're comparing two things.

Business is *slower* today than it was yesterday.

Use a *superlative* adjective when you're comparing three or more things.

Business is the *slowest* it's been all week.

Several adjectives have irregular comparatives and superlatives; they don't end in *er* or *est.* The following table illustrates a few:

Adjective	Comparative	Superlative
good	better	best
little	less	least
bad	worse	worst

Absolute adjectives

Some adjectives are absolute; they either *are* or *aren't.* For example, one thing can't be more complete than something else. Either it's complete or it's not. Following are some adjectives considered absolute:

complete	correct	dead	empty
genuine	parallel	perfect	right
round	stationary	unanimous	wrong

Express the comparative and superlative forms of absolute adjectives by adding "more nearly" or "most nearly."

Jason's assumption was more nearly correct than Jim's.

Compound adjectives

In many cases, you use a hyphen to join together two adjectives so they form a single description. Use a hyphen only when the compound adjective comes before the noun, not after.

Before the noun: a part-time job; a two- or three-year lease

After the noun: a job that's part time; a lease of two or three years

Here are two exceptions:

1. Eliminate the hyphen when you generally think of the words as a unit; for example, *post office address* and *life insurance policy.*

2. Don't put a hyphen between adjectives if the first one ends in *est* or *ly;* as in *newly elected officer* and *freshest cut flowers.*

Articles

Use *the* to refer to a specific article and *a* or *an* to a nonspecific item. Use *a* when a consonant sound follows the *a* (*a* hot dog, *a* three-week trip); use *an* when a vowel sound follows (*an* onion, *an* illness, *an* heir, *an* X-ray).

Adverbs

Just as an adjective can add pizzazz to a noun, an adverb spices up a verb. An adverb modifies a verb, an adjective, or another adverb. An adverb answers one or more of these questions: How? When? Why? How much? Where? To what degree? Adverbs take different forms for the positive, comparative, and superlative, just as adjectives do.

Adjectives ending in *ly* may also function as adverbs — depending on what they're modifying.

Adjective:	Her handwriting is legible.
Adverb:	She writes legibly.
Adjective:	The professor's talk was brief.
Adverb:	The professor spoke briefly.

Double Negatives

If you've ever said, "I don't want no liver," what you said is that you do want liver. Two negatives equal a positive. Never use two negative words to express one positive idea.

Correct:	I can hardly believe what I just heard.
Incorrect:	I can't hardly believe what I just heard.

Conjunctions

A conjunction connects two or more words, phrases, or clauses that are equal in construction and importance. Common conjunctions are *and, or, for, so, but, nor,* and *yet.*

For information about punctuating sentences that contain conjunctions, see Appendix A.

Nouns

The noun — although critical to every sentence — is probably the least sexy part of speech. The noun doesn't create any emotion or add flair to your thoughts; it's merely a *person, place,* or *thing.*

A proper noun is specific and is capitalized. A common noun isn't specific and isn't capitalized.

> ***Proper nouns:*** New York City; Marlborough High School; Main Street

> ***Common nouns:*** the city; the school; the street

A collective noun is a group. When the group is acting as a unit (company, council, audience, faculty, union, team, jury, committee, and so on), use a singular verb. When members of the group are acting independently, use a plural verb.

> ***Acting collectively:*** The family is going on vacation.

> ***Acting individually:*** The family are going on separate vacations.

Prepositions

A preposition shows the relationship between words and sentences. Here are some common prepositions:

above	about	across	after	along
among	around	at	before	behind

below	beneath	beside	between	beyond
by	down	during	except	for
from	in	inside	into	like
near	of	off	on	since
to	toward	through	under	until
up	upon	with	within	without

Pronouns

A pronoun is a word that substitutes for a noun. Do you recall being unkind to a substitute teacher? Treat your pronouns well, and you'll atone for all the substitute teachers you made cry.

A pronoun substitutes for a noun. Use a pronoun to eliminate awkward wording. The pronoun must agree with the noun it replaces in person, number, and gender.

Singular pronouns

Certain pronouns are always singular and take singular verbs and pronouns, including: anybody, anyone, anything, each, either, everybody, everyone, everything, much, neither, nobody, nothing, one, somebody, someone, something.

> *Everyone*, including Pete and Jane, has *his* and *her* problems.

> *Neither* Gary's nor Bob's proposal *is* acceptable.

Who and whom

Who-and-whom cowards can mumble these words hoping the listener won't notice their indecision. Writers don't have that luxury. But it is possible to think of *who* and *whom* in easy terms!

When you can substitute he/she/they, use *who*. And when you can substitute her/him/them, use *whom*.

> The company needs a person *who* knows the new software. (*He/she* knows the new software.)

> Are you the person to *whom* I spoke yesterday? (I spoke to *her/him*.)

Verbs

The verb is the most important part of a sentence because it expresses an action, condition, or state of being. The verb makes a statement about the subject and can breathe life into dull text.

Dangling participles

If your participles dangle, it's nothing to be ashamed of. The condition's curable. A *dangling participle* is nothing more than a verb that doesn't clearly or logically refer to the noun or pronoun it modifies. Participles can dangle at the beginning or end of a sentence. The following shows how to undangle a participle:

> ***Dangling:*** While attending the meeting, the computer malfunctioned. (*Who* attended the meeting?)
>
> ***Correct:*** While James attended the meeting, the computer malfunctioned.

Were and was

Have you ever fantasized about being someone else? The English language provides a verb for those fantasies. "I wish I *were*. . ." The verb *were* is often used to express wishful thinking or an idea that's contrary to fact. *Was,* on the other hand, indicates a statement of fact.

> She acts as if she *were* president of the company. (Wishful thinking.)
>
> If Charles *was* at the airport, I didn't see him. (He may have been there.)

Was is the past tense of is. Why am I mentioning the obvious? Because people mistakenly use *was* for the present tense when referring to something that's already happened.

> ***Correct:*** I thoroughly enjoyed the book — even though it *is* 950 pages long.
>
> ***Incorrect:*** I thoroughly enjoyed the book — even though it *was* 950 pages long.

Split infinitives

The present tense of a verb preceded by *to* is called an infinitive. Don't put a modifier between *to* and the verb or you split the infinitive and sometimes confuse and distract your reader.

>*Correct:* The instructor wants *to read* all the papers carefully.

>*Incorrect:* The instructor wants *to* carefully *read* all the papers.

It's a good thing I wasn't asked to proofread Gene Roddenberry's original *Star Trek* script or we'd never have heard "To boldly go. . . ."

Subject and verb agreement

One of the most basic rules in grammar is that the subject and verb of a sentence must agree. Both must be singular or both must be plural. Although most situations are pretty straightforward, the following demonstrate situations that may be a little tricky:

- ✔ Don't be fooled by interrupting phrases.

  >*Correct:* The software, despite the new installation manuals, still takes several days to install.

  >*Incorrect:* The software, despite the new installation manuals, still take several days to install. (The subject is *software*.)

- ✔ *Many a, many an,* and *each and every* always take a singular verb.

  >Each and every computer *has* a modem.

  >Many a man *is* denied this chance.

- ✔ *None, some, any, all, most,* and *fractions* are either singular or plural, depending on what they modify.

  >Half the shipment was misplaced. (The subject, *shipment*, is singular.)

  >Half the boxes were misplaced. (The subject, *boxes*, is plural.)

- ✔ When referring to the name of a book, magazine, song, company, or article, use a singular verb even though the name may be plural.

  >*Little Women* is a great classic.

  >Wanderman & Greenberg is a fine team of attorneys.

- ✔ When referring to an amount, money, or distance, use a singular verb if the noun is thought of as a single unit.

> I think *$900 is* a fair price.
>
> There *are 10 yards* of fabric in that dress.

✔ When *or* or *nor* is used to connect a singular and plural subject, the verb must agree in number with the person or item closest to the verb.

> Neither Jim nor his *assistants were* available.
>
> Neither the assistants nor *Jim was* available.

Gerunds

A gerund is a word or phrase whose root is a verb and which ends with *ing*. Gerunds start out as verbs, but act as nouns. When a gerund is preceded by a noun or pronoun, the noun or pronoun takes the possessive form.

> I don't like *your giving* me such short notice.
>
> *Ted's yelling* is quite irritating.

Commonly Confused Constructions

Figuring out the correct usage for phrases that include prepositions can often mangle the mind. Table B-1 can help straighten you out.

Table B-1	Confusing Phrases
Phrase	*Example*
accompany by (a person)	The teacher was *accompanied by* her student.
accompany with (an object)	The bicycle was *accompanied with* assembling instructions.
account for (something or someone)	I can't *account for* Peter's behavior.
account to (someone)	The cashier had to *account to* the manager for the error.
compare to (show similarity)	You can *compare* this restaurant *to* any one with four stars.
compare with (examine for similarities and differences)	She *compared* his writing *with* Poe's.

(continued)

Table B-1 *(continued)*

Phrase	*Example*
convenient for (suitable)	Will Sunday be *convenient for* you?
convenient to (close)	The new theater should be *convenient to* you.
correspond to (agree with)	The merchandise doesn't *correspond to* what was advertised.
correspond with (write letters)	I *correspond with* Aunt Raye.
differ about (something)	We *differ about* ways to accomplish that project.
differ from (be unlike)	I *differ from* you in many ways.
differ with (someone)	I *differ with* you over the outcome of the project.
different from (never use *different than*)	This computer is not too *different from* my last one.
talk to (address)	The speaker *talked to* the audience for two hours.
talk with (discuss)	I *talked with* the speaker after he finished.

Appendix C

Abridged Abbreviations

• •

A lot of fellows nowadays have a B.A., M.D., or Ph.D. Unfortunately, they don't have a J.O.B.

— Antoine "Fats" Domino, singer

Abbreviations are useful for a variety of reasons: to avoid repetition, save space, or conform to conventional usage. Leading authorities can't agree on the capitalization or punctuation for many abbreviations; therefore, there are few set rules. For the most part, it's wise not to abbreviate unless you have a reason to do so. Having said that, here are some guidelines to cover variations, exceptions, and peculiarities.

I present the abbreviation guidelines in alphabetical order.

Acronyms and Initialisms

An *acronym* is a combination of the first letters of several words that you pronounce as a word itself: laser (light amplification by stimulated emission of radiation) and OPEC (Organization of Petroleum Exporting Countries) for example. An *initialism* is also a combination of the first letters of words, but you pronounce an initialism as separate letters, like I - B - M (International Business Machines) and F - D - I - C (Federal Deposit Insurance Corporation).

In business, industry, education, and government, acronyms and initialisms are often used among people who work together. That's fine, as long as your reader can easily understand your frame of reference. Keep in mind that the reference may not be comprehensible to those outside your magical kingdom. And, certain acronyms can mean different things to different people. For example, the ABA to an attorney is the American Bar Association; to a banker, the American Banking Association; to a bowler, the American Bowling Association; and to a bookseller, the American Booksellers' Association.

My son's friend used to impress his classmates by telling them that his father was head of the CIA. Everyone was awed. His dad was the head of the Culinary Institute of America, not the Central Intelligence Agency.

Alphabet soup

Don't feed your readers alphabet soup. I attended a meeting recently with what I refer to as the alphabet people. Those attending were the CEO; COO; CFO; VP of HR; VP of MIS; and, oh yes, B.J., the Pres.

Abbreviate acronyms and initialisms after you spell them out the first time, unless you're absolutely sure that your reader will understand your reference.

> The National Association of Manufacturers (NAM) will hold its annual meeting in July. At that time, NAM will outline its agenda for the year.

> The FDA did not give its approval to the drug you mentioned. (Most people know what FDA means.)

Companies and Organizations

Styling varies widely in organizational names. Treat the name as the company or organization treats it. Check the company's Web site or letterhead for an accurate picture. If you can't check it out, write it out.

Compass Points

Abbreviate compass points when they appear after street names. Spell them out when they appear before street names.

Latin Words and Phrases

Words derived from Latin are commonly abbreviated. Use lowercase and don't italicize them. Check out Table C-1 for these abbreviations.

Table C-1	Latin Abbreviations
Abbreviation	*Meaning*
c. or ca.	*(circa)* about
e.g.	*(exempli gratia)* for example
et al.	*(et alii)* and others
etc.	*(et cetera)* and so forth
ibid.	*(ibidem)* the same
i.e.	*(id est)* that is
pro tem	*(pro tempore)* for the time being
ss.	*(silicet)* namely (often used in affidavits)
viz.	*(videlicit)* namely

I suggest that people refrain from using Latin abbreviations because they're often written or read improperly. For example, many people confuse *i.e.* and *e.g.* They're not interchangeable.

Laws and Bylaws

Write the complete law or bylaw at first mention: "The reference appears in Article I, Section 2." Thereafter, use the abbreviation: "See Art. I, Sec. 2."

Metric System

The United States is probably the only country in the universe that isn't using the metric system. Some of the more popular metric abbreviations are shown in Table C-3.

Table C-3	Metric Abbreviations
Abbreviation	*Unit*
km	kilometer
hm	hectometer
dam	dekameter
m	meter
dm	decimeter
cm	centimeter
mm	millimeter
l	liter
cl	centiliter
ml	milliliter
MT or t	metric ton
kg	kilogram
hg	hectogram
dag	dekagram
g or gm	gram
dg	decigram
cg	centigram
mg	milligram

Write out metric measurements unless you're certain your reader will understand your abbreviated form.

Periods

To use a period or not to use a period: That is the question. Here are the answers.

✔ In general, use periods for academic degrees, but not for professional references.

> Thomas Greenberg, Ed.D.; Richard L. Hodge, CPA

✔ Use a period after most abbreviations formed by omitting all but a few letters of a word.

> mfg. (for manufacturing); avg. (for average)

✔ Omit the period from abbreviations made up of initial letters that constitute an acronym, initialism, or compound word.

> ROI (return on investment) and GNP (gross national product); but f.o.b. (free on board) and a.k.a. (also known as)

Postal Abbreviations

The United States Postal Service requests that the two-letter state abbreviations — without periods — be used on all mail. Table C-2 gives the abbreviations for U.S. states and territories.

Table C-2		U.S. Postal Service Abbreviations			
Location	*Abbreviation*	*Location*	*Abbreviation*	*Location*	*Abbreviation*
Alabama	AL	Georgia	GA	Maryland	MD
Alaska	AK	Guam	GU	Massachusetts	MA
Arizona	AZ	Hawaii	HI	Michigan	MI
Arkansas	AR	Idaho	ID	Minnesota	MN
California	CA	Illinois	IL	Mississippi	MS
Canal Zone	CZ	Indiana	IN	Missouri	MO
Colorado	CO	Iowa	IA	Montana	MT
Connecticut	CT	Kansas	KS	Nebraska	NE
Delaware	DE	Kentucky	KY	Nevada	NV
District of Columbia	DC	Louisiana	LA	New Hampshire	NH
Florida	FL	Maine	ME	New Jersey	NJ

(continued)

Table C-2 *(continued)*

Location	Abbreviation	Location	Abbreviation	Location	Abbreviation
New Mexico	NM	Puerto Rico	PR	Vermont	VT
New York	NY	Rhode Island	RI	Virginia	VA
North Carolina	NC	South Carolina	SC	Virgin Islands	VI
North Dakota	ND	South Dakota	SD	Washington	WA
Ohio	OH	Tennessee	TN	West Virginia	WV
Oklahoma	OK	Texas	TX	Wisconsin	WI
Oregon	OR	Utah	UT	Wyoming	WY
Pennsylvania	PA				

Appendix D

Spelling Superbly

- -

Nothing you can't spell will ever work.

— Will Rogers

If you're frustrated with English language spelling, be glad we don't have words such as *Wirtschaftstreuhandgesellschaft*, the German word for "business trust company." Perhaps that's no consolation because English certainly has its own perplexities. For example, check out some of the words in the English language that end with the "er" sound and see how differently they're spelled: burgl*ar*, writ*er*, aviat*or*, glam*our*, ac*re*, murm*ur*, inju*re*, mart*yr*. Is it any wonder we all scratch our heads when it comes to spelling?

If you remember a few basic rules, you can overcome many of the spelling difficulties you may have. Just keep in mind that there are exceptions to every rule.

Butt, eye half Spill-Czech

Now that we have spell checkers, why worry about spelling?

I have a spelling checker.

It came with my PC.

It plane lee marks four my revue

Miss steaks aye can knot see.

— Author Unknown

Despite all the advances in technology, the need to spell is alive and kicking. Spell checkers don't identify all spelling errors. They can't discriminate between homophones (they're, their, there) or commonly confused words (proceed, precede). And they can't know that you mean *our* instead of *out*. Only humans can do that.

Plurals

How simple things would be if we could walk around like befuddled children saying, "My feets hurt." Plurals aren't that simple.

The following list demonstrates different ways to make plurals by adding *s* or *es*.

- ✔ Form the plurals of most nouns by adding an *s:* automobile*s*, flower*s*, leg*s*.

- ✔ Pluralize words ending in *s, x, z, ch,* or *sh* by adding *es:* bunch*es*, business*es*, Sanchez*es*.

- ✔ Pluralize words ending in *y* when *y* is preceded by a vowel by adding an *s:* chimney*s*, journey*s*, kidney*s*.

- ✔ Pluralize words ending in *y* when *y* is preceded by a consonant by changing the *y* to *i* and adding *es:* academ*ies*, arm*ies*, beneficiar*ies*.

Handle words ending with *o* like so:

- ✔ Pluralize words ending in an *o* preceded by another vowel by adding an *s:* cameo*s*, studio*s*.

- ✔ Pluralize words ending in an *o* preceded by a consonant by adding *es:* veto*es*, hero*es*, echo*es*.

- ✔ Pluralize musical terms ending in *o* by adding an *s:* piano*s*, soprano*s*, solo*s*.

When compound words aren't hyphenated, they work as regular words. For example, just add *s* to make *letterheads* and *handfuls*. With a hyphenated compound word, make the main part of the word plural, as in *sisters-in-law* and *editors-in-chief*.

Making some words plural requires changing the vowel and/or the form, like child*ren*, g*ee*se, and ox*en*. Other words require no change at all because singular and plural forms are the same — deer, mathematics, news, sheep, and series.

You usually pluralize words ending in *f* or *fe* by changing the *f* to a *v* and adding *s* or *es:* kni*ves* and li*ves*, for example.

You pluralize many foreign words with origins in Greek or Latin by changing the ending. Check out the table below for the most common examples.

	Change this	*To this*
sis to *ses:*	analysis	analyses
um to *a:*	datum	data
us to *i:*	radius	radii
on to *a:*	criterion	criteria

The Final E

To e or not to e, that is the question.

- ✔ Drop a final *e* preceded by a consonant when the suffix starts with a vowel. Excuse becomes *excusable;* argue, *arguable;* and desire, *desirous.*
- ✔ Retain the final *e* when the suffix begins with a consonant. Move becomes *movement;* care, *careless;* and resource, *resourceful.*

The Final Y

If you want to know y, here's y.

- ✔ Retain the final *y* when the *y* is preceded by a vowel, so that employ becomes *employs* and attorney becomes *attorneys.*
- ✔ When the final *y* is preceded by a consonant, change the *y* to *i* and add the suffix. Easy becomes *easily;* salary becomes *salaries;* and angry becomes *angrily.*

IE and EI

Perhaps Old MacDonald had the right idea: E I E I O. He didn't need to learn this jingle. If you learn it, however, you'll be able to spell most of the *ie* and *ei* words.

> Put *i* before *e,* (yield, field)
> Except after *c,* (deceit, receive)
> Or when sounded like *a,*
> As in *neighbor* or *weigh.*
> And except *seize* and *seizure,*
> And also *leisure.*
> *Weird, height,* and *either,*
> *Forfeit* and *neither.*

Pluralisms

We'll begin with a box and the plural is boxes, but the plural of ox is oxen, not oxes.

Then one fowl is a goose, but two are called geese, yet the plural of mouse should never be meese.

You may find a lone mouse or a whole set of mice, but the plural of house is houses, not hice.

If the plural of man is always called men, shouldn't the plural of pan be called pen?

If I speak of a foot and you show me your feet, and I give you a boot, would a pair be called beet?

If one is a tooth and the whole set are teeth, why shouldn't the plural of booth be called beeth?

Then one may be that and three would be those, yet hat in the plural wouldn't be hose. And the plural of cat is cats, and not cose.

We speak of a brother and also of brethren, but though we say mother, we never say methren.

Then the masculine pronouns are he, his, and him; but imagine the feminine she, shis, and shim.

So English I fancy that, I'm sure you'll agree, is the funniest language you ever did see.

Note: The author of this poem is anonymous. If you can identify him or her, you may win a copy of Webster's original dictionary signed by Webster shortly after his death.

Doubling the Final Consonant

This section answers that ageless question: To double, or not to double.

- ✔ Double the final consonant if the word has one syllable or has its accent on the last syllable. The table shows some common verbs.

crop	cropped	cropping
admit	admitted	admitting
plan	planned	planning

- ✔ Double the final consonant in a word ending in a single vowel followed by a single consonant.

allot	allotted	allotting
prefer	preferred	preferring
transfer	transferred	transferring

- ✔ Don't double the final consonant if the word has three or more syllables: congealed, benefited.

REMEMBER

Then there are words where the consonant may be either singled or doubled: canceled, traveller.

Super Stumpers

These super stumpers are the way they are — just because they are. Tables D-1 and D-2 list the correct spelling and usage of some tricky words and expressions. The abbreviations in the table are fairly standard ones: *n* for noun, *v* for verb, *adj* for adjective, *adv* for adverb, *conj* for conjunction, *prep* for preposition, and *pron* for pronoun. In addition, letters or words in **bold-face** indicate common letter(s) that can help you remember both the correct spelling and correct usage.

Table D-1	Puzzling Pairs
Word	*Usage*
accept (v)	to take
except (prep)	other than
ad (n)	short for advertisement
add (v)	to increase
addition (n)	something added
edition (n)	published work
adverse (adj)	hostile
averse (adj)	unwilling
advice (n)	recommendation
advise (v)	to give an opinion
affect (v)	to influence
effect (n/v)	result; to bring about
already (adv/adj)	previously
all ready (adj)	all prepared
alright	slang for *all right*
all right	entirely correct
altar (n)	part of church
alter (v)	to change
altogether (adv)	entirely
all together (adv)	everyone in one group
among (prep)	comparison of three or more
between (prep)	comparison of two
amount (n)	refers to things in bulk or mass
number (n)	refers to countable items

(continued)

Table D-1 *(continued)*

Word	Usage
appraise (v)	to estimate
apprise (v)	to notify
assistance (n)	help
assistants (n)	those who help
bare (n)	naked; no more than
bear (v)	to carry
beside (prep)	alongside
besides (prep)	in addition to
biannual (adj)	twice a year
biennial (adj)	every two years
brake (n/v)	device for stopping motion/to stop
break (n/v)	fracture; to breach
canvas (n)	course cloth
canvass (v)	to solicit
choose (v)	to select
chose (v)	past tense of choose
coarse (adj)	rough
course (n)	direction; series of studies
complement (n/v)	that which completes; to complete
compliment (n/v)	expression of praise; to praise
correspondence (n)	letters
correspondents (n)	those who write letters
device (n)	a plan
devise (v)	to plan
disburse (v)	to pay out
disperse (v)	to scatter
dual (adj)	double
duel (n)	formal fight
elicit (v)	to draw out
illicit (adj)	illegal
eminent (adj)	well-known
imminent (adj)	immediate
ensure (v)	to make certain
insure (v)	to protect against

Word	Usage
farther (adj)	greater distance
further (adv)	to a greater degree
faze (v)	to embarrass
phase (n)	stage of development
fewer (adj)	modifies plural nouns
less (adj)	modifies singular nouns
formally (adv)	in a formal manner
formerly (adv)	at a former time
forth (adv)	forward
fourth (n)	follows third
forward (adv)	ahead
foreword (n)	preface in a book
incite (v)	stir to action
insight (n)	clear understanding
knew (v)	past tense of know
new (adj)	not old
know (v)	to understand
no (adj)	not any
lay (v)	to place an object down
lie (v/n)	to recline; untruth
lead (n/v)	heavy metal; to guide
led (v)	past tense of lead
maybe (adv)	perhaps
may be (v)	might be
miner (n)	one who works in a mine
minor (n)	person under legal age
moral (n)	lesson relating to right and wrong
morale (n)	spirit
overdo (v)	do to excess
overdue (adj)	past due
passed (v)	past tense of pass
past (n)	time gone by
patience (n)	endurance
patients (n)	persons receiving treatment

(continued)

Table D-1 *(continued)*

Word	Usage
peace (n) piece (n)	state of calm portion
peer (n) pier (n)	equal wharf
persecute (v) prosecute (v)	oppress institute legal proceedings
personal (adj) personnel (n)	private staff
principal (n/adj) principle (n)	sum of money; school official; main; first in rank rule
respectfully (adv) respectively (adv)	in a respectful manner in the order listed
role (n) roll (n)	part in a play; function register or list; small bread
should of should have	improper English proper English
stationary (adj) stationery (n)	fixed in place paper products
than (conj) then (adv)	comparison expressing exception at that time; next
undo (v) undue (adj)	open; render ineffective improper; excessive
waive (v) wave (n)	forego gesture; surge of water
weather (n/v) whether (conj)	atmospheric condition; to come through safely if; in case
who's (contraction) whose (pron)	who is; who has possessive of who
your (pron) you're (contraction)	belonging to you you are

Table D-2	Troublesome Triplets
Word	**Usage**
adapt (v)	to adjust
adept (adj)	skilled
adopt (v)	take as your own
access (n)	right to enter; admittance
assess (v)	to set a value
excess (n/adj)	extra
capital (n/adj)	official city of a state; money; serious; chief
capitol (n)	building that houses state legislature
Capitol (n)	building in Washington, DC
cite (v)	to summon
sight (n)	that which is seen
site (n)	location
council (n)	assembly
counsel (n/v)	attorney; to advise
consul (n)	foreign representative
its (pron)	belonging to it
it's (contraction)	it is
its'	no such word
loose (v)	to set free
lose (v)	to suffer a loss; to mislay
loss (n)	something lost
right (adj/n)	correct; just privilege
rite (n)	formal ceremony
write (v)	to inscribe
suit (n/v)	clothes; to please
suite (n)	set of rooms
sweet (adj)	having a sugary taste
their (pron)	belonging to them
there (adv)	in that place
they're (contraction)	they are
to (prep)	toward
too (adv)	also
two (adj)	numeral

Booby Traps

Table D-3 presents the "spelling demons" hit parade.

Table D-3		Booby Traps	
abbreviation	absence	accept	accessible
accommodate	accompanied	acknowledge	acquaintance
across	advantageous	affect	affiliated
a lot	already	ambiguity	anonymous
apparent	appreciate	appropriate	argument
arrangement	attendance	bankruptcy	beginning
believable	beneficial	benefited	benign
bookkeeping	bulletin	business	calendar
campaign	cancel	cannot	category
cemetery	changeable	clientele	coming
committee	competition	concede	confident
conscientious	controversy	convenience	corroborate
criticism	defendant	depreciate	description
desirable	difference	disappoint	disbursement
discrepancy	dissatisfactory	dissipate	effect
eligible	embarrass	endeavor	endorsement
enthusiastic	environment	equipped	especially
exceed	excellent	except	exercise
exhaust	existence	experience	explanation
extension	extraordinary	familiar	feasible
February	foreign	forty	government
grateful	guarantee	handwritten	height
immediate	inasmuch as	incidentaliy	independence
independent	insistent	interpret	jeopardize

jewelry	judgment	knowledge	laboratory
leisure	library	license	lien
likable	litigation	loose	lose
maintenance	mandatory	mediocre	mileage
minimum	miscellaneous	misspell	municipal
necessary	occasion	occurred	omission
opportunity	opposite	original	paid
pamphlet	parallel	paralyze	perseverance
persuade	physician	possession	practical
precede	preferred	procedure	prosecute
privilege	psychology	pursue	questionnaire
really	receive	reference	repetition
separate	sheriff	similar	sincerely
subpoena	succeed	successful	sympathy
techniques	unanimous	unnecessary	until
vacuum	Wednesday	withheld	yourself

Just for fun

1. Can you think of a word in the English language that has three consecutive double letters?

2. Can you think of a word that has four consecutive vowels?

3. Can you think of a word that has 28 letters?

1.Bookkeeper or bookkeeping 2. Sequoia or queue 3. Antidisestablishmentarianism

Answers

Index

• Symbols and Numbers •

{ } (brackets), 261
: (colons), 255
, (commas), 252–253
( ) (parentheses), 257
. (periods), 254
; (semicolons), 255–256
' (apostrophes), 259–260
/ (bars, shilling lines, slant lines, slashes, virgules), 261
— (em-dashes), 256–257
! (exclamation points), 255
- (hyphens), 260–261
? (question marks), 254
" (quotation marks), 258–259
7 Habits of Highly Successful People, The, 9

• A •

absolute adjectives, 265
academia, forms of address, 225
acronyms, abbreviations and initialisms
  companies and organizations, 274
  compass points, 274
  definition, 273
  Latin words and phrases, 274–275
  laws and bylaws, 275
  metric system, 275–276
  periods in, 276–277
  postal, 277–278
  U.S states and territories, 277–278
  writing, 274

action words. *See also* pizzazz
  employment letters, 115–116
active voice, 79–80
address changes, e-mail, 239–240
addresses
  on envelopes, 25
  inside address, 34–36
  international mail, 232
  in letterhead, 19
adjectives, 263–266
adverbs, 266
ambiguity, avoiding, 76–77
American Paper Institute, 246
apologies, 180
apostrophes ('), 259–260
appearance. *See* visual impact
application letters, 108
Aristotle, on persuasion, 50
articles (grammar), 266
attachments
  e-mail, 194, 237
  letter, 41
attention line, 36
audience, defining, 48–50

• B •

Bair, Jeffrey, 235
Baldridge, Letitia, 209, 219
bars (/), 261
bc notation, 41
Bean, L.L., definition of a customer, 131
blind copy notation, 41
block letter style
  definition, 63
  example, 65

body of the letter, 38–39
boilerplate
    definition, 39
    employment letters, 109
boondoggles, 85
brackets ({ }), 261
broadcast letters, example, 116
broadcasting a request for a job, 114–115
Brothers, Dr. Joyce, 139
Brown, Jerry, 193
Browne, Sir Thomas, 33
bulk mail, 95–96, 228
bulleted lists, 70
Business @ The Speed of Thought, 247
business cards
    designing, 22–23
    global savvy, 24
    instead of a letter, 23–24
    Japanese etiquette, 24
    using the back side, 23
business titles
    inside addresses, 34
    letterhead, 19
Business Writing For Dummies, 37, 204
bylaws
    acronyms, abbreviations and
        initialisms, 275

● *C* ●

canceling an event, 190
capital letters, in e-mail messages, 83
Carbone, Louis, 127
cc notation, 41
certificate of mailing, 228–229
certified mail, 229–230
chain letters, 240
charities, soliciting for, 201
chatty tone, 73
Churchill, Winston, 263

clichés, avoiding, 83
clutter, office, 243–248
collection letters, 144–148
colons (:), 255
commas (,), 252–253
company names
    acronyms, abbreviations and
        initialisms, 274
    in addresses, 35
comparative adjectives, 265
compass points, abbreviating, 274
Complete Guide to Executive Manners,
    209, 219
complimentary closing
    e-mail, 39
    letters, 39
    multi-page letters, 68
compound adjectives, 265–266
computerized postage, 233
conciseness, 73–75
condolences, 171–172
congratulations, 178–179
conjunctions, 267
conservative stationery, 18
contemporary stationery, 18
contractions, 70–71
conversational tone, 73
Cosby, Bill, 211
courtesy copies, 41
cover letters
    definition, 193–194
    for resumes, 108
Covey, Stephen R., 9
credit buying
    collection letters, 144–148
    denying credit, 143–144
    extending an offer of credit, 140–141
    granting credit, 141–142
    pros and cons, 140
    reviving inactive accounts, 144

customer, definition, 131
customer claims, processing
  benefits of, 130
  denying an adjustment, 135–137
  example, 137
  following up, 134–135
  granting an adjustment, 132–134
  replying promptly, 131–132
customer claims, writing
  example, 136
  following up, 130
  gathering information, 128
  tone, 128–130

● *D* ●

dangling participles, 269
dashes (—), 256–257
dates
  format, 33–34
  translating, 84
Dear Sir or Madam, 36–37, 220
delivery method
  determining, 51
  noting in the letter, 34
domestic mail service, 227–231
Domino, Antoine "Fats", 273
double negatives, 266–267
drafting a letter
  preparing for, 57
  reviewing the draft, 58–59
  writing the draft, 57

● *E* ●

E. Growers Plain Words, 263
ECPA (Electronic Communication
  Privacy Act), 240
editing *versus* proofreading, 85
Edwards, Robert C., 93

elected officials, forms of address,
  37, 223
Electronic Communication Privacy Act
  (ECPA), 240
e-mail
  acknowledging a mail order, 166
  address changes, 239–240
  addresses in letterhead, 19
  all capital letters, 83
  attachments, 194, 237
  chain letters, 240
  complimentary closing, 39
  distribution, choosing, 50
  between doctor and patient, 241
  ECPA (Electronic Communication
    Privacy Act), 240
  emergency messages, 51
  filing, 239
  flames, 238
  get-well wishes, 172–173
  graphics, 71
  invitations, 185–189
  job applications, 114
  long messages, 237
  multi-page messages, 68
  posting to a Web site, 238
  posting to an intranet, 237
  praising others, 202
  priority, 239
  privacy, 240
  sales promotions, 100
  salutations, 37
  shotgunning, 236
  signature files, 40
  subject lines, 38, 53, 236–237
  tone, 83, 238
  trimming headers, 240
  uppercase, 83
  white space, 62
embossing stationery, 22
em-dashes (—), 256–257

employment letters (employees)
  action words, 115–116
  application letters, 108
  boilerplate, 109
  broadcast, example, 116
  broadcasting, 114–115
  cover letters for resumes, 108
  declining a job offer, 121–122
  denying a request for interview,
    196–197
  do's and don'ts, 108–109
  ending paragraph, 112
  example, 113
  length, 110–112
  letterhead, 110
  listing accomplishments, 115
  mail merges, 111
  middle paragraph, 111–112
  opening paragraph, 110
  resigning from a job, 124–125
  sending electronically, 114
  thanks for the interview, 117
  timing, 112
employment letters (employers)
  acknowledging a resume, 118
  extending a job offer, 119
  managing a merger, 197–199
  rejecting a candidate, 120
  terminating an employee, 121
  welcoming a new employee, 122–123
enclosure notations, 41
encouragement, 170–171
engraving stationery, 22
envelopes
  addressing, 25
  bulk mailing, 95–96
  folding letters for, 26–27
  grabbing attention, 97
  international addresses, 232
  mailing labels, 96
  personalizing, 95–96
  presorted, 96
  sales letters, 95–96
  teasers, 95
euphemisms, 82
examples
  announcing a merger, 198
  bad headlines, 56
  bad proofreading, 87–90
  block letter style, 65
  broadcast letters, 116
  customer claims, 136–137
  employment letters, 113, 116
  full-block letter style, 64
  invitations, 189, 191
  letter format, 42
  letterhead, 28–31
  letters of request, 160–161
  memo announcing a merger, 198
  memos, 197–199
  modified-block letter style, 65
  readable layout, 14–16
  sales letters, 103–104
  semiblock letter style, 66
  simplified letter style, 67
exclamation points (!), 255
express mail, 231
extending an offer of credit, 140–141

• F •

favors
  asking, 174–175
  refusing, 176
fax numbers, in letterhead, 19
faxing job applications, 114
filing e-mail messages, 239
finish, stationery, 21
firing an employee, 121
first class mail, 228
first drafts. *See* drafting a letter
flames (e-mail), 238

foreign language translations
  dates, 84
  geographic expressions, 84
  goodbye, 39
  please, 153
  thank you, 153
formal invitations, 188
formal tone, 73
forms of address
  academia, 225
  Dear Sir or Madam, 36–37, 220
  elected officials, 37
  general salutations, 220–221
  government officials, 223
  job title, 36
  judges, 37
  military ranks, 221–223
  religious leaders, 224
  unknown gender, 35, 37
  To Whom This May Concern,
    36–37, 220
  women, 37
full-block letter style
  definition, 62
  example, 64

• G •

Gates, Bill, 247
gender
  neutrality, 80–82
  unknown, forms of address, 35, 37
geographic expressions, translating, 84
gerunds, 271
get-well wishes, 172–173
gifts
  acknowledging, 177–178
  offering, 176
  refusing, 178
glamour stationery, 18
global savvy, definition, 4
going away, 173–174

government officials, forms of address,
  37, 223
grain, stationery, 21
grammar
  absolute adjectives, 265
  adjectives, 263–266
  adverbs, 266
  articles, 266
  comparative adjectives, 265
  compound adjectives, 265–266
  confusing phrases, 271–272
  conjunctions, 267
  dangling participles, 269
  double negatives, 266–267
  gerunds, 271
  nouns, 267
  positive adjectives, 265
  prepositions, 267–268
  pronouns, 268
  quiz, 264
  split infinitives, 270
  subject and verb agreement, 270–271
  superlative adjectives, 265
  verbs, 269–271
  were and was, 269
  who and whom, 268
graphics, 71
greetings. *See* salutations

• H •

headers
  e-mail, trimming, 240
  memos, 210
headlines in letters
  bad examples, 56
  emphasizing, 69
  format, 38–39
  getting attention with, 53–54
  sequencing for bad news, 55–56
  sequencing for good news, 54–55

holiday wishes, 180–181
Hugo, Victor, 74
humor, 82, 211
hyphens (-), 260–261

• *I* •

idioms, 84
informal invitations, 185–186
in-house notation, 34
initialisms. *See* acronyms, abbreviations
    and initialisms
international mail, 231–232
interviews
    denying a request for, 196–197
    thank-you letter, 117
intranets, posting messages, 237
invitations, extending
    canceling an event, 190
    contents, 184–185
    e-mail, 186
    examples, 189, 191
    formal, 188
    informal, 185–186
    RSVP, 185
    semi-formal, 187–188
    timing, 188
invitations, responding to, 190

• *J* •

Japanese business card etiquette, 24
jargon
    in letters, 83
    in memos, 210
job candidates, rejecting, 120
job interviews
    denying a request for, 196–197
    thank-you letter, 117
job title, form of address, 36

jobs
    applying for, 108
    broadcasting a request for, 114–115
    declining an offer, 121–122
    extending an offer, 119
judges, form of address, 37

• *K* •

Kennedy, Joyce Lain, 115
KISS (Keep It Short and Simple)
    principle, 73–75
Kitt, Etta, 37
kudos, 178–180

• *L* •

Landers, Ann, 183
Latin words and phrases, 274–275
laws
    acronyms, abbreviations and
        initialisms, 275
letter format
    attachments, 41
    attention line, 36
    bc notation, 41
    blind copy notation, 41
    block style, definition, 63
    block style, example, 65
    body, 38–39
    business titles, addressee, 34
    cc notation, 41
    company addresses, addressee, 35
    company names, addressee, 35
    complimentary closing, 39
    courtesy copies, 41
    dates, 33–34
    delivery method, 34
    enclosure notations, 41
    example, 42

full-block style, definition, 62
full-block style, example, 64
headlines, 38–39
in-house notation, 34
inside address, 34–36
line spacing, 38–39
mailing notation, 34
modified-block style, definition, 63
modified-block style, example, 65
multi-page letters, 68
names, addressee, 34
pc notation, 41
photocopy notation, 41
postscripts, 41
reference initials, 40
salutations, definition, 36
salutations, forms of address, 36–37
salutations, punctuation, 37
semiblock style, definition, 63
semiblock style, example, 66
signature block, 40
simplified style, definition, 63
simplified style, example, 67
subject line, 37–38
typist identification, 40
white space, 62
letter tone. *See* tone
letter types
    See also credit buying
    See also employment letters
    See also invitations
    See also letters of request
    See also mail order
    See also memos
    See also personal business letters
    announcing a new business, 200
    complaints. *See* customer claims
    cover letters, 193–194
    follow up to customer visit, 106
    praising others, 202
    querying a publisher, 213–218

sales proposals, 202–204
    transmittal letters, 193–194
letter writing
    history of, 10
    steps in. *See* Six-Step Process
letterhead
    addresses, 19
    business titles, 19
    designing, 19–20
    e-mail addresses, 19
    employment letters, 110
    examples, 28–31
    fax numbers, 19
    logos, 19
    multi-page letters, 68
    names, 19
    personal business letters, 169
    phone numbers, 19
    Web addresses, 20
    when to avoid, 20
lettering process, stationery, 21–22
letters
    drafting. *See* drafting a letter
    folding for envelopes, 26–27
    versus memos, 209–210
letters of request
    denying the request, 195–197
    examples, 160–161
    for money, 201
    for permission to reprint, 204–205
    to renew membership, 199–200
    replying to, 156–159
    solicitation for charities, 201
    writing, 153–156
line spacing in letters, 38–39
lists
    bulleted, 70
    guidelines for, 69
    numbered, 70
    parallel structure, 70
logos, letterhead, 19

• M •

mail merges, 111
mail order, filling an order
   acknowledging the order, 165–166
   delays in shipping, 167
   incomplete order information, 166
   shipping partial orders, 167
   substitutions, 167
mail order, placing an order, 163–164
mailgrams, 231
mailing labels, 96
mailing notation, 34
memo reports, 211
memos
   announcing a merger, example, 198
   constructive complaints, 211
   giving bad news, 210
   headers, 210
   jargon, 210
   versus letters, 209–210
   sense of humor, 211
   signature lines, 212
metric measurements
   abbreviations for, 276
   in global correspondence, 84
   and global mail order, 164
military rank, forms of address, 221–223
modified-block letter style
   definition, 63
   example, 65
money, asking for, 201

• N •

names
   inside addresses, 34
   letterhead, 19
   unknown gender, 35, 37
Nancy, Ted N., 153
negative words, 78

news reporter's approach to letter
   writing, 52
nouns, 267
numbered lists, 70

• O •

On Dreams, 33

• P •

Paper Direct, 18
paper quality, stationery, 20–21
paperless office, 248
parentheses (( )), 257
passive voice, 79–80
pc notation, 41
PC Postage, 233
periods (.)
   in acronyms, abbreviations and
      initialisms, 276–277
   as punctuation, 254
personable tone, 73
personal business letters
   apologies, 180
   condolences, 171–172
   congratulations, 178–179
   definition, 169
   favors, asking, 174–175
   favors, refusing, 176
   get-well wishes, 172–173
   gift, refusing, 178
   gifts, acknowledging, 177–178
   gifts, offering, 176
   going away, 173–174
   holiday wishes, 180–181
   kudos, 178–180
   letterhead, 170
   words of encouragement, 170–171
personalizing sales envelopes, 95–96
phone numbers in letterhead, 19

photocopy notation, 41
pictures, 71
pizzazz, words and phrases, 98–99,
    115–116
plurals, spelling, 280, 282
positive adjectives, 265
positive tone
    benefits of, 77–78
    in job applications, 112
positive words, 77–78
post office. *See* U.S. Postal Service
postage, computerized, 233
postscripts
    definition, 41
    sales letters, 101
Powers, John, 167
prepositions, 267–268
presorted mailings, 96
printing, stationery, 21–22
priority mail, 231
privacy, e-mail, 240
pronouns, 268
proofreading
    bad examples of, 87–90
    boondoggles, 85
    versus editing, 85
    exercise, 90
    guidelines for, 85
P.S.
    definition, 41
    sales letters, 101
punctuation
    apostrophes ('), 259–260
    bars (/), 261
    brackets ({ }), 261
    colons (:), 255
    commas (,), 252–253
    complimentary closing, 39
    dashes (—), 256–257
    effect on meaning, 71, 251–252
    em-dashes (—), 256–257

exclamation points (!), 255
hyphens (-), 260–261
parentheses (( )), 257
periods (.), 254
question marks (?), 254
quotation marks ("), 258–259
salutations, 37
semicolons (;), 255–256
shilling lines (/), 261
slant lines (/), 261
slashes (/), 261
spacing after, 255
virgules (/), 261

• Q •

question marks (?), 254
quotation marks ("), 258–259

• R •

rag content, stationery, 20
reader-focused sentences, 78–79
recycling office paper, 246
redundancy, avoiding, 74–76
reference initials, 40
registered mail, 230
religious leaders, forms of address, 224
reporter's approach to letter writing, 52
resigning from a job, 124–125
resumes
    acknowledging receipt of, 118
    cover letters, 108
Resumes For Dummies, 115
Revson, Charles, 163
Rogers, Will, 279
RSVP, 185
Rubin, Karen, 243
Russell, David L., 169

• S •

sales letters
  benefits *versus* features, 99–100
  call for action, 100
  envelopes, 95–97
  examples, 103–104
  length, 100
  mailing lists, compiling, 105–106
  planning a campaign, 94–95
  postscripts, 101
  price of offering, 100
  SASE (self-addressed stamped
    envelope), 101
  tactics to avoid, 101
  tone, 93–94
  words with pizzazz, 98–99
sales proposals, 202–204
salutations
  definition, 36
  e-mail, 37
  forms of address, 36–37
  general forms of address, 220–221
  punctuation, 37
SASE (self-addressed stamped
  envelope), 101
Sassoon, Vidal, 107
self-addressed stamped envelope
  (SASE), 101
semiblock letter style
  definition, 63
  example, 66
semicolons (;), 255–256
semi-formal invitations, 187–188
sequencing
  for bad news, 55–56
  for good news, 54–55
*7 Habits of Highly Successful People,
  The,* 9
sexism, avoiding, 80–82
shilling lines (/), 261
shotgunning e-mail, 236

signature block, 40
signature files, e-mail, 40
signature lines, memos, 212
simplified letter style
  definition, 63
  example, 67
Six-Step Process
  1. getting started, 47–53
  2. headlines and sequencing, 53–56
  3. writing the draft, 56–59
  4. visual impact, 62–72
  5. setting the tone, 72–84
  6. proofreading, 85–90
slang, 83
slant lines (/), 261
slashes (/), 261
spacing
  after punctuation, 255
  between lines, 38–39
spell checkers, 279
spelling
  doubling final consonants, 282
  final "e", 281
  final "y", 281
  ie *versus* ei, 281
  plurals, 280, 282
  spell checkers, 279
  tricky words and phrases, table of,
    283–289
spicing up a letter. *See* pizzazz
split infinitives, 270
standard paragraphs, 39
Start Up Sheet, 47–53
stationery. *See also* envelopes;
  letterhead
  conservative, 18
  contemporary, 18
  creating your own, 18–22
  definition, 17
  embossing, 22
  engraving, 22
  finish, 21

glamour, 18
grain, 21
image categories, 18
lettering, 21–22
Paper Direct, 18
paper quality, 20–21
printing, 21–22
rag content, 20
suppliers, 18
thermography, 22
watermarks, 21
weight, 20
subject and verb agreement, 270–271
subject lines
   definition, 37–38
   e-mail, 38, 53, 236–237
superlative adjectives, 265

• T •

templates, 39
terminating an employee, 121
thermography, stationery, 22
To Whom This May Concern, 36–37, 220
tone
   active voice, 79–80
   ambiguity, avoiding, 76–77
   chatty, 73
   clichés, 83
   conciseness, 73–75
   conversational, 73
   customer claims, 128–130
   dates, 84
   e-mail, 83, 238
   euphemisms, 82
   formal, 73
   gender neutrality, 80–82
   geographic expressions, 84
   global savvy, 83–84
   humor, 82
   idioms, 84
   jargon, 83

KISS principle, 73–75
metric measurements, 84
passive voice, 79–80
personable, 73
positive *versus* negative, 77–78
reader-focused sentences, 78–79
redundancy, avoiding, 74–76
sales letters, 93–94
sexism, avoiding, 80–82
slang, 83
wordiness, avoiding, 74–76
writer-focused sentences, 78–79
trade shows, as source of mailing list, 105–106
transmittal letters, 193–194
Twain, Mark, 61
typist identification, 40

• U •

uppercase letters, in e-mail messages, 83
U.S. Postal Service
   abbreviations for states and territories, 276
   alternatives to, 232
   bulk mail, 228
   certificate of mailing, 228–229
   certified mail, 229–230
   computerized postage, 233
   cutting costs, 233
   domestic mail service, 227–231
   express mail, 231
   first class, 228
   international addresses, 232
   international mail, 231–232
   mailgrams, 231
   PC Postage, 233
   priority mail, 231
   registered mail, 230
   size limits, domestic mail, 228
   size limits, international mail, 232

• V •

Vanderbilt, Cornelius, 74
verbs, 269–271
virgules (/), 261
visual impact
    block style, 62–67
    contractions, 70–71
    crowding, 68
    graphics, 71
    headline emphasis, 69
    letter styles, 72
    lists, 69–70
    multiple pages, 68
    white space, 62, 71

• W •

Walters, Dotty, 45
was *versus* were, 269
watermarks, stationery, 21
Web addresses in letterhead, 20

Web sites, posting messages, 238
weight, stationery, 20
welcoming a new employee, 122–123
were *versus* was, 269
white space
    e-mail, 62
    letters, 62, 71
who, what, when, where, why,
        and how, 52
who *versus* whom, 268
women, forms of address, 37
wordiness, avoiding, 74–76
writer-focused sentences, 78–79
writer's block, 47
Writer's Market, 217
writing a draft. *See* drafting a letter
writing letters. *See* letter writing

Notes

Notes

Notes

Notes

Notes

Notes

IDG BOOKS WORLDWIDE
BOOK REGISTRATION

We want to hear from you!

Visit **http://my2cents.dummies.com** to register this book and tell us how you liked it!

✔ Get entered in our monthly prize giveaway.

✔ Give us feedback about this book — tell us what you like best, what you like least, or maybe what you'd like to ask the author and us to change!

✔ Let us know any other *...For Dummies*® topics that interest you.

Your feedback helps us determine what books to publish, tells us what coverage to add as we revise our books, and lets us know whether we're meeting your needs as a *...For Dummies* reader. You're our most valuable resource, and what you have to say is important to us!

Not on the Web yet? It's easy to get started with *Dummies 101*®: *The Internet For Windows*® *98* or *The Internet For Dummies*®, 6th Edition, at local retailers everywhere.

Or let us know what you think by sending us a letter at the following address:

...For Dummies Book Registration
Dummies Press
7260 Shadeland Station, Suite 100
Indianapolis, IN 46256-3917
Fax 317-596-5498

TM

BESTSELLING BOOK SERIES